Women Philosophers

Women Philosophers

Genre and the Boundaries of Philosophy

Catherine Villanueva Gardner

A Member of the Perseus Books Group

Excerpts from Miriam Brody Kramnick, ed., *A Vindication of the Rights of Women,* Harmondsworth, Middlesex: Penguin Books, 1983. p. 13, 40, 41, are reprinted by permission of Penguin Books, Ltd.

Copyright © 2004 by Westview Press, A Member of the Perseus Books Group

Published in 2003 by Westview Press, A Member of the Perseus Books Group, 5500 Central Avenue, Boulder, Colorado 80301–2877, and in the United Kingdom by Westview Press, 12 Hid's Copse Road, Cumnor Hill, Oxford OX2 9JJ.

Find us on the world wide web at www.westviewpress.com

Westview Press books are available at special discounts for bulk purchases in the United States by corporations, institutions, and other organizations. For more information, please contact the Special Markets Department at the Perseus Books Group, 11 Cambridge Center, Cambridge, MA 02142, or call (617) 252–5298, (800) 255–1514 or email j.mccrary@perseusbooks.com.

A Cataloging-in-Publication data record for this book is available from the Library of Congress.

ISBN 0–8133–4133–7 (paperback); 0–8133–6610–0 (hardcover)

The paper used in this publication meets the requirements of the American National Standard for Permanence of Paper for Printed Library Materials Z39.48–1984.

10   9   8   7   6   5   4   3   2   1

Contents

Acknowledgments

I would like to thank the women philosophers with whom I have been fortunate enough to study, in particular Cora Diamond.

I would also like to thank those who encouraged me to write this book: Sylvia Gardner, Marion Carrigan, Charles Dunlop, and Barbara Haskins; and those who helped in its production: Lori Lookliss my research assistant, Terry Swier from the University of Michigan–Flint library, Sarah Warner my acquisitions editor, and the University of Michigan–Flint for funding the project.

And last, but not least, I would like to thank Luis Villanueva for all the help and encouragement he has given me and will, no doubt, give me in the future.

Catherine Villanueva Gardner

Preface

On the Teaching of *Women Philosophers*

Since the initial publication of this book, I have been asked to consider how the text might be useful in introducing women philosophers from the history of philosophy into classrooms. I realized that—if I am sincere in my desire to recapture women philosophers—I should consider both how *Women Philosophers* could be a general resource for such teachers and the ways in which it could be used as a classroom textbook.

I believe *Women Philosophers* is useful for our classrooms in three interconnected ways: it introduces the work of women philosophers; it analyzes their exclusion from the philosophical canon; and it considers what is required for their inclusion. I shall first discuss this in fairly general terms and then show how this could play out in the construction of actual courses both in philosophy and in women's studies.

First—and most obviously—this book provides an introduction to and an analysis of the work of some women philosophers who could be integrated into courses on philosophy or women's studies. Until recently, not only was there little or no critical work on women philosophers from the history of philosophy, but many people were ignorant of their very existence. The history of women philosophers is a surprisingly rich one. Mary Ellen Waithe has brought to our attention the life and works of around one hundred women philosophers ranging in time from the twentieth century to ancient Greece and Rome.[1] While some of these philosophers wrote on the nature of women or argued for their social equality, the majority of them are concerned with the whole gamut of philosophical subject areas from epistemology to moral philosophy.

Much of the initial work of gathering information on women philosophers has now been done, and work is now beginning on in-depth analyses of the writings of these philosophers. In this book I aim to contribute to the further recovery of five women moral philosophers for our philosophical canon: the eighteenth century historian and philosopher Catharine Macaulay, the eighteenth century feminist Mary Wollstonecraft, the nineteenth century novelist George Eliot, the medieval French writer Christine de Pisan, and the thirteenth century mystic Mechthild of Magdeburg.

Even though the recapturing of women philosophers from our past is an important moment in both philosophy and women's history, it can also be an awkward moment for us as teachers. Whether we are working within philosophy properly speaking, or within women's studies more generally, we may be unsure how to include these women philosophers into our courses. We have not necessarily studied about them ourselves, and there is still—at present—a limited amount of information available to us.

Part of our uncertainty about how to include women philosophers comes from the fact that we now recognize that the history of philosophy most of us studied as undergraduate and graduate students is an inaccurate account of the history of our discipline. Setting the account straight is not simply an issue of historical accuracy. It is also important for philosophy itself. For in philosophy (perhaps more than other disciplines) we study the history of our discipline, and we wish to have conversations that cross that history. Moreover, we may have been limited in our exposure to different types of philosophical writing, and are thus unsure how to deal with the work of philosophers who do not write in forms that we now think of as standard philosophical forms. Yet it is often the case that women philosophers employ such non-standard forms.

How then are we to include women philosophers from the history of philosophy into our courses? What we should avoid—as Mary Ellen Waithe argues—is just adding in a few women and stirring.[2] Adding in one woman here or there—as Waithe points out—gives the mistaken impression that these women were the rare (and rarified) exceptions. Instead we need a broader understanding of how these women became lost or—if they were not entirely lost from sight as in the case of Mary Wollstonecraft—what was it about their philosophy that kept it remaining visible. It seems clear that women philosophers *cannot* be included into our philosophy courses without changes in our teaching of the history of philosophy itself and without hard questions being asked about the construction of the discipline of philosophy. Nor can these women philosophers be included into women's studies courses more generally if we do not also explore the numerous social and cultural factors that combined to their neglect.

When we examine the works and lives of many women philosophers we find that they were not necessarily undervalued and ignored during the period in which they lived and wrote. Indeed, many of them were highly respected by their male contemporaries. If we do not accept some kind of "cream rising" theory of canon formation, then we need to find an explanation for this phenomenon. It is certainly true that some women philosophers have disappeared as a result of direct sexist suppression: i.e., this philosophy cannot be any good, look who wrote it. But this kind of explanation is not sufficient to account for the disappearance of so many women philosophers, nor can it account for why they remain undervalued or marginalized even after they have been rediscovered. Instead we must recognize—and explore the ways that this has happened—that philosophy itself has been defined in such a way that the work of women philosophers has been excluded and may still remain undervalued or not properly understood in the present.

Thus, the clearly necessary inclusion of women philosophers brings with it a variety of questions about their initial exclusion. These two elements—specific discussion of the work of these women philosophers and questions about their exclusion—are integral to any course that aims to introduce women philosophers to students. It is here that I find the second way *Women Philosophers* will be of use in the classroom. It offers both an account of the philosophical arguments of five different women philosophers, and it brings out some of the specific reasons they have been forgotten or devalued. Specifically, I explore the way they wrote and the apparent connection to the status of being philosophers.

This then is the third and final way *Women Philosophers* will be of use in the classroom, and I believe it is also its most important contribution. For I show not only how it is that these five women philosophers have been excluded from the history of philosophy, but I also show what is needed for them to be *included*. Specifically, I show how we are to read the work of these five philosophers, and—by implication—how the work of other philosophers can be read. Moreover, I argue that our lack of ability to deal with certain lost forms and styles of writing is ultimately *our loss*.

When I began to interpret the work of my chosen philosophers, I found that I needed first to address the issue of how to approach their writings. Their works do not have the formal and stylistic hallmarks which characterize what we now think of as "standard" philosophy. Rather than being argumentative treatises, these works take the form of allegorical stories, letters, or novels. Moreover, this is not unique to the particular philosophers I had chosen to interpret but is surprisingly frequent in the writings of other women philosophers. Some obvious examples here include Sor Juana Ines de la Cruz, Hildegard of Bingen, and Marie le Jars de Gournay.

I recognize that there is no essential or necessary connection between sex and genre that explains the prevalence of women writing in what are—from the standpoint of contemporary philosophy anyway—nonphilosophical genres. But we must not ignore the fact that there are connections between sex and genre. Given the restrictions women experienced not only in their access to education, but in their entrance into the public world of publishing, we can see that it was far easier for women to write within the more accepted "feminine"—and thus devalued—genres: novels, poetry, devotional works, or "advice" letters. Unfortunately it has become all too easy to confound both sex and gender, and genre and content, and to claim that the philosophical works produced by women are of little value and are typically only concerned with the private and the domestic.

What I started to see as I began interpreting the work of these five philosophers was that, given the accepted boundaries of philosophical writing today, we do not have the analytic and conceptual tools immediately at hand to interpret these other forms of writing—even if it is allowed that the content of a work may have value or interest. What then happens is that we may feel justified in ignoring or marginalizing the work of these women philosophers. The Anglo-American analytic tradition trains us to read purely for content. Style and form are discussed only if and when they obscure comprehension. Moreover our moral philosophical tradition aims for the impartial, the reasoned, and the universally applicable. Yet novels, letters and poetry, by their very nature, are more intimate, more personal, more particular. Indeed they seem to lend themselves better to dealing with moral concerns—such as emotions or relationships—that are often devalued within this tradition. It was when I realized this that the project grew in my mind.

I was no longer satisfied simply to show how the form of the work of some women philosophers has contributed towards their being neglected, misunderstood, or undervalued. Nor did I merely want to try and show that these forms are "not a problem." Instead I decided to demonstrate that an analysis of the genres of the particular women philosophers I was examining is vital to a productive understanding of their work. Rather than aiming to extract *what* they say from the *way* they said it, I argue that we must recognize that the form in which they wrote was not only inextricably connected to the content but even at times an essential part of the philosophical arguments themselves.

In order to take this approach, I hold that we must ultimately be prepared to offer criticism of accepted approaches to philosophical analysis, and the boundaries of philosophical investigation. And this comprises the second—more general—part of the project. For instance we must recognize that the particular form a work takes can be philosophically important, and we must understand the notion of argument not as something that can necessarily be subtracted from a text and broken down into premises and a conclusion, but nonetheless as constituting a piece of coherent reasoned thought. Ultimately, this means that we must question whether our model of philosophical investigation of a text is the only model. I argue that this questioning constitutes a challenge to our conception of moral philosophy *itself*, for–as I claim–our model of assessment is bound up with what we take philosophy to be.

The actual structure of the book can allow flexibility in how much of my overall argument is included into a course. While the work forms an argumentative whole, it breaks down into chapters that can be read independently of each other without any particular loss of comprehension. Moreover, each chapter is divided into sections which would allow a further division of the material. Within each chapter I explore the thought of each philosopher, and I conclude by offering an analysis of how to read the work of that philosopher. Thus the book can be read for the specific analyses that combine to make up the first part of my project or it can be read in its entirety for both parts of my project.

In this way then, I believe *Women Philosophers* is useful in the classroom context because it goes beyond offering an introduction to the work of five women philosophers. Not only does it offer an answer to the necessary adjunct question of how their work became lost, but it aids the inclusion—and discussions about this inclusion—of these women because it shows how to read their work. And, obviously, this latter point is not something that is confined to these particular philosophers. Given the prevalence of women philosophers writing in non-standard philosophical forms, teachers who wish to include other women philosophers in their courses need to engage with this question of how they are to be read.

How might this inclusion then look in the classroom setting? Within the discipline of philosophy, there are many different ways of structuring courses to include women philosophers. The main possibilities include: as a separate "stand-alone" course, within a particular historical period, within a particular philosophical field, or as part of a general history course. *Women Philosophers* is potentially useful for any of this type of course.

In the case of a stand-alone course, students are typically introduced to a chronological range of women philosophers from all eras of philosophy: ancient, medieval, modern, contemporary. Obviously, an in-depth examination of their philosophy can provide a useful introduction or supplement to the primary texts. Moreover, the examination in *Women Philosophers* of how the written form of their philosophy contributed to the exclusion of some women philosophers can provide a running theme for a stand-alone course that is solely focused on examining women philosophers. It also raises further themes such as how—if their thought had not been excluded—their work might have shaped the discipline of philosophy itself.

As *Women Philosophers* provides an analysis—at least in part—of how the history of philosophy came to be constructed, it could provide a useful element for any general history of philosophy course that includes women philosophers. Moreover—in the case of Macaulay and Wollstonecraft—it can also offer an account of the ways that mainstream philosophical ideas were appropriated for their feminist arguments. In addition, *Women Philosophers* could be used as a component—read as a pair with a male contemporary or individually—of either a course on eighteenth century philosophy (with the chapters on Mary Wollstonecraft and Catharine Macaulay) or a course on medieval philosophy (with the chapters on Christine de Pisan and Mechthild).

As all the women philosophers discussed in *Women Philosophers* wrote on moral philosophy, it could be of use for a course in moral philosophy either as an addition to a mainstream history of moral philosophy course or one that is focused on feminist ethics. *Women Philosophers* can offer an alternative picture of the history of moral philosophy (although it would be a mistake to think of these women philosophers as forming a tradition). It can offer a challenge to the received picture by pointing to the biases that underlie the construction of what I call the dominant model of moral philosophy. In the book I demonstrate not only how the ideals of the dominant model—such as impartiality or universality—reflect the concerns of certain groups and are thus not objective or neutral, but also that these ideals require certain modes or forms for their written expression or presentation which are then designated as properly philosophical. Moreover, I argue that these forms themselves—because of the content they can best express—can serve to reinforce the dominant model.

In addition, for a feminist ethics course, *Women Philosophers* does not just simply offer the possibility of foremothers for feminist theorizing. It shows how their work could be of potential interest to modern day theorizing. On a general level, their work can provide material for discussions within modern day feminist ethics about the existence of women's moral voices and the revaluing of previously devalued aspects of human moral life. On a more specific level, we can find parallels with present day concerns in Eliot's emphasis on concreteness for morality, or the partiality and particularity in Christine de Pisan's work. Yet the work of these historical philosophers can also challenge theorizing in modern day feminist ethics. For instance, it is not just that philosophers like Wollstonecraft, Eliot, and Mechthild place the emotions as central to their moral thought, they also recognize that such a move requires a reconceiving of the emotions. For example, on Wollstonecraft's account of sensibility it is not merely a feeling, but is necessarily connected with the liberation of women and the improvement of society.

Women Philosophers could provide important primary material for the type of women and philosophy course that engages with questions such as do women philosophize differently from men?; is there a women's philosophical voice or voices?; and are there issues that are of particular interest to women philosophers? Typically, such courses pair texts by male philosophers *about* women with texts *by* women philosophers.

Women Philosophers could provide a third element to this type of course through its detailed analysis of the arguments of some key women philosophers. Moreover in the cases that there does appear to be something different about philosophy done by women, it allows further questions to be brought to bear on this issue: in what ways such differences can be attributed to the social circumstances within which these women philosophers were writing.

Needless to say, the classroom use of *Women Philosophers* need not be restricted to the discipline of philosophy. It could be a component of women's studies courses. In particular, it would be of interest to courses in women's literature as four of the five philosophers covered wrote fiction or poetry. And while Christine de Pisan, Wollstonecraft and Eliot are often mainstays of such courses, Mechthild would be an unusual addition. *Women Philosophers* could also be of interest to courses in the history of feminism as it engages with germinal feminist or proto-feminist figures such as Wollstonecraft, Macaulay, and Christine de Pisan. In both these cases, the questions I raise about the prevalence of women philosophers writing in certain forms and the devaluation of those forms would be important.

Perhaps the central way to make classroom use of this book effective is to capitalize on the fact that this material has been previously unavailable whether literally or because it has been defined as non-philosophical. Students are often intrigued and excited by the newness of this material, and by the fact that there is often so little information available on these women philosophers. Thus an important component of classes that include books like *Women Philosophers* can be an independent research project. This can be research on a particular philosopher, or on the connections between a philosopher and her male contemporaries. It can be research on the social limitations on women writing during a particular historical period, or a comparison of their work in philosophy with women's contributions in other disciplines and areas such as the arts or sciences.

Ultimately, I think *Women Philosophers* is of use in the classroom setting because it introduces the work of some women philosophers in such a way that we can see their potential to be part of our "living" philosophical conversation. They are neither musty curiosities nor figures to be resurrected merely to "set the record straight."

Notes

1. Mary Ellen Waithe, *A History of Women Philosophers*, 4 Vols. (Dordrecht: Kluwer, 1987–1995).
2. Mary Ellen Waithe, "On Not Teaching the History of Philosophy." *Hypatia* Vol. 4. No. 1: 132–8.

1

Introduction

Preliminaries

Perhaps the best way to provide an introduction to this work is to start with an account of how it began. Inspired by Mary Ellen Waithe's four-volume work *A History of Women Philosophers*, I wanted to learn more about our philosophical foremothers; and I wondered what, if anything, their work may have to offer modern theorizing in feminist ethics. I decided to interpret a varied selection of moral philosophers from our all but forgotten past that would both contribute to our understanding of their work and perhaps even encourage other philosophers to interpretive work of their own. Yet as I began reading, my philosophical toe was stubbed time and time again on a particular aspect of the work of these women philosophers, for the particular works that I was interested in took the form of novels, poetry, or letters.[1] Specifically, Catharine Macaulay wrote using the epistolary genre, Mary Wollstonecraft and George Eliot both wrote fiction, Mechthild of Magdeburg wrote poetry, and Christine de Pisan wrote allegory. Moreover it seemed that a significant number of women philosophers from our past employed these, or similar, forms. But as a philosopher from what is typically called the Anglo-American tradition, I did not have the analytic and conceptual tools immediately at hand to read philosophy in these other forms of writing. I had been trained to read purely for argumentative content and to discuss style and form only if and when they obscured comprehension. Like many of us, I am most comfortable with what Alasdair MacIntyre has called "that most eccentric latecomer of all philosophical genre forms, the article contributed to a professional journal" (MacIntyre 1995, 32).

The moral philosophical tradition within which I (like many of us from English and American universities) have been trained to work stresses the impartial, the coolly reasoned, and the universally applicable. But novels, letters, and poetry, by their very nature, are often more intimate, more personal, more particular. Indeed during the seventeenth and eigh-

1

teenth centuries certain collections of letters written by women were popular simply because of the voyeuristic thrill of reading someone else's private correspondence. Some novels and poetry may seem uncomfortably personal to those of us used to dealing with the abstract and impersonal arguments of the type of modern moral philosophy that is influenced by such philosophers as Kant and Mill. Indeed, it may even seem that these forms of writing are more appropriate to describe the particular, concrete nature of human emotions and daily life, rather than to give an account of the abstract, universal truths we are supposed to aim for in philosophy.

From the standpoint of this tradition of moral philosophy then, it appears that the work of women philosophers which takes the form of novels, letters, or poetry can have little philosophical significance for us; perhaps it can never be more than a curiosity. Specifically, they can never be forms of the philosophical genre; and I shall use the term "form" throughout as a "catch-all" term for the types of work I am discussing. Yet surely we would like to have at least the opportunity of including the work of some of our philosophical foremothers in our future explorations of feminist ethics. I realized that if we are to work towards including the work of these philosophers properly, then one thing we must do is to look further into the reasons for the assignment of non-philosophical status to certain forms. Something that is all the more pressing in the light of the fact that the employment of these forms seems to be prevalent in the work of women philosophers from the history of philosophy. And while I do not intend to argue that male philosophers did not use these forms, I suspect that the issue of the non-philosophical status of these forms may be a more pressing concern for work of women philosophers, for it seems possible that the sex of an author can get played into the way a work is initially perceived and categorized.

The Exclusion

It is unlikely that the exclusion of women from the realm of philosophy in one way or another is anything novel. Even though it is historically irresponsible to make blanket statements about the sorts of social pressures that may have restricted the ability of the women philosophers I study or their contemporaries to write philosophy, there can be little doubt that they would have been limited in their access to educational or publishing opportunities. They could also have expected to encounter hostile public reception of their work (as Mary Wollstonecraft did), and restrictions in the arenas—both disciplinary and actual—within which they could express their opinions. These social pressures may well have (directly or indirectly) informed the choice of form by these philosophers, although I would want to stress here that there is no essential connection here between form and sex. I find illuminating here Waithe's suggestion that "social pressures sometimes acted against women writing at all, sometimes especially against more philosophic kinds of writing. . . . As a result, women writers may have deliberately chosen an oblique approach, and this may be one motive for some of the philosophic forms they adopted" (Waithe 1989, 2, xxx).

However, even though there may have been social pressures that at times affected the range of forms that women employed, this does not mean that the forms they did use were not deliberately chosen, or that they were not conscious of the form they were using. As we shall see, this is far from the case with the work of George Eliot or Christine de Pisan. Furthermore in looking at the history of women writing, we need to be careful of the claim that certain types of work—novels poetry, etc.—have always had questionable philosophical status. For if such a claim were true, it would support the notion that the philosophical status of a form is a "given." In the later part of the eighteenth century and throughout the nineteenth there was a distinction between "feminine" and "masculine" genres of written discourse. The feminine genre included novels, letters, verse, and other similar "light" work. These lighter genres were considered suitable for the subject matter of interest to women and to their weaker intellectual capabilities. But despite this division it is important to notice that ultimately it was "the *sex* of the author [that] played a fundamental role in determining the import of a particular text for readers: women venturing into topics and genres gendered masculine were uniformly condemned; men venturing into topics and genres gendered feminine were seen as conferring new dignity and seriousness on them" (Kelly 1993, 12, italics used for emphasis).

However my interest in rediscovering women philosophers is not an enterprise in the history of philosophy in this way. My focus is not on tracing the history of the exclusion—and the extent of this exclusion—of women from philosophy, nor on how to rewrite the history of our discipline in order to include their work. This is not to say that such work, for example Eileen O'Neill's "Disappearing Ink," is not of the utmost importance to the study of women philosophers from the history of philosophy. Nor is it to forget the fact that we are inheritors of a tradition that was—at least in part—created through an exclusion of the work of women philosophers. But my interest is in what an interpretation of the work of some of these philosophers can offer modern ethical, specifically feminist, theorizing. I would like them to become part of our modern dialogue, for in this way they can become revalued or "rediscovered" not just through an interpretation that demonstrates the quality of philosophical thought but through putting this thought (or at least some of it) to use.

Yet in order to do this I realized that my first step would more often than not be to justify how and in what ways some of the work I was interested in interpreting was *in actuality* philosophical work. Initially there did not seem to be any serious obstacle to my goal of interpreting the work of my five chosen philosophers. If they were truly works of philosophy then I—as an objective critical reader—had been trained to separate out the arguments from their problematic forms and begin my interpretation from there. But despite bringing all my objectivity and critical thinking skills to bear on some of these works, this approach did not allow me to deal with the type of case where the form *is* part of the argument of the work. A case, for example, where the self-reflection or emotion that the actual form (and not just the content) of a work produces in the reader is part of its overall argument, seems not just difficult, but impossible to analyze as a work of philosophy in this way.

Yet I did not want to conclude from this that work of this type must automatically be categorized as "non-philosophical" or, at best, as containing "a few interesting insights." Instead I decided to question what lay behind this apparent philosophical failure of certain forms to be part of the philosophical genre. I realized that it is our modern way of drawing boundaries between disciplines, of having fixed limits to the philosophical genre, that can prevent us appreciating and understanding the works of women philosophers such as Catharine Macaulay, George Eliot, and the others considered in this book. I began to understand that this classification of some forms as part of the philosophical genre, and the exclusion of others, is not a "given" or somehow independent of modern conceptions of what moral philosophy is.

But I further realized that a discussion of these limitations, and an argument for the philosophical status of the forms within which these philosophers wrote, does not simply entail mandating that traditional Anglo-American moral philosophy should be opened up to include these other types of form. For I began to see the connections between what forms "count" as philosophical forms or as part of the philosophical genre and this model of moral philosophy that is dominant in modern moral theorizing. And I started to see that these connections are constructed in such a way as to prevent the inclusion of certain other types of forms as philosophical writing. I realized therefore that the first part of my task in interpreting my chosen philosophers would be to expose those connections in order to show *how* and *why* certain forms become excluded—and will remain so—on this model of moral philosophy.

To say that the exclusion of certain forms from this model is simply because they are not "philosophical" is to beg the question. It is, moreover, to imply that their exclusion is somehow value-neutral, or objective. This is to remain willfully ignorant of the biases that have underpinned the creation of our Western ethical tradition. It is to assume—mistakenly—that the choice of one type of form, rather than another, as having philosophical status is somehow value-neutral. I believe that the devaluation or exclusion of these forms can be traced back to the male bias in what I shall call the dominant model of moral philosophy.

The Dominant Model
of Moral Philosophy

Thus, the first step in examining how and why these forms are excluded as properly philosophical forms is to get clear about the content and structure of what I have been referring to as the dominant model of moral philosophy.[2] By this I mean the model that has been dominant (particularly in the twentieth century) in our moral theorizing, and my purpose in calling it a "model" rather than a "view" or "conception" is to draw attention to its components and construction.[3] To call it the dominant model is not to say that there have been no alternatives or critiques; rather its dominance, to use Margaret Urban Walker's succinct phrasing, "shows in its prevalence in shaping professional work and training, its embodiment in the structures of courses and texts, its secure seating in prestigious institutions, and its conspicuous presentation in central venues of publication and discussion" (Walker 1998b, 18).

While this model offers a way of distinguishing the realm of the philosophical from the non-philosophical, it is no one theory. It is, however, possible to identify certain central features of this model, features that can be found underpinning much of contemporary moral theorizing in, for example, neo-Kantian, utilitarian, and contractarian theories. There have been many contemporary challenges and alternatives for a variety of ethical perspectives to this model, but there has not been complete agreement, even among feminist philosophers, on what features are problematic and why. For the purposes of my discussion, I am focusing just on the structure or construction of this model and the interconnections between its different components, as well as on the apparent male-bias inherent in this model.

This dominant model of moral philosophy operates on certain basic assumptions about what is included in the field of morality—and thus the subject of moral philosophy.[4] Its foundational assumption is that we can state both neutrally and in advance what morality consists in, although—as Iris Murdoch has argued—this definition of the initial area of study is in fact framed by our moral judgments (see Murdoch, 1956). This initial delineation of the sphere of the "moral" from which the philosophical task of traditional Western ethics begins has historically been that which reflects the moral concerns of men (or a particular class of men). This bias should come as little surprise given the ways that, historically, it has been denied that women have the capacity for full moral agency; or the ways that spheres associated with women, such as childcare, have been devalued. Nor should it come as a surprise that this initial delineation of the sphere of the moral has the *appearance* of being value neutral. For, given the way in which this exclusion of women and their moral concerns has taken place, there appears to be no other suitable alternative.

Although it may be more subtle or implicit, this bias is still present today with the dominant model's initial delineation of the scope of morality. Even though the exclusion of women and women's experience is not as explicit as on some historical moral theories, their exclusion is implicit in that the moral concerns and activities that make up the initial sphere of morality are typically not central—and can even be quite alien—for the moral world of many women. For the dominant model places an emphasis on concerns associated with activities in the public sphere and on concerns associated with the "social roles, and character ideals associated with socially advantaged men," such as administrative roles and ideals of justice (Walker 1998a, 364). This initial scope of morality reflects the concerns of these types of roles: dealing with unknown others, with one's peers, or with people with whom one has a social or professional relationship; as well as concerns about the moral responsibilities of these roles: decision-making that may have to apply to more than one case and of providing justification for self and others of those decisions. These are the sorts of concerns that lend themselves well to being addressed or dealt with through the creation and use of sets of rules, principles, or beliefs—albeit, perhaps, unrefined and unsystematized—for agent behavior.

Given this initial delineation of the concerns or field of morality, the specific theoretical task set for the moral philosopher, and the resulting characteristics of the philosophical theory produced, become clear. The typical task of the moral philosopher is then to formulate and test this moral data and produce a systematized body of moral propositions, concepts, and principles that together offer the moral agent a rationalized moral theory that s/he can use to guide her/his moral choices, and against which the agent can refine or revise his/her previously held (unreflective) moral views. This will require not just that the moral data is clarified, but that it is reduced and abstracted from its original format, for in this way the principles drawn from it can be used by all agents.

This model will then place a reliance on certain capacities both for the moral theorizing of the philosopher and for the moral decision-making of the agent. Whatever shape the resulting theory takes—perhaps one founded on a supreme principle of morality, or a system of rules that any rational person will follow—the moral philosopher will have arrived at this theory through a certain type of rational scrutiny and analysis of the original moral data, for example a logical analysis of its interrelations. In order for the moral agent to use this theory to make specific moral decisions or to solve concrete cases, the agent needs to be able to pick out the general features of these decisions or cases. This isolation of these general features is important for it makes these decisions and cases "theory ready": it has removed extraneous information that might serve to hinder the proper application of the appropriate theoretical moral elements such as moral rules or principles. Essentially, the "moral" has been separated off from the "non-moral." Both the analysis of the general features, and the application of the appropriate theoretical element to guide decision-making or to resolve concrete cases, require specifically rational capacities on the part of the agent for assessment, derivation, deduction, etc.

Given this reliance of the dominant model on these types of capacity for the practical moral life of the agent, it is evident that notions of the sphere of the properly rational have little or no place for the involvement of emotional responses or certain kinds of imaginative understanding in moral decision-making. On this type of dualistic division between emotion and reason, these types of emotional response and understanding—even such superficially "good" ones such as a sympathetic understanding of others—can affect or even distort the processes of the making of rational (and thus moral) judgments. Even in cases where the moral agent is required, as for example on R. M. Hare's account, to have some kind of imaginative identification with others and to acquire their actual preferences in order to make a universal prescription, this identification is accomplished not through some sort of sympathetic involvement with the actual preferences of others; but instead through an abstract calculation of the idealized preferences of others: the preferences they would have if they were thinking rationally.[5]

According to this dominant model, when an agent makes a particular moral choice, or solves a particular moral problem, this choice or solution needs to be applicable to all people in all similar situations. Once the general features of the choice or problem have been isolated, whatever decision or solution is generated by the moral theory in one case will apply to all similar cases. Indeed this is one of the main aims of the reduction or abstraction of the original moral data. To say that, for example, one general principle counts in one case, but another counts in an identical case, conflicts with the consistency and rationality that are paradigmatic of moral theorizing on the dominant model. This universality of both theory and practice connects back to the need for an impersonal approach in moral activity, and the (rational) capacities needed for such an approach, for our love or hatred of others can create partiality in our actions towards them.

While these theoretical features such as impartiality, universality, sys-
tematization, and abstraction may not be problematic in themselves,
making them central ideals lends itself to a certain picture of the proper
way of doing moral philosophy. Walker calls this picture "theoretical-ju-
ridical," for the activities of "the" moral agent are like those of a judge or
a manager making judgments in legal or administrative contexts; judgments that are law-like, impartial, and principled (see Walker 1998b). She
argues that this picture "suggests either the reciprocal positions of par-
ticipants or competitors in a rule-structured practice, or the positions of
those with authority to apply law or policy impartially to cases . . . positions and operations like this [however] characterize roles, offices, and
activities that are historically reserved to men in Western societies"
(Walker 1998a, 364).

This picture of moral philosophy, in its turn, reaffirms the validity of
these theoretical features and these central concerns for doing moral philosophy. When this type of theory is applied to practical moral concerns,
it applies most successfully to concerns related to male-associated
spheres of activity and interest. An issue such as our particular love for
and our relationship to our children does not have the features or characteristics that allow a useful or interesting application (or perhaps even
any application at all) of this type of theory. The conclusion can thus be
drawn that this issue, and others like it, are not properly part of significant moral discourse. The narrowness, exclusivity, and self-affirming nature of the dominant model of moral philosophy finds its source in its initial delineation of the scope of morality. This phenomenon is something
that is brought to our attention (albeit as part of a non-feminist argument) by Murdoch in "Vision and Choice in Morality," when she states
that a "narrow or partial selection of phenomena" of this kind "may suggest particular techniques which will in turn seem to lend support to that
particular selection; and then a circle is formed out of which it is hard to
break" (Murdoch 1956, 33).

Philosophical Genre and
the Dominant Model

Just as the ideals, theoretical features, and objectives of the dominant
model of moral philosophy are not objective, neutral, or ahistorical, what
are to count as philosophical genre forms are not a neutral "given," or
even an ahistorical "given." Instead the ideals of the dominant model of
moral philosophy get played out in the designation of certain forms as
"philosophical" or "non-philosophical." Such aspects of moral theorizing
as, for example, impartiality, universality, or rule formulation, require
certain modes or forms of written expression and presentation; forms

that are suited to the expression of the moral concerns and judgments of (to use Walker's image again) judges and administrators. The treatise, the essay, and—above all—the modern journal article would seem to be best suited for the dissemination of the moral philosophy of the dominant model and are thus designated "philosophical." Indeed these types of philosophical presentation are so common that many of us may not have even questioned this designation.

The expected—and required—response of the reader to a work of moral philosophy on the dominant model is a concern to "develop certain ideas, to work out their consequences and systematic relations, to see their rational justification. The training a reader of philosophy needs will develop in him the capacity to grasp, formulate, and examine critically the philosophical ideas present in a text" (Diamond 1995, 370). In order to achieve this, we must not allow the way the author says something (and thus the author him or herself) to distract us from what s/he is saying. Form and style must be separable from content and only become a subject for discussion when they obscure comprehension. On the dominant model, the literary skills of the author do not have any bearing on the cogency of his or her arguments, as Cora Diamond states, "Failure of style as *philosophical* failure has then no place" (Diamond 1995, 372).

But it is not that these forms are designated as "philosophical" simply because that is what they are, or even just because they are the best suited to the philosophical theorizing of the dominant model. Certain aspects of these forms *themselves* reinforce or uphold the ideals of the dominant model, as well as having their philosophical status reinforced by it. The ideal of the independent, impersonal moral agent making uniform judgments from an impartial point of view is embodied in the objective critical reader who is not swayed by the particular personality of an author or their rhetorical blandishments. The ideal of philosophical argument as rational, deductive, and logically analytic is the standard by which the cogency of argument in a text is measured; if this argument includes or relies on literary skill then—by implication—it includes appeals to the emotions or the imagination. For on the dominant model, the aim of moral philosophy is to eliminate extraneous information that can be a source of error, not to include such information by insisting on the potential philosophical significance of the presentation of a work. Indeed the concern on the dominant model would be that such an insistence can make the reader vulnerable to errors in judgment.

In contrast, non-philosophical status is assigned to poetry, novels, and letters on this model. But we must recognize that this designation is not because they are somehow unphilosophical in themselves, nor is it simply because these forms would be unsuitable for presentation of the sort of work done within the theories of the dominant model, although it is true that most administrators are not given to wax poetic. These types of form seem to be at odds with the dominant model because in their own way they can be seen to uphold the importance of, or give validity to, certain moral concerns that are devalued on the dominant model. For example, they are open to the possibilities of being more intimate, more personal, indeed they may not only include the emotions of the author, but involve them on the part of the reader. What we must recognize is that what may appear to be "the" philosophical genre is in fact just one possibility, and I intend to show that there are other possibilities throughout this work.

Thus it would appear that not only are there connections between what forms "count" as forms of the philosophical genre and the model of moral philosophy dominant in modern theorizing, but that these two notions are mutually reinforcing. If so, then in order to offer interpretations of work that employs forms that have been given "non-philosophical" status, we shall need to question not only this "non-philosophical" designation, but this model *itself*. We must ultimately be prepared to offer criticism of accepted approaches to philosophical analysis and the boundaries of philosophical investigation. Yet once we begin to break out of the circle by questioning how we do moral philosophy, then we shall also start to question what moral philosophy properly is. Ultimately we must question whether the model of philosophical investigation of a text that comes from the dominant model of moral philosophy is the only model, a questioning that constitutes a challenge to this conception of moral philosophy itself, for our model of assessment is bound up with what we take philosophy to be.

In order to offer these criticisms, and to ask these questions, I need to do more than simply discuss in the abstract the philosophical status of certain forms. Instead I need to examine actual work that raises these issues. Obviously an examination of the "standard" philosophical genre, while it may show the reasons why these forms are given philosophical status, will not demonstrate the problems with this designation. Rather I need to examine works that can call into question their supposedly non-philosophical form, and thus ultimately the dominant model of moral itself. Thus I focus on interpreting work that can specifically show other possibilities for the philosophical genre, as well as the way that these possibilities can form a critique of the dominant model of moral philosophy. And it is, therefore, through my interpretation that I offer my arguments; although I want to stress that this does not mean that the work can only be done by interpreting the philosophical writing of women philosophers. In this way we can see how the "rediscovery" of the five women philosophers I have chosen can be of importance for modern feminist ethical theorizing. Although, and this is something I make clear in the concluding chapter, this does not mean that I believe that their interest is limited to this use.

**Five Forms,
Five Philosophers**

There were many other philosophers that I would have liked to have included in this work, Sor Juana Ines de la Cruz, Hildegard of Bingen, Marie le Jars de Gournay, Catherine of Siena, to name but a few. It may also have been interesting to do a comparison with the work of philosophers who did write in more traditional philosophical forms. However the central aim of this book is to offer interpretations of the work of specific moral philosophers that—in virtue of its form—can be used to present a challenge to what I have been calling our modern dominant model or view of moral philosophy. To this end, I focus on interpreting five women moral philosophers, each of whom has written a work in a different form that poses particular questions and challenges to this dominant model of moral philosophy. The essence of my approach is to interpret their work and to show that despite—or even because of—its form it is philosophical, and how an exclusion of this work is a loss to the philosophical enterprise; as well as to offer different possibilities for what "the philosophical" can mean.

Rather than deal with these philosophers chronologically, I chose to place them in an order such that the arguments and conclusions of one chapter build on those of previous chapters, thus presenting an increasing challenge to our dominant moral view. It is important to stress at this stage that although I create an argument based on the work of these five philosophers, each chapter must be recognized as an individual unit. These philosophers are as different as they are similar, and, more importantly, I do not want mistakenly to give the impression that they are part of some kind of philosophical tradition.

The first step in my argument is to show quite simply that we cannot ignore philosophical genre, or the issues raised by it. In the case of *Letters on Education*, the little known philosophical work of the eighteenth-century historian Catharine Macaulay, it is quite clear what forces have led to the claim that this work does not contain a sustained philosophical argument. I suggest that the neglect and apparent misinterpretations of the *Letters* would seem to be underpinned by assumptions generated by the form of the work. It would appear that because this work was written in the form of personal advice or instructional letters to a female friend, it has not been considered to be able to contain any systematic philosophical argumentation or theory. Instead it has been considered that the central philosophical content of the *Letters* is mainly confined to its contribution to the Enlightenment debate on education; specifically Macaulay's work is considered distinctive within this debate because of the way that she outlined a system of practical education that was for both sexes.

I then show that a supposedly "non-philosophical" form such as personal advice letters need not prevent the work from containing a self-contained, sustained, and systematized philosophical thesis. Once we have moved past our expectations (and prejudices) of what form a moral philosophical plea for the equality of women should take, we can see that Macaulay's work clearly contains a deliberate and fully worked out systematized argument for the equality of women based on her ethicoreligious principles. Macaulay's true philosophical contribution then, is not as a participant in the Enlightenment debate on education, but as the writer who predated Wollstonecraft in offering a self-contained, sustained argument for the equality of women (albeit a rather rarified one).

If what is to count as "philosophical" genre forms is not a "given," then we need to understand how they become designated as such, and this is something that I start to bring out with an examination of the allegorical work *The Book of the City of Ladies* by the medieval writer Christine de Pisan. For Macaulay's *Letters on Education*, once we get past our expectations of philosophical form, it is non-problematic to produce a philosophical reading of her argument for the equality of women. In the case of *The Book of the City of Ladies*, however, we cannot "get past" the form; it is part of Christine's moral "defense" of women itself. If we ignore the allegorical form of this work we shall not only neglect important aspects of Christine's moral thought, but fail to recognize how the form of the work is—for her—not incidental, but intimately connected to its moral truth.

The allegorical city, like all allegories, works on different levels. As a symbol in an allegory the city means something both literally and as a trope. Thus it is both a city or community, and it signifies—as I demonstrate—the possibility of women's moral agency. I show that de Pisan is not simply presenting arguments for the moral capacities of women, she is also inviting her readers into the allegory of the city in order that they too can develop their capacity for morality. In short, to read the book is to be aided in the way that the inhabitants are aided by the protective walls of the city. What this then means is that ultimately the philosophical success or failure of the arguments of *The Book of the City of Ladies* will not only depend on Christine's literary abilities, but also on the way the reader approaches her allegory. In this way Christine shows us possibilities for philosophical readership and authorship other than those of the dominant model of moral philosophy.

As we shall see with Wollstonecraft, Eliot, and Mechthild, other forms and other moral views may require different types of involvement from both reader and author. However, from the standpoint of the dominant model, a text which has its form as part of its content, and that thus requires a particular way of reading it, does not fall within the boundaries of "the philosophical." What we need to recognize is that this is not because the allegorical form of *The Book of the City of Ladies* is "unphilosophical" *per se*, but because of the way that the moral ideals of the dominant model get played out in the categorization of form.

In the following chapter, I show that even when a woman philosopher is known for her writing of a "standard" philosophical treatise, this can still create problems for interpretations of her work. Mary Wollstonecraft's *A Vindication of the Rights of Woman* is viewed—due to our current philosophical interests—as an Enlightenment treatise. Unfortunately, however, this categorization has meant that significant aspects of her moral thought, as well as her other works (in particular her fiction), have been neglected or misunderstood. Central to Wollstonecraft's view of morality, and thus central to *A Vindication of the Rights of Woman*, is a complex notion of a genuine, non-artificial sensibility. A reading of all of Wollstonecraft's works shows how, for her, this sensibility becomes intertwined with the creative imagination, moral and social progress, and the equality of women. Yet this notion of sensibility is not simply the subject of her work, it is also a part of her work in the sense that it is expressed through the form of her work. In this case form meaning a particular style of writing, a style of writing that is in evidence in *A Vindication of the Rights of Woman*.

But in order to accept this role played by sensibility in Wollstonecraft's philosophical thought, we are required to reconsider—not only our preconceptions that she was a writer of Enlightenment treatises—but also the way we treat philosophical arguments in a text. If we treat the complex issue of the sentiment of sensibility and its expression simply as another argumentative point, or as just a tool in political polemic, we then run the risk of giving too narrow an interpretation of Wollstonecraft's work. It becomes increasingly clear that we must be able to allow for the fact that sensibility is not simply argued for in her work, but it is inextricably in her writing and thought. But in order to do this we must smudge the boundaries—as Wollstonecraft herself does—between creative or imaginative writing on the one hand and reasoned or philosophical writing on the other. This will obviously require us to consider not only where the boundaries of moral philosophy lie, but how clear cut they can be.

I continue with a fuller exploration of some of the issues raised in the discussion of Wollstonecraft with an examination of the work of George Eliot, the nineteenth-century British novelist who has been described as a "philosopher whose genre was fiction" (Waithe 1991, 3: 255). What interests me here is how this has been understood, because it sheds light on the expectations of philosophy that come from the dominant model, the narrow boundaries that this model draws around the discipline, and the way these curtail our abilities to read the text.

Much of the work done on the philosophical aspects of Eliot's novels has been aimed at drawing out an explicit philosophical theory from Eliot's fiction; indeed it is frequently claimed that there is a deliberate reproduction on Eliot's part of some or all of the theory of an "established" philosopher such as Spinoza or Comte. To treat Eliot's novels in this way is to focus on the philosophical accuracy of Eliot's reproduction of a particular philosopher's ideas, a question which calls for an evaluation in terms of (among other things) logical consistency and accuracy. Yet the fictional "arguments" and "evidence" used to support the novel's theorizing are, by their very nature, unable to withstand such an examination. Such an approach will ultimately ignore much of the moral view expressed in her novels, specifically it will ignore the importance of the connection between what Eliot says with the way she says it.

This type of philosophical assessment of a work is not the only one possible, nor need it be the only one that is valuable or informative. Eliot's own account of the moral value of literature can provide us with a way of reading Eliot's novels for their philosophical aspects; a way of reading that can produce a fruitful account of Eliot's moral thought. Once we have recognized that there is no one predetermined approach that counts as a "philosophical assessment" of a work, then we are in a position to see that it is where the boundaries of moral philosophy are drawn that generates a particular view of what is to count as philosophical assessment, a view which—in its turn—reinforces these boundaries.

The final philosopher I consider is Mechthild of Magdeburg and her mystical work *The Flowing Light of the Godhead*. The central problem raised by the form of this work is how we are to deal with the ambiguity of its authorship, for Mechthild claims that it is God who wrote the book: it takes the form of a message from God. However the book is (obviously) also written by Mechthild, and accordingly takes the form of a spiritual and moral autobiography. Even more problematically, God claims in *The Flowing Light* that the book somehow contains him, and the physical book itself represents him. Through a study of this problematic form we find a way to understand how the book can be all these things. Yet if the author or the authorial voice of *The Flowing Light* is not tied into an individualistic concept of the self, this brings with it interesting epistemological implications, something that we find resolved when we understand it as part of a systematic and consistent moral epistemology at work in *The Flowing Light*.

Both this way of writing and its underlying concept of knowledge are no doubt somewhat alien to the modern philosopher. And in order to give coherence to these notions, we must recognize the connections between Mechthild's moral epistemology and the conceptual scheme of her world. Similarly if we find this claim problematic or incoherent, we must recognize that this may be due to a clash of her conceptual scheme with ours, rather than any fundamental incoherence in Mechthild's writing or her moral epistemology. While it would be nonsensical to try to replace our scheme with hers, an examination of it is useful for it illuminates the contingency of our own definitions of philosophy.

In the conclusion I pull together the different ways that what I have been calling the dominant model of moral philosophy fails to deal with the work of these women philosophers, and I isolate the common failures of interpretation. I contend that these common failures are produced by the narrowness of the paradigmatic approach of this model to philosophical investigation, and I have focused on the way that this gets played out in the particular area of philosophical genre. I consider the significance of this narrowness and suggest that it goes beyond the mere exclusion of certain philosophical work on the grounds of its presentation. This narrowness of approach stems directly from the original—problematic—view of the moral world of the dominant model. Finally, although my focus is specifically on the issue of philosophical genre, I do conclude by briefly indicating the ways in which the recovery of the philosophical thought of certain women moral philosophers has the potential to contribute to feminist ethical thought.

Notes

1. My focus is on philosophical genre, and I am interested in what types of work fall into this class. Accordingly, I shall use "form" as a catch-all term for these types of work so as to avoid confusion.

2. I draw the use of this term from Virginia Held who writes of "the dominant" moral tradition (Held, 1999).

3. It is tempting to call this model "masculine," however, Alison Jaggar has shown that it is more productive to talk of the Western tradition in terms of male-bias (see Jaggar 1991).

4. Much of my account has been drawn from my thinking through of Cora Diamond's work on moral philosophy, in particular "Anything but Argument" and "Having a Rough Story About What Moral Philosophy Is," both in Diamond

(1995). Although I am not certain that she will be completely happy with the use to which her work has been put.

5. See Bernard Williams, *Ethics and the Limits of Philosophy*. (Cambridge, Mass.: Harvard University Press, 1985).

2

Catharine Macaulay's
Letters on Education: What Constitutes a
Philosophical System

Before I begin to show specifically how what I have been calling the modern dominant model of moral philosophy excludes certain forms of philosophical writing, as well as the loss to our philosophical endeavors that would accompany such an exclusion, I want to demonstrate a simpler point. I want to question the foundational assumption that a sustained philosophical thesis or argument can only take place within certain types of form such as the treatise or essay. I do this through a questioning of its corollary that a work that does not take this type of "philosophical" form cannot be a sustained work of philosophy. Perhaps at best, this corollary continues, this type of work can offer a few philosophical insights. In this way, therefore, this chapter is somewhat different from the other chapters in the book, as my focus is on the expectations of its philosophical content produced by the epistolary form of Catharine Macaulay's work *Letters on Education*. Indeed at the risk of belaboring my point, I spend time in the introductory pages to this chapter giving a lengthy overview of modern commentaries on Macaulay's work, analyzing and, at times, speculating about the assumptions that drive their interpretations.

It would appear that these commentators have assumed that because the *Letters* is in the form of personal advice or instructional letters to a female friend (a genre typically associated with women authors), it cannot contain any systematized philosophical thought. This assumption seems driven not only by the actual structure of the work, but also by the associations produced by the sex of the author. However, once we have become aware of these problematic assumptions and associations, it is easy to read Macaulay's *Letters on Education*—despite its non-standard form for philosophy—*as* a work of moral philosophy. I believe a proper interpretation of Macaulay's work is important, not simply because of the way that she offers a sustained, self-contained argument for the equality of women based on her ethicoreligious system, but also because this argument predates Mary Wollstonecraft's polemical argument for female equality in *A Vindication of the Rights of Woman*.

Biography

Catharine Macaulay was born in 1731 in Kent as Catharine Sawbridge. As there is little biographical information available about her early years, it is hard to know how much education she had as a child.[1] What is certainly clear is that by her twenties she was well read in history and philosophy. Indeed it is interesting to note that in an account of Macaulay at age 26, she is described as "having formed a most extraordinary system" from "the Spartan laws, the Roman politics, the philosophy of Epicurus, and the wit of St. Evremond" (quoted in Hill 1992, 11). She married George Macaulay in 1760, and in 1763 she published the first volume of her best known work: *The History of England, from the Accession of James I to that of the Brunswick Line*. The reaction to the first volume was one of enthusiasm, something at which we should not be surprised as not only was her *History* seen as a Whig answer to Hume's history, but "it was the first republican history of the seventeenth century based on an extensive knowledge of hitherto unused tracts of the 1640's and 1650's" (Hill 1992, 30). The final—eighth—volume was finished twenty years later. The end of Macaulay's period of fame coincided with her second marriage to William Graham in 1778, a marriage that accorded scandal and horror, for not only was there as class difference (he was a surgeon's mate), but he was 26 years her junior. However, according to Bridget Hill in *The Republican Virago*, Macaulay's reputation was already fading for her Whig supporters, for the later volumes clearly demonstrated her republicanism and more radical political views.

   Macaulay also wrote the first volume of another proposed two-volume work: *History of England from the Revolution to the Present Time in a Series of Letters to a Friend* (1778). It is written in the form of a letters with a conversational tone, and it also signals a similar change in Macaulay's style of writing in her other work. While this other history drew criticism both for its scholarship, and its lack of in-depth analysis, it is interesting to note that it was not criticized for lacking a sustained thesis. Macaulay also wrote political pamphlets: *Loose Remarks on Certain Positions to be Found in Mr. Hobbes's 'Philosophical Rudiments of Government and Society'* (1767); and *Observations on a Pamphlet Entitled 'Thoughts on the Cause of the Present Discontents'* (1770); *Short Sketch of a Democratic Form of Government in a Letter to Signor Paoli* (1769); and *Address to the People of England, Scot-*

land, and Ireland on the Present Important Crisis of Affairs (1775). Of these, the first two were published anonymously, perhaps because politics was an even greater male preserve than history, and Macaulay could only truly venture into it once her scholarship had been acknowledged. She also wrote a defense against contemporary attacks on literary copyright: *A Modest Plea for the Property of Copyright* (1774), and a response to Archbishop King's reconciliation of the existence of evil with the notion of a benevolent and omnipotent God: *Treatise on the Immutability of Moral Truth* (1783).

Letters on Education

Letters on Education—Macaulay's only work of philosophy—was published just five years before *A Vindication of the Rights of Woman*, and the work is an acknowledged influence on Mary Wollstonecraft; indeed Wollstonecraft herself states that when she first thought of writing the *Vindication*, she "anticipated Mrs. Macaulay's approbation" (Wollstonecraft 1983, 207).[2] In the form of "advice" letters to a female friend or student who Macaulay names "Hortensia," Macaulay discusses the subjects of equal education, government, and morality. It seems to be generally accepted by commentators on Wollstonecraft that Macaulay's ideas on equal education and her critique of Rousseau's theory of sex-complementarity are developed by Wollstonecraft into her clarion call for equality. While it was Macaulay who argued that "there is but one rule of right for the conduct of all human beings," it was Wollstonecraft who turned it into an early feminist slogan (Macaulay 1974, 201).

In "Catharine Macaulay's *Letters on Education* (1790): An Early Feminist Polemic," Florence Boos offers a detailed account of the aspects of Macaulay's *Letters* that reappear in Wollstonecraft, and are thus presumably the results of Macaulay's influence. In particular, Boos notes that both writers explore the notion of co-education, the importance of physical exercise for girls, and deplore sexual double standards. Above all Boos argues, it is letters 21 to 24 of part 1, that are "the most striking sources for Wollstonecraft's *A Vindication of the Rights of Woman*" (Boos 1976, 71). In these letters, Macaulay argues that there is one principle of virtue for both sexes, and that an education will aid—rather than hinder—a woman in her social duties. Moreover Macaulay attacks the misogynist opinions of Chesterfield and Rousseau, the very same writers who were attacked by Wollstonecraft in a "fuller, more energetic refutation" five years later (Boos 1976, 74).

Yet despite Macaulay's formative influence on the writer of the *Vindication*, the *Letters* were largely ignored when they were published and remain neglected today. The lack of interest by Macaulay's contemporaries may have occurred because, as Florence Boos suggests, the *Letters* were "swiftly buried in the reaction which succeeded the radicalism of the early 1790's; few early nineteenth century readers were interested in Enlightenment prescriptions for educational reform" (Boos 1976, 65). Given the current interest in "rediscovering" women philosophers, Macaulay's neglect in the present is not so easily explained. And here the second explanation offered by Boos as to why the *Letters* have remained ignored appears to provide our answer: the form of the work. Quite simply the *Letters* seems uncohesive, without any linking themes or principles.

Boos points to the fact that Macaulay's work in actuality "contains three separate books, each well-written (*sic*) and unified, but unlikely to appeal to the same reader" (Boos 1976, 65). Indeed Boos further claims, that part 1 in effect is the "real" letters on education; and she suggests that "Letters on Society" would have been a more accurate title for the second part, as it looks at forms of government and takes issue with various social problems such as the slave trade. Boos also holds that part 3 of the *Letters* is simply a revision of Macaulay's work on religion and morality, *Treatise on the Immutability of Moral Truth*, containing her responses to contemporary theodicies. However, as we shall see, while Boos is correct in identifying the form of the *Letters* as the cause of their neglect, her understanding of this cause is ultimately part of the problem. For it is not the form of the work *per se*, but the expectations and assumptions generated by this form that are problematic for the interpretation of the *Letters*.

It would appear that Macaulay's influence on Wollstonecraft should, at the very least, be a call for a more complete investigation of her work. Yet on a closer examination of the work of these two philosophers, it seems that—again due to the form of the *Letters*—Macaulay loses out in the comparison. Wollstonecraft's pioneering feminist writing in *A Vindication of the Rights of Woman* has become—either explicitly or implicitly—our yardstick for eighteenth- and nineteenth-century work on the equality of women. In comparison with Wollstonecraft, Macaulay's work—while expressing what we would call feminist concerns—has not been considered to offer a comprehensive argument for the liberation of women. Thus we find, for example, Miriam Brody Kramnick in her introduction to Wollstonecraft's *Vindication* claiming that while Macaulay, like Wollstonecraft, argued for the education of women, and for the existence of one moral rule for both sexes, her interests lay in a variety of topics. Kramnick states that "the issue of female emancipation was not a central concern for Macaulay, who wrote like a feminist but did not write the feminist manifesto. Macaulay is concerned equally with the management of infants and the education of princes. It was for Mary Wollstonecraft to take the argument of natural rights and make their application to women the subject of a *sustained* argument" (Wollstonecraft 1983, 40, italics used for emphasis).

Later I intend to question the assumptions that lie behind this kind of categorization of Wollstonecraft's *A Vindication of the Rights of Woman* as the yardstick of early feminist philosophy, and to suggest that this categorization may even create difficulties for interpretation of Wollstonecraft's *own* work. But for the present I wish to focus on what constitutes the difference between the "sustained" argument of Wollstonecraft, and the "collection" of concerns of Macaulay. I find that there are two obvious differences. First, even though Wollstonecraft's work covers a variety of different issues related to the emancipation of women—from national education, to motherhood, to criticism of contemporary female manners—her interest in these issues, and her arguments pertaining to them, are underpinned by the central thesis of the book: the rights of women. Macaulay in the *Letters*, on the other hand, apparently treats the issue of natural rights simply as one issue among many.

While the equation of the argument for natural rights with an argument for the equality of women is clear enough to need no further comment, we do, however, need to recognize that it might not exhaust all the possibilities for cogent arguments for female equality. Macaulay is in fact offering a sustained and consistent argument for the equality of women, albeit of a rather idiosyncratic kind. The answer to why Macaulay's argument in the *Letters* has been missed, or has seemed non-existent compared to the argument for equality found in Wollstonecraft's *Vindication*, can be found in the second difference between the two works: their form. Such misconceptions about the content of Macaulay's work, I hold, stem directly from expectations of the shape or appearance a self-contained, sustained moral argument for the equality of women should take: a designated "philosophical" form. Unlike the Enlightenment treatise which is the supposed form of Wollstonecraft's *Vindication*, a collection of letters on apparently diverse topics does not appear to be an adequate vehicle for such an argument. Thus Boos is correct in identifying the problem with the *Letters*; what she has missed, however, is that the form in itself is not the problem.

An examination of modern critical work on Macaulay shows how a conception of the *Letters on Education* as a collection of comments on a diverse series of topics gets played out in interpretations of the philosophical content of the work. As we have already seen, Boos offers documentation of the influence of the *Letters* on Wollstonecraft's *Vindication*, however she also takes pains to emphasize the differences between the intellectual quality of the two writers' views. For Boos, Macaulay is the more restrained of the two in her criticism of the situation of women, as

well as less radical in her view of the conditions necessary for social reform. Macaulay "glances backward" at de Genlis and Fénelon in letter 25
on the importance of a proper education for an ideal prince; whereas
Wollstonecraft dismisses the possibility of social reform from an enlight-
ened monarchy (Boos 1976, 75). Wollstonecraft recognized that class oppression was inextricably bound up with the oppression of women, and
accordingly the *Vindication* is also an attack on "the pestiferous purple
which renders the progress of civilization a curse" (Wollstonecraft 1983,
99). Boos notes that Wollstonecraft is to be commended for demanding
social reform and the rights of women, while Macaulay's *Letters* "merit
notice for their original opinions on *an idiosyncratic range* of social questions" (Boos 1976, 64–65, emphasis added). Thus, although the germ for
the radical social reforms of the *Vindication* can be traced back to the *Letters*, "it remained," states Boos, "for Wollstonecraft to emphasize
Macaulay's feminism as a separate topic" and "associate with it the revolutionary belief in human equality" (Boos 1976, 75).

Boos's evaluation of Macaulay's *Letters* is reiterated in "Catharine
Macaulay: Historian and Political Reformer," co-authored with William
Boos. Again Macaulay is praised for her revolutionary views of sexual
egalitarianism; Boos and Boos even go so far as to suggest that Macaulay
is the first writer to produce a sustained indictment of the assumption
that there are innate sexual differences. What will prove significant for an
account of the *Letters* is the separation that Boos and Boos see between
the feminist aspects of Macaulay's arguments and the other strands of
the *Letters*. Boos and Boos see the issue of educating women equally with
men treated as a separate argument from the way we learn: "*In addition*
to its revolutionary prescription of sexual egalitarianism, Part I of the *Letters* offers a thorough discussion of the relationship between learning and
society" (Boos & Boos 1980, 56, emphasis added). This separation of
ideas is echoed in the conclusion: "Catharine Macaulay remains a significant but unacknowledged contributor to feminist thought *and* persua-
sive advocate for human liberation and social justice" (Boos & Boos 1980,
63, emphasis added).

Bridget Hill, in *The Republican Virago*, also treats the *Letters* as a diverse
collection. She suggests that the only reason the *Treatise* was included in
the *Letters* is because Macaulay was delighted by a particularly glowing
review of them (see Macaulay 1974, vii). Hill—like Boos and Boos—also
does not find that Macaulay is writing a work focused on female equality:
"Her *Letters on Education* range over a wide variety of subjects; nursing
and infant care, the upbringing, training, and education of children; slavery, capital punishment and public executions, the need for improved
care of prisoners and the better management of prisons; the importance
of personal cleanliness, the treatment of animals, and the conditions of

slaughter-houses. The diversity of contents may reflect awareness that time was running out for her. She wanted to express her ideas on a host of questions before it was too late" (Hill 1992, 158).

For Hill, the "main thrust" of the "bewildering variety of ideas" contained in the *Letters* is towards education (Hill 1992, 160). Indeed Hill claims that the *Letters* marks a change in Macaulay's political outlook: "She was now convinced that progress, whether political or social, could only come about through the extension and improvement of education" (Hill 1992, 162–63). But such progress is not to be understood in terms of an improvement in the political or sexual position of women. Hill states that political equality was, for Macaulay, impossible unless the electorate was educated: "Any progress for women, she implied, relied on their receiving more and a better education" (Hill 1992, 160). Hill emphasizes that while Macaulay was clearly sympathetic to women, she regarded herself principally as a historian and a political polemicist; indeed, it seems to demonstrate Macaulay's intellectual priorities that only *Letters on Education* focuses on women.[3]

The Problems of
the Epistolary Form

If I am going to maintain that the *Letters on Education* contains a sustained argument for female equality, I need first to understand what seems to be underpinning claims that it does not. An initial reading of the *Letters on Education* would certainly seem to support the assertion that the *Letters* does simply consist of a collection of arguments on the various themes of education, sexual equality, and social justice. The early letters in part 1 are concerned with the upbringing and care of infants and small children; Macaulay discusses such topics as the benefits of a lively nurse for children, the advantages of learning needlework (for both sexes), and suitable reading matter for young children. In letter 4, she gives advice on the suitable nutrition for infants and young children. In a typical mixing of health and moral advice, Macaulay discusses the use of gravy for infants: "When I recommended the use of gravy for sucking infants, Hortensia, it was merely on the notion of its being the best corrector of the acidities of human milk, and not with the view of bringing them up to be devourers of animal substances" (Macaulay 1974, 38). Indeed, she believes that a mainly vegetarian diet is most suitable for the stomachs of children, a belief bolstered by a sense of the cruelty of meat eating: "the cruel necessity which our wants impose on us, to inflict that fate on other beings which would be terrible to ourselves, is an evil of sufficient weight were the use of animal diet confined within as moderate limits as the present state of things will admit" (Macaulay 1974, 38).

The later letters of part 1 discuss adult social and moral behavior. Macaulay expounds on such topics as fashion, politeness, sobriety, flattery, and male rakes. It is in these later letters that we also find Macaulay's views on female education and the question of innate sexual differences. Yet these letters on women appear to be isolated comments, as the letter immediately following them contains a discussion on the education of princes. The overall impression of part 1 seems accurately described by Boos as collection of letters "discussing an ideal pattern of instruction from infancy onward, with digressive comments on the proper environment for young people, the equality of the sexes, and romantic love" (Boos 1976, 65). It would also appear that the volume as a whole contains, as Boos maintains, three separate parts: the first on education; the second on society, detailing the defects and successes of ancient civilizations; and the third a revision of Macaulay's earlier *Treatise*.

Viewing the *Letters* as a collection of different interests is not simply reinforced by the form of the work, it would seem to be generated by it. Indeed an initial reading of the work scarcely invites an examination for a sustained argument of any kind. Not only are the three parts apparently separate, but—as is characteristic for the epistolary genre—the letters within each part are typically self-contained and can be separated from the other letters with no apparent loss of intelligibility. It would then seem that while there can be "philosophical insights" or "points of interest" that can be gained from the *Letters*, they may not be able to contain a sustained philosophical argument.

However while the epistolary form may not be conducive to the production of a sustained philosophical argument, there is nothing about its *structure* that would prevent it. Even though each letter is a unit in itself, it is still part of the larger unit of the book. We must then look elsewhere for our explanation as to why it has been assumed that *Letters on Education* does not contain a sustained philosophical argument. The first answer seems obvious and is something that I have already indicated: it does not take the "standard" form of a work of philosophy. But this is to assume that philosophical genre forms are a "given," somehow independent of ways of doing and conceiving of philosophy—an assumption that I am questioning throughout this work. The second answer is related to the first, but is considerably more complex. The expectations raised by the epistolary form—especially when it is written by a woman—link it firmly to the private sphere and, more particularly, to "feminine" discourse, i.e. non-philosophical discourse. This then appears to generate assumptions not only about the content of the work but about its appropriate classification.

According to Gustave Lanson's standard account of the epistolary form in his *Essais de Méthode*, what is important in the philosophical letters of the eighteenth century is that they show us the person behind the theories; and, what he describes as, the ever-changing flow of life itself that lies under the rigid connectivity of their ideas. If this is so, then it would seem clear that the epistolary form is far more closely connected to the sphere of private life rather than the public sphere of philosophical discourse. Moreover there is a close connection between the letter and natural social conversation, an association which Lanson finds to be one of the charms of the well-written letter. Even more unfortunately, the association of women with the ability to converse well, means that the epistolary form has become associated with the forms of writing suitable for women, and thus (whether legitimately or not) to be classified as "feminine" (and therefore devalued) discourse. This association is clear in Lanson's nineteenth-century account of the relationship between the ability of women to be pleasing or charming in conversation and their ability to write better letters than men. Indeed he claims that the reason why Fénelon and Voltaire, among others, wrote such charming letters is because they had what he thinks of as a womanly sensibility.

Certainly during the eighteenth century, according to Gary Kelly in *Women, Writing, and Revolution*, the letter was "well established as a predominantly feminine discourse, conventionally seen as informal, immediate, personal, private, and domestic, and thus suited to the supposedly more emotional character, limited education, domestic interests, and quotidian experience of women" (Kelly 1993, 39). These expectations about the epistolary form are reinforced by the kinds of epistolary works that were typically produced by women writers. One example is the "elegant" collection of letters offering ladies of rank models of elegant letter writing on interesting and instructive subjects. Such collections could be entertaining or amusing (in a refined way), and thus improvement could come without too much exertion on behalf of the reader. The instruction offered by these collections is in small manageable doses, so that the reader need not be taxed by having to trace the course of an argument through an entire work.

It is not evident whether these associations and expectations affected the reception of the *Letters* by Macaulay's contemporaries; they certainly do not appear to have affected the best known review of her work by Mary Wollstonecraft in the *Analytical Review*. While Wollstonecraft does go through the work commenting on the arguments of different letters, she clearly treats it both as a whole and as being more than a discussion of education. In the opening lines of her review, Wollstonecraft comments on the fact that Macaulay's consideration of the subject of education appears to cover a far wider range of issues than is typical in works of this type. Wollstonecraft also recognizes that while the first letter may appear what she terms "desultory," it in fact "contains many observations strictly connected with the main subject" (Wollstonecraft 1989, 7:309). In this Wollstonecraft is absolutely correct, the first letter provides an introduction to Macaulay's views on virtue, on society, and on divine benevolence, in short what I find to be the ethicoreligious system present in her work. This is not to say that Wollstonecraft sees the same argument that I do in the *Letters*, but it is provocative to find that the passages she quotes are often those that I have found make the central points of Macaulay's argument.

It is not clear, however, that the expectations of content generated by the letter form have not influenced the assumptions underpinning *modern* approaches to Macaulay's work. Boos, for example, implies that the title *Letters on Education* is misleading, as not all of the work is on education, indeed Boos describes letters that do not appear to be related to the education or instruction for infants and young people as "digressive." The assumption here is that Macaulay means education in the sense of the sort of instruction and upbringing that women would be in a position to give in their roles as mother, nurse, or governess. What is also interesting is that Boos and Boos appear to assume that it is these matters which truly interest Macaulay, or at least more so than the topics of government and social reform. Indeed they comment on the change in style in part 2 of the *Letters* (the part devoted to topics related to society and government) when Macaulay discusses more traditionally "feminine" topics such as gardening and cooking: "The prose style warms noticeably when she turns to [these] more practical forms of 'art'" (Boos & Boos 1980, 59). This makes an interesting contrast to Wollstonecraft's review of the *Letters* in which she praises the way that these subjects are "traced with a philosophic eye" (Wollstonecraft 1989, 7: 317).

But it is not just that certain expectations about the letter form and its authorship appear—at least in part—to underpin interpretations of *Letters on Education*, they also appear to have affected its classification. I suspect, the typical categorization of *Letters on Education* as educational theory rather than moral philosophy has been—at least in part—influenced by the sex of its author. Works by male authors in the epistolary genre do not seem to suffer the same fate so easily, indeed their entry into the genre can even endow it—at least in the case of their own work—with an increased level of seriousness. One example of this could be Rousseau's *La Nouvelle Heloise*. Unfortunately once a work has been classified, then commentators are more likely to explore its contribution to that particular field, than to question its initial classification. In Macaulay's case this classification as a work of education and nothing else has proved to be particularly pernicious, as some forms of the epistolary genre have become associated with the conduct manuals for women that flourished in the eighteenth and nineteenth centuries.

During the late eighteenth century the conduct book or advice manual appeared in a new guise as letters of advice written by an older woman for a younger woman. Lady Sarah Pennington seems to have started this trend when she wrote *An Unfortunate Mother's Advice to Her Absent Daughters* (1761), advising them of the importance of marriage in a woman's life and how to bear its trials. Hester Chapone's *Letters on the Improvement of the Mind* (1773) addressed to a girl of fourteen echoed in some ways Pennington's view of marriage and the importance of bearing its trials. Although she also held the need for some level of education for girls so that they would be properly prepared for the married state.

The most recent edition of Macaulay's *Letters on Education* is as part of collection on female education. This in itself may not be cause for complaint, until we see the other works that are part of this collection. Hester Chapone and Jane West are the other female writers. West's *Letters to A Young Lady* (1806) is little more than a guide to women's domestic duties.[4] Even though it is quite encyclopedic in its range of information, in the words of the collection's editor, "Piety is much enjoined, both as essential for salvation and as comfort in what West was quite prepared to see, echoing Chapone and Pennington, as a life of trials, especially in marriage" (Todd 1996, 1:xxiii). The male writers include James Fordyce's *Sermons for Young Women* (1766) and John Gregory's *A Father's Legacy to His Daughters*, both of whom were criticized by Wollstonecraft in *A Vindication of the Rights of Woman*. Even though the editor of the collection distinguishes Macaulay in her introduction from the other members of this collection in that Macaulay is seen to hold that women should be educated to be citizens and not just wives, it seems clear that Macaulay is considered to be part of an ongoing discussion about the relationship between female education and female duties: marriage and the domestic life.

Admittedly, my claim about the assumptions behind these commentators' approaches to an interpretation or classification of the *Letters* is somewhat speculative. But the expectations and associations generated by the form of the *Letters* do appear to provide the most rational expectation for its neglect in the present and its classification with epistolary conduct manuals. For it appears that, due to its structure, the *Letters* does not appear to be able to contain a sustained philosophical argument. While, due to the association of the epistolary genre (particularly when authored by women) with "feminine" or domestic concerns, it appears that Macaulay's interests do not lie in this direction anyway. In sum, therefore it would appear that the *Letters* seems only to contain a few interesting philosophical insights. Conceived thus, it seems unlikely that the *Letters* can offer anything in the way of systematized and sustained philosophical thought. Indeed it is hard not to conclude that, unlike Wollstonecraft, Macaulay was not offering a sustained argument for the equality of women; nor did she seem to recognize the connection between this equality and social reform.

Yet commentators are not skeptical about the content of Macaulay's *History* in the same way that they are about the content of the *Letters*, although the latter has no less an impressive display of learning and intellectual ability than the former. We need to move past the expectations (and prejudices) produced by the form of Macaulay's work. Once we have done this, we shall be in a position to see that the concept of education outlined in the *Letters* is a far more wide ranging one: it is nothing less than the moral and mental perfection of human beings in accord with the divine plan. Furthermore, once we examine the letters of part 1, in which Macaulay discusses the situation of women, in the context of parts 2 and 3 which explain her view of the progress of humankind, we shall be able to see how the equality of women is interconnected with the philosophical ideas underpinning Macaulay's view of social and political reform. Indeed it will be clear that Macaulay's work contains a deliberate and fully worked out systematized argument—albeit of a rather unusual or unexpected kind—for the equality of women based on her ethicoreligious principles. Offering this interpretation is valuable not just in the way it reclaims Macaulay's philosophical work in *Letters on Education*, but also because the possibility of this interpretation allows us to see beyond the assumption that philosophical work must take the form of such standard forms as the treatise, essay, or journal article.

Macaulay's Work

Even a fleeting glance at Macaulay's life and work seems to support the need for a reexamination of the *Letters on Education*. Macaulay's best-known work, *History of England*, comprehensive and detailed, and 3549 pages in length, demonstrates her knowledge of political philosophy and contains criticism of the work of Hobbes, Hume, Burke, and others. Her *History*, in turn, drew fire from Hume. Hume's letter in the *European Magazine* is a criticism of Macaulay's political interpretation of the facts, not of her abilities as a thinker or a historian. Macaulay's carefully argued response to this letter in the same magazine provoked the perhaps partisan editorial comment, "it is unnecessary to observe, that this celebrated scotch (*sic*) historian, in the present correspondence, is manifestly inferior to the lady, at least in argument" (*European Magazine* 1783, 332). Not only is it clear from this exchange that Macaulay was actively involved in English politics, but Macaulay can be credited, Hill argues, with shaping radical ideas in England, France, and The United States.

As the first historian in the eighteenth century to attempt a republican history of the seventeenth century, she deserves more study than she has so far received. Her *History*—and its popularity—illustrates how vital the seventeenth century still was to both Commonwealthmen and Wilkites. It makes the point that any understanding of eighteenth-century radicalism must start from the seventeenth century. Her influence on radical ideas in England, and the contribution she made to the changing nature of radicalism in the last three decades of the eighteenth century, made her *History* and political polemic of no small importance. Her role in familiarizing Americans with the history of the seventeenth century and reinforcing their conviction that events of that earlier century were being replayed in their time . . . has not been lost on American historians who have recognized her importance. That her writings also had relevance for many French patriots in the early years of the Revolution is less well known. (Hill 1992, 250)

Clearly there is a disparity between Macaulay the politically involved historian and Macaulay whose only role in early feminist (or protofeminist) thought is supposed to be as the tame conservative influence on Wollstonecraft. Furthermore, it is curious that the respected writer of sustained attacks on the work of others would have failed to appreciate the importance of sustained arguments in her own work.

Macaulay was part of a large group of eighteenth-century intellectuals who were influenced by Locke's *An Essay Concerning Human Understanding*. The denial of innate ideas and the argument for the human mind as a *tabula rasa*, were perhaps the most eagerly embraced of his views by such writers as Johnson, Cowper, Chesterfield, and Gray. Part of the appeal of Locke's attack on the doctrine of innate ideas was its implication for intellectual or mental equality. Using the influences of Locke, Macaulay could have devoted her time merely to explaining and thereby excusing the character and conduct of the eighteenth-century woman; but as she says herself, she is no "apologist for the conduct of women" (Macaulay 1974, 214). Instead, Macaulay sets herself the task of arguing for the equal education of women, an argument that, I claim, ultimately develops into an argument for equality itself.

Macaulay states in the preface to *Letters on Education* that an understanding of the mind is necessary for the moral improvement of human beings, for without such an understanding we shall not be able to formulate a principled, uniform system of education that can produce moral excellence. Macaulay explicitly declares her Lockean foundations for this understanding of the mind in the introductory first letter. What we are and, more important for Macaulay, whether we are good or bad is not inherited or innate but is purely the effect of our environment: "There is not a virtue or a vice that belongs to humanity, which we do not make ourselves. . . . There is not a wretch who ends his miserable being on a wheel, as the forfeit of his offences against society, who may not throw the whole blame of his misdemeanors on his education; who may not look up to the very government, by whose severe laws he is made to suffer, as the author of his misfortunes; and who may not with justice utter the hardest imprecations on those to whom the charge of his youth was entrusted, and to those with whom he associated in the early periods of his life" (Macaulay 1974, 11).

If crime and vice are effects of environment and education, Macaulay argues, then careful and correct education and parenting are vital. Macaulay cautions parents to remember "that the misery or bliss of your posterity, in a great measure depends upon yourselves, and that an inattention to your duty, may draw on your head the guilt of many generations" (Macaulay 1974, 14). It should be, therefore, no surprise to find that the majority of the early letters are devoted to discussions of infant care and juvenile education, as every aspect of a child's environment can affect the development of the childish mind.

What is interesting about Macaulay's account of the education of children is that it extends beyond a typical account of discipline and the parental role as moral exemplar. As we have already seen, Macaulay's advice on the healthfulness of a mainly vegetarian diet for children is not directed solely at the physical health of the child; the eating of meat and the moral development of the child seem inextricably linked. Macaulay holds that meat eating "must naturally tend to weaken that sympathy which Nature has given to man, as the best guard against the abuse of the extensive power with which she has entrusted him" (Macaulay 1974, 39). The role of education and environment in cultivating sympathy is constantly emphasized throughout part 1. It is only in part 2, however, when Macaulay argues that sympathy is the source of all human virtue, that its importance is clearly brought out. While this may be a potential weakness for the coherence of the arguments of part 1, it points towards the existence of a continued argument running through the different parts of the *Letters*.

Macaulay does not restrict her discussion to those aspects of a child's life that could seem to have a direct effect on moral development. She also stresses the necessity of a calm and consistent environment, which will affect more indirectly the development of moral character. Harsh discipline of a child, she believes, produces an environment in which the child's mind is often disturbed and "violently shaken by rigorous sensations." This results, in later life, in an adult in whom "the temper becomes fretful and impatient, and the spirits are thrown into disorder by every thwarting incident which occurs" (Macaulay 1974, 98).

The significance of these aspects of the early letters of part 1 starts to become clear when we examine letters 21 to 23. A close examination of these three crucial letters allows Macaulay's comments on child care to be read as part of an argument for the equality of women, for it is in these letters that Macaulay argues for the connection between moral principles and education that will produce moral excellence in the Lockean mind. In this way, we can start to see that—far from being digressive as Boos claims—the letters on the equality of the sexes and the proper environment for young people are part of a larger argument concerning moral excellence.

In letter 21, Macaulay discusses the need for moral education: without an understanding of the principles of morality and the law, one can never attain moral excellence, or contribute to legal reform. This attention to moral education is vital if Macaulay plans to follow Locke in dismissing the existence of innate moral principles and replacing them with an educated morality grounded on reasoning. But Macaulay's work here is not merely derivative of Locke's. Her recognition that moral principles are not universally applied is clearly based on the third chapter of the first book of Locke's *Essay,* but her central concerns are the reasons this is true. According to Macaulay, people's lack of knowledge of the principles of morality is the reason their "notions of right and wrong are loose, unconnected, and inconsistent" (Macaulay 1974, 198). Without proper moral education, "even those who bear the specious title of philosophers are apt to be dazzled by the brilliancy *(sic)* of success, and to treat qualities and characters differently according to the smiles and frowns of fortune" (198–99). To avoid the inconsistencies of which we are all so guilty (when, for example, we find the crime of murder in a poor man to be statecraft in a leader), Macaulay argues that morals must be taught on "immutable principles": principles that are not innate but are grounded in reason.

It is one thing, Hortensia, to educate a citizen, and another to educate a philosopher. The mere citizen will have learnt to obey the laws of his country, but he will never understand those principles on which all laws ought to be established; and without such an understanding, he can never be religious on rational principles, or truly moral; nor will he ever have any of that active wisdom which is necessary for co-operating in any plan of reformation. But to teach morals on an immutable fitness, has never been the practice in any system of education yet extant. Hence all our notions of right and wrong are loose, unconnected, and inconsistent. Hence the murderer, in one situation, is extolled to the skies; and in another, is followed with reproach even beyond the grave. (Macaulay 1974, 198)

These immutable principles seem to play a dual role in the education of the child. Their primary function is to provide the individual with a consistent set of moral guidelines, but Macaulay also seems to suggest that these principles ultimately produce a consistent environment in which to educate a child. Without a consistent environment, the good work of the parent may become undone at any moment. As we have seen, this consistent environment for the child is constantly emphasized in the early letters. Given the role that these immutable principles play in the education of children, and, as we shall see, their status as the foundations of Macaulay's argument for the equal education of women, it may seem a weakness in Macaulay's work that she does not describe in detail how the immutable principles of morality are to be established or give examples of the principles themselves in the first part of the *Letters*. Indeed, not until part 3 does Macaulay explain her focus on the function of these principles. Yet, again, this apparent weakness of one part of the *Letters* is also further support for my contention that Macaulay intended its three parts to be read as a whole.

Three deceptively brief arguments are given in letter 21 for the equal education of men and women. The first is based on the consistency of moral principles. Macaulay claims "That there is but one rule of right for the conduct of all rational beings; consequently that true virtue in one sex must be equally so in the other, whenever a proper opportunity calls for its exertion; and, *vice versa*, what is vice in one sex, cannot have a different property when found in the other" (Macaulay 1974, 201, Macaulay's emphasis). The moral education of both sexes must be the same, and it is clear that by this Macaulay means a general principled education rather than the sexes sharing a moral education but having a separate general education.

Macaulay's second reason for the equal education of women is that "true wisdom, which is never found at variance with rectitude, is as useful to women as to men; because it is necessary to the highest degree of happiness, which can never exist with ignorance" (1974, 201). Contrary to Rousseau's arguments in *Emile*, she implies, keeping women in ignorance will not secure their virtue or their happiness. This second argument also seems to hint at the utility of educating women: the wise woman will benefit society. This seems plausible considering Macaulay's comments earlier in letter 21 on the necessity of wisdom for social reform. The final argument addresses the injustice of keeping women in ignorance when wisdom is necessary to enter the next world: "Lastly, That as on our first entrance into another world, our state of happiness may possibly depend on the degree of perfection we have attained in this, we cannot justly lessen, in one sex or the other, the means by which perfection, that is another word for wisdom, is acquired" (1974, 201–2).

Thus Macaulay intends to connect the development of moral excellence with the need for the equal education of women. Moral excellence, because of the form of the mind, can be produced only through a consistent education grounded on immutable principles; and any attempt at producing this moral excellence will invariably entail a call for equality of education. To deny women the same education as men is to deny the consistency of moral principles and to ignore our own interest in a morally excellent society. To deny them any kind of education, furthermore, is not only to remove the possibility of their happiness in this world and the next, but to act with injustice.

Although Macaulay's arguments for the equal education of women seem consistent, a tension is apparent between these reasoned arguments for the promotion of women and her occasional tirades against the behavior of her contemporaries. In letter 22, Macaulay expresses her disdain for anyone who still believes that there are innate character differences between the two sexes; she declares that the "particular foibles and vices" displayed by women "originate in situation and education only" (Macaulay 1974, 206). Yet earlier in the same letter, she castigates women for their complicity in their own subjugation: "suffer them to idolize their persons, to throw away their life in the pursuit of trifles, and to indulge in the gratification of the meaner passions, and they will heartily join in the sentence of their degradation" (Macaulay 1974, 205). Macaulay recognizes that her reader may be shocked by this "fit of moral anger" and that the reader may cry that she "expected an apology, instead of a libel, on women," but Macaulay does nothing to reply to this charge (Macaulay 1974, 214). The reader is left unsure as to why, although Macaulay can trace all the sources of these women's vices to their situation and education, they are still held, in some way, morally accountable for their behavior.

This tension seems to indicate a certain recalcitrant or conservative quality in Macaulay's work. Although she clearly recognizes the reasons that women remain oppressed, she seems to be making no *demand* for any kind of societal reform. Instead, Macaulay appears to be content to wait "till that period arrives in which women will act wisely," suggesting that meanwhile we should "amuse ourselves in talking of their follies" (Macaulay 1974, 207). Moreover, this tension stems directly from ideas that are central to Macaulay's work. The emphasis she places on the immutability of moral principles requires that judgment of people's behavior must not vary depending on who they are. Macaulay could not help but observe that the compliance of women prolonged their degradation, and therefore she was bound to criticize this as harshly as she criticized behavior in men that also maintained women's oppression. Men prefer "to give up the advantages we might

derive from the perfection of our fellow associates, than to own that nature has been just in the equal distribution of her favours" (Macaulay
1974, 204–5). But she adds that we should mark how readily women as-
sent to this situation, "not from humility I assure you, but merely to
preserve with character those fond vanities on which they set their
hearts" (Macaulay 1974, 205).

A comparison with Wollstonecraft's comments in the *Vindication of the
Rights of Woman* may be useful here in understanding Macaulay's criticisms of women. Wollstonecraft also offers scathing criticism of these
same women while recognizing the social forces that produced their
vices; but her comments can be understood within the framework of a
call for social reform. Wollstonecraft sneers at a woman of fashion she
used to know who considered "a distinguishing taste and puny appetite
the height of all human perfection" (Wollstonecraft 1983, 130). Wollstonecraft remembers seeing this woman "neglect all the duties of life,
yet recline with self-complacency (*sic*) on a sofa, and boast of her want of
appetite as a proof of delicacy" (Wollstonecraft 1983, 130). Seeing women
in this deplorable state, says Wollstonecraft, shows that "it is time to effect a revolution in female manners—time to restore them to their lost
dignity—and make them, as a part of the human species, labour by re-
forming themselves to reform the world"(Wollstonecraft 1983, 132). If
Macaulay, like Wollstonecraft, is arguing for some kind of general social
reform, then her criticisms of women could also be understood as implied criticisms of the social structures that produced these women and
as challenges to these women to self-reform.

It is here that we must let go of the assumptions about Macaulay's
work produced by its relationship to that of Wollstonecraft. Simply because Wollstonecraft incorporated Macaulay's arguments for equal education into a call for a total reform of the position of women, we should
not assume, without further investigation, that Macaulay's *Letters on Education* contains no similar arguments. Instead of looking for—and fail-
ing to find—an argument for the equality of women grounded in a claim
for their rationality, we should look to Macaulay's discussion of the development of moral excellence as the possible ground of a sustained argument for the equality of women. But in order to recognize the existence of this argument, we must put to one side the expectations
generated by the form of Macaulay's work. While a work of the epistolary form may lead us to assume that her concept of moral excellence
will be closer to the preachings of the typical conduct book for the improvement of the female reader, we need to recognize that instead it is
part of a complete ethicoreligious system that necessitates an argument
for the equality of women.

The Argument for Women

Macaulay does indeed suggest that the time is ripe for change. Men, she has noticed, "have relaxed in their tyranny over women," so much so that if women were able to make intelligent use of the little power they do possess, "they might carry every point of any importance to their honour and happiness" (Macaulay 1974, 207). This passage implies that Macaulay was not blinkered to the possibilities of some kind of change. Although we are accustomed to expecting an argument for equal education to be part of a more general plan of reform for the position of women, and we may expect to find such an argument only in an essay or treatise, we should consider whether Macaulay's ideas on education and morality were actually intended to produce, by themselves, some kind of reform in the position of women.

What Macaulay really might be offering is a discussion of social reform, but of a perhaps unexpected kind: it is a discussion of the moral reform of the human mind. This mental reform appears to work in two ways. On a practical level, an improvement in the general level of virtue could certainly bring about some kind of social reform. If men and women have an understanding of the workings of legal reform and the need for equality in our treatment of others, both characteristics that will be produced by a proper moral education, then they might work toward some change in the position of women. Even though Macaulay recognizes that her plans for education may be available only to the ruling classes, their improved virtue, she claims in the preface, "would be felt in the improved virtue of all the subordinate classes of citizens" (Macaulay 1974, v–vi). Thus it would seem that Macaulay's final letter in part 1 on the education of princes is neither a digression from her arguments for the equality of women nor an expression of the desire to maintain the societal status quo; instead, it appears to be a pragmatic recognition of how change could take place.[5]

On a more theoretical level, Macaulay's guidelines for education seem to entail the need for a consistent society in which that education could take place. If ideas are not innate but are to be learned through rational exercise of the mind, then the pupil will learn best in a society that demonstrates consistency in its principles and judgments. The argument for equal education in the *Letters* also acknowledges the need to give women an equal position in society, as this will be the best way to produce a suitable environment for the education of both sexes. Simply allowing women equal access to the same learning as men without an environment conducive to mental development will deny them the same chance for moral excellence. Not only will women's unequal position in society affect their education, it will ultimately affect male moral excellence, too. If women remain uneducated, or if they are educated but their position in society is allowed to remain unaltered, then it is doubtful that men can achieve moral excellence in this inconsistent and unjust environment. Indeed, the opening comments of letter 24 appear to refer to this construction: "After all that has been advanced [in letters 21–23], Hortensia, the happiness and perfection of the two sexes are so reciprocally dependent on one another that, till both are reformed, there is no expecting excellence in either" (Macaulay 1974, 216).

Thus part 1 of Macaulay's *Letters on Education* can be understood as a sustained discussion of the topic of social reform, rather than a collection of comments on a variety of subjects. Indeed once we have "looked past" its epistolary form, the subject of the *Letters* and the presence of this sustained discussion could hardly be more obvious. Looking past the form allows us to see that the *Letters* should not be classified simply as a work on education, they are also a work of moral philosophy, as well as an opportunity to examine the individual letters for their connections rather than their differences. Macaulay's view of social reform is a kind of moral reform of the human mind that requires principled education, a consistent environment, and equality both in the education and the position of women. Like Wollstonecraft, Macaulay is criticizing the social structures that produced the indolent lady of fashion, and she does challenge women to self-reform. Both the inconsistency of the social structures that oppress women and the seeming acquiescence of women to this oppression must be overcome to produce moral growth of both the individual and society. Unlike Wollstonecraft, however, both Macaulay's criticism and her challenge stem not from a wide-ranging call for justice but from a particular view of morality, a view that is further developed in the other parts of the *Letters*.

The Second and Third Parts of
Letters on Education

Appearances to the contrary, part 2 of the *Letters* is not separate from part 1, but is rather an extension of it in that it discusses the role government should play in the moral growth of the individual and society. In part 1 Macaulay states explicitly that government is also responsible for the moral development of an individual. She stresses the importance of proper moral education for the legal reforms necessary to produce the morally excellent society. In part 2, she offers an account of the source and development of human virtue, an account that provides the philosophical justifications for the views on education and the equality of women in part 1.

Government, Macaulay contends, plays an educational role in the development of what she calls duties of benevolence that fall to citizens or members of society. Macaulay now makes explicit what she only alluded to in the final letter of part 1: that it is the task of the higher classes, once properly educated, to frame laws that will "enlighten the understandings (*sic*) of the citizens in the essentials of right and wrong" (Macaulay 1974, 237). The importance of this role of government becomes clear when we see the relationship Macaulay perceives between the laws of a society and the moral development of its citizens.

To understand this relationship, we need first to examine Macaulay's concept of virtue. In letter 8 of part 2, Macaulay gives the most explicit statement in all of her letters of her notion of virtue: "All human virtue [is] found to proceed from equity; consequently, if the principle of equity itself owes its source in the human mind to the feelings of sympathy, all human virtue must derive its source from this useful affection" (Macaulay 1974, 275). Macaulay believes that humans bear a natural sympathy: when we see pain or unhappiness in another, our feelings of sympathy enable us to imagine ourselves in the other's place. This sympathy leads to our acquiring the ideas of equity and an understanding of the utility of benevolence. By equity, Macaulay means the forbearance of our own gratification in respect to the needs and wants of others (including, it would seem, animals). While equity finds its source or inclination in our original sympathetic feelings for others, it becomes recognized as the principle for all virtue only through its approval by reason; Macaulay is clear that morality is to be rational and principled. While sympathy is natural to all human minds, it will lie latent "till put into motion by the influence of some corresponding impression" (Macaulay 1974, 276). Moreover, it is not enough for this sympathy to be activated; it must be fostered: "[its] growth and prevalence in a great measure depends on the repetition of those impressions which are in their nature adapted to affect [it]" (Macaulay 1974, 276). With this account of the source of human virtue, it is clear why Macaulay constantly emphasizes in part 1 that the education and upbringing of children should aim toward the development of their sympathy.

Macaulay holds that the prime sources of these impressions are law, example, precept, and custom. Therefore it is government's responsibility to use these sources properly, to produce "that improvement on which true civilization depends" (Macaulay 1974, 276). Sympathetic feelings, if properly nurtured, will help lead the way to a morally excellent society.

It is known, that the power of custom over the mind arises from such a repetition of the same impression, as acts to the weakening or destroying [of]

the force of every impression of a contrary tendency. Could we therefore, by
the spirit of our laws, exclude from society the operation of every impression which partook of the smallest tincture of cruelty, and did we encourage
the operation of every impression which had a benevolent tendency, it appears probable, that we should exalt the sympathizing feeling to a degree
which might act more forcibly than the coercion of rigorous laws—to the re-
straining all acts of violence, and consequently all acts which militate
against the public peace. (Macaulay 1974, 276–77)

Macaulay is so convinced of the connection between laws and the development of a morally excellent society that she offers suggestions for
how such necessities as the slaughter of animals for food and the execution of criminals can be carried out so as to produce the appropriate impressions in the mind of the public. For executions, "the ceremonies that
attend this melancholy act, should be made as aweful (*sic*) as possible,"
but the execution itself should be in private so as to prevent any impression that may prove too much of a shock to the sympathetic or "contribute
to steal [steel] the hearts of the more insensible" (Macaulay 1974, 279).

Although Macaulay does not discuss the importance of legal reforms
regarding the position of women, it is unlikely that she was unaware of
the specific implications about women of part 2 of the *Letters*. On the
basis of her arguments in both parts 1 and 2, she seems to believe that
laws regarding the political and social position of women must be reformed to create a consistent and morally positive environment for the
development of all the citizens of a particular society. Yet it is here, perhaps, that a weakness in Macaulay's views may lie. While these legal reforms would have the aim of benefiting women, we can see that their
overall aim would include the moral reform both of women and of society as a whole. This implies, unfortunately, that granting rights to
women equally with men would depend not so much on recognizing
gross injustice as on acknowledging the potential moral benefits for both
women as individuals and society as a whole. Thus it is possible that
Macaulay's views could justify leaving in place laws that a modern
reader would consider oppressive to women.

These implications of Macaulay's views are borne out by her earlier
outline of an ideal form of democratic government in *Letter to Signor
Paoli*, the only work other than the *Letters* in which Macaulay (briefly)
discusses the position and education of women. There, Macaulay emphasizes the prevention of an "aristocratical accumulation of property"
(Macaulay 1767, 36). She believes that such an accumulation would lead
to corruption and a disproportionate distribution of power, ultimately
destroying any democratic government (the only kind that Macaulay believes would produce moral reform). Thus we find Macaulay, in a dis-

cussion of the inheritance of property, recommending that estates should be divided equally between all male heirs and that women should be barred from bringing dowries in marriage. Although Macaulay includes, as a condition of the reforms, a provision for the proper education of female offspring, these proposed reforms clearly do nothing to promote the position of women, and indeed could even take away the little economic power women had at that time (see Staves 1989). Yet while these apparent implications of Macaulay's views cannot, perhaps, be excused, an examination of part 3 of the *Letters* provides a rationale for them.

In the final letters of part 2, Macaulay addresses the crucial question of the moral principles on which government will base the laws necessary to produce moral improvement in society. In letters 12 and 13, Macaulay stipulates that the morally excellent society, the well-ordered society, is the society based on Christian principles. Although Macaulay is well aware of the corrupt societies that have evolved under Christian rule, she argues that these are cases of abuse of religious sentiment, and states that we should ask instead "whether the [religious] sentiment itself, when rendered as pure as the disinterested reason of man is capable of making it, is, or is not, useful to the rectitude of morals, and consequently to the happiness and good order of society" (Macaulay 1974, 323).

Macaulay also addresses one of the potential philosophical objections to the use of religious principles in the government of society: that human laws are sufficient to produce a well-ordered society. In reply, she argues that laws without the backing of religion cannot always influence the agency of humans; furthermore, even the most virtuous of minds may fall into indifference or despair at the thought of a universe that is not ordered. Macaulay also points out the positive side to a society based on religious principles: the recognition that we are governed by a mind of pure moral excellence will produce in us the desire to be virtuous.

It is important to notice that in Macaulay's philosophy, the role that religious principles play in society is, above all else, a practical role. Macaulay states that the government should ensure that religion is taught as the practical way to moral improvement and that the notion of religious faith is demystified. The fundamental tenet that should be taught is that humans are naturally moral creatures, who, using their reason properly, will continue to develop and improve on their propensity for virtue.

On the instructions to the people, government would do well to prescribe the following rules: That all the mysteries of faith, and such metaphysical arguments as are disputable, be carefully avoided by the preachers. That they should enter largely, and dwell particularly, on the practical doctrines of the Christian religion. That they should represent man as a creature endued with powers capable of meliorating (*sic*) his own natural situation, and that of the greater part of the brute creation. They should insist that the powers of human reason can never be so properly employed, as when they are enlarging the boundaries of good, and narrowing the empire of evil. (Macaulay 1974, 334–35)

The role that a practical and demystified religion plays in the ordering of a morally excellent society is the link between the first two parts of the *Letters* and the third and final part. Part 3 appears to comprise the "observations on religious and metaphysical subjects" promised in the full title of the *Letters*. It can be read as a separate work discussing such topics as the origin of evil, the divine perfections, and free will and necessity.[6] Of the eighteen letters it contains, the first nine provide a critical discussion of Bolingbroke's views on the attributes of God and the characteristics of human nature, and six form a reply to the doctrine of free will. Yet these letters also contain Macaulay's arguments for the existence of an afterlife (and its relationship to human virtue) and for moral necessity (and its connection to education), which provide crucial foundations for many of the arguments in the two earlier parts of the *Letters*. Indeed, Macaulay herself states, with reference to part 3, that her main reason for reprinting her earlier *Treatise on the Immutability of Moral Truth* here is that "the principles and rules of education now laid before the public, are founded on the metaphysical observations contained therein" (Macaulay 1974, vi). Moreover, she claims, "A full persuasion of the equity and goodness of God, with a view to the purity and benevolence for which the precepts of our religion are so eminently distinguished, has been the author's sole guide in forming her instructions [for education]" (1974, iii). Clearly then, for Macaulay, part 3 of the *Letters* lays the groundwork for the arguments and the moral principles which are to unify the work. Thus Hill's suggestion that the *Treatise* was reprinted only due to its favorable reviews appears unfounded. This reason is listed last, and—given the hesitant and conciliatory tone of the preface—it appears to function more as a way of giving authority to her presence in this particularly masculine preserve of moral and religious philosophy.

Macaulay begins part 3 with a discussion of the existence of moral evil. Evil, for Macaulay, cannot be necessary, for that would contradict her belief in an omnipotent and wholly good God. Instead, Macaulay believes that God allows evil to be present in the world because this will ultimately produce greater happiness than if evil were not to exist at all. Macaulay believes that the creature who is as perfect as possible will not achieve as much happiness on the whole (and it must not be forgotten that Macaulay sees perfection as necessary for happiness) as the creature who starts in a lesser state and gradually draws nearer to the goal of perfection. We are driven to strive for this perfection not because of self-love or self-interest, but because our reason dictates the wish to imitate (however faintly) the divine virtues; indeed, the pleasure we receive from knowing we are imitating God, and his pleasure at this, is a further motivation for our behavior. The standard for our behavior is the divinely authored invariable rule of right, the immutable principles, for all moral agents.

Macaulay clearly shows how she believes the immutable principles that play a vital role in the arguments for the equality of women are established. The "metaphysical" underpinnings for Macaulay's argument, moreover, are visible in letter 21 of part 1, in which she contends that keeping women in ignorance will deprive them of the possibility of aiming for perfection and thus prevent their happiness. Human beings' increased perfection, and thus, happiness, is evidently part of the divine plan for the world; therefore, denying women these possibilities would appear to contradict human nature itself, a nature that is part of the divine plan.

Macaulay does admit in part 3 that the virtuous person will not always receive happiness in this life. Because an omnipotent, perfectly just, perfectly benevolent divine being will reward virtue (and punish vice), this must therefore mean that there is a future life in which virtue finds its just reward: "But even the virtuous man cannot always by his virtue obtain happiness in this life, or avoid ending his short existence in a condition of misery; therefore, this is a state of trial aptly fitted for the exercise and improvement of that virtue which will find its fruition by an enlarged and more permanent enjoyment of its excellence in another state. But if there be no other state for man to enjoy the undisturbed exertion of his intellectual faculties, virtue is defrauded of its just expectations, God is not omnipotent, or he is a being physically determined to evil" (Macaulay 1974, 380). While this is a rather insubstantial argument for the existence of an afterlife, it is important for the argument in letter 21 of part 1 that to deny women education may be to remove the possibility of their happiness in the next world. Assuming that readers of the *Letters* share Macaulay's faith, they should agree that a refusal to educate women equally with men would again appear to be a direct contravention of the divine plan for human beings.[7]

If, however, the increased perfection of humankind is part of the divine plan, we must ask whether humans have free will; whether they are free to chose the path to perfection. Macaulay argues that humans are bound by moral rather than physical necessity. Once we understand good, we must choose it; in this we follow God, who sees what is perfect and, in his infinite wisdom, chooses perfection. Indeed, Macaulay claims that God's own subjection to moral necessity "is the peculiar glory of the divine character" (Macaulay 1974, 462). To argue that humans have a free will and are not determined in this way accords neither with our nature nor with the path of virtue: "The nearer approaches which all finite creatures make to the perfections of their creator, the more they will be brought under the blessed subjection of being necessarily determined in their volitions by right principles of conduct" (Macaulay 1974, 462).

Given Macaulay's belief in moral necessity, the role of education in the moral development of the human mind takes on a particular urgency. To follow the path of perfection, we must understand the "immutable principles." Moreover, it is not enough that we merely learn the right principles of conduct; we must have "the knowledge also of the mechanism of the human mind, which includes the knowledge of its discipline," for this will be "not only an (*sic*) useful but a necessary auxiliary in the contest between wisdom and folly, between the dictates of the understanding and the tumultuous desires of the passions" (Macaulay 1974, 426). Returning to part 1 of the *Letters*, we can see why Macaulay focuses on demonstrating the mechanism of the human mind and how it can be educated, rather than giving an account of the actual rules of conduct for humans.

The Argument of
Letters on Education

Thus it would appear that the second and third parts of the *Letters* should be read in conjunction with the first part. The second part continues the first with a discussion of the development of sympathy and the consistent environment, both of which are necessary for moral excellence, and shows how they contribute to the development of this excellence. Part 3 provides the general metaphysical foundations for the *Letters* as a whole, and operates explicitly in letter 21 of part 1, in which Macaulay argues for the equal education of women.

It becomes clear then that there is an ethicoreligious system running throughout the *Letters* that unifies the apparently divergent contents of the three parts. It is also evident that Macaulay's arguments for the equality of women are founded on the principles of this system, producing a self-contained, sustained argument for women's equality. Yet while the *Letters* can now be seen as a sustained work of philosophy rather than a collection of Macaulay's opinions on a diverse range of topics, the examination of part 1 in conjunction with parts 2 and 3 once again raises the question of Macaulay's intellectual priorities. The arguments in part 1 for the equal education of women may now seem merely incidental to a more general discussion of social and political reform, a reform based, moreover, on a particular religious view. Nevertheless, an examination of this brand of ethicoreligious reform can provide the key to judging Macaulay's arguments for the equality of women.

A dominant theme throughout all of Macaulay's historical and political writings is the doctrine of "postmillennialism."[8] Blending Enlightenment notions of progress with her own religious beliefs, Macaulay held that God's plan for the world was a gradual improvement in human nature and society leading to a period of perfection on earth heralding the Second Coming.[9] Macaulay envisioned this period to be one "when the *iron* sceptre of *arbitrary* sway shall be broken; when *righteousness shall prevail* over the whole earth, and a *correct* system of equity take place in the conduct of man" (Macaulay 1790, 21, Macaulay's emphasis). Humans do not play a passive role in this plan; both individually and collectively, they can work, through the use of their reason, toward improvement. Thus the role of education in developing and perfecting reason is of central importance for carrying out the divine plan.

In Macaulay's political and historical work, the doctrine of postmillennialism is an underlying assumption, but it is not explored or defended. Her *History of England* is a moral history, an examination of the progress (and regress) of humankind produced through both the collective contribution of governments and the roles of key individuals. For Macaulay, the fighting of the parliamentary army (of the Long Parliament) was "not a trade in blood, but an excertion (*sic*) of principle, and obedience to the call of conscience, and their conduct was not only void of insolence, but benevolent and human" (Macaulay 1768, 4: 181–82). Oliver Cromwell, by contrast, is criticized for allowing his self-interest to contribute to the destruction of a potentially morally progressive government, a criticism that indicates what Macaulay saw as the vital role of moral character in determining the course of English history. In the *Letters on Education*, however, Macaulay does seem to provide an examination of the moral views underlying her historical and political works. Clearly, parts 1 and 2 explain how education will perfect human reason and human society, while part 3 expands on the religious foundations for her "perfectionist" doctrine.

If the *Letters* is a philosophical discussion of Macaulay's "perfectionist" view, how are we to understand the assertion that part 1 offers a sustained argument for the equality of women? It may appear that the arguments for the equal education of women are incidental to Macaulay's central doctrine of perfectionism. Yet this is to misunderstand Macaulay, and to assume that, like Wollstonecraft, she had to be writing a political polemic. Macaulay is offering a moral vision; not a vision of the end of injustice but a vision of a morally excellent society that would require the equality of women. Whether Macaulay argued for the equality of women merely because it was a condition for the morally ordered, well-governed society is open to question. What remains clear, however, is that given Macaulay's philosophical and political views, both equal education and the equality of women are not only unavoidable but divinely ordained.

Conclusion

Could Macaulay have written another *Vindication*? It would seem not. Macaulay clearly recognized the connection between social reform and the equality of women, but such reforms as she envisaged were more for the individual development of the female mind than for some kind of wholesale social change. If the position of women did not restrict moral progress, it would seem that Macaulay would have accepted women's suffering as one of the evils of an imperfect world. Yet although Macaulay did not write like Wollstonecraft, she did offer a sustained and consistent argument for the equality of women, albeit of a rather idiosyncratic kind. The *Letters* can and does contain the sort of sustained argument based on the principles of a self-contained philosophical system that is uncontroversially identifiable as the argument of a philosophical work.

Yet—as I have tried to show in this chapter—it is not simply that Macaulay does not offer the same type of argument as Wollstonecraft for the equality of women that may lead commentators to believe that the *Letters* does not contain a self-contained, systematic, and sustained argument for this equality. The actual structure of the work itself seems to encourage the view that it does not contain such an argument. Moreover, there are certain expectations about the content of the *Letters* that are generated because it is a work in the epistolary genre. In particular, it may be assumed that the content of this type of work will be more concerned with subjects of a more domestic or private nature, such as the moral instruction of young people; an assumption that seems further compounded by the fact that the author is a woman.

But perhaps nothing much seems to hang on this. All it seems I have shown is that Macaulay's work is initially a little hard for the modern reader to interpret. Once we have moved beyond certain expectations generated by its form: we have learned to "read past" it, neither the form nor the content of Macaulay's work seem particularly problematic. But this is not an issue simply about the epistolary form *per se*, it points to something far deeper. It becomes clear from an examination of Macaulay's *Letters on Education* that we must pay attention to the issue of philosophical form. For we must recognize the forces at work that designate certain forms as "philosophical," or that (as in Macaulay's case) create or reinforce associations between certain forms and certain spheres of moral concern. If we come to the study of the work of women philosophers from the history of philosophy before we have examined these forces carefully, we may find that we have certain expectations of a work produced by its form that are prejudicial to an interpretation of that work. Once we start to realize that what is to count as "philosophical" genre is not a "given," then we are in a position to start questioning the biases—and the ideals which come from those biases—that have produced the exclusion of the work of women moral philosophers from the history of philosophy on the grounds of the "non-philosophical" form of their work.

Having shown with Macaulay's *Letters on Education* that a work of sustained philosophical argumentation need not take place within certain forms designated as "philosophical," I want to start exploring possibilities for philosophical genre forms that are different from these designated forms. Thus in the next part of my argument, I examine a work whose form is integral to an understanding of its philosophical content. This examination allows us to see the way that the ideals of the dominant model of moral philosophy get played out in the rejection of this work as "philosophical"—for there is no doubt that it will be rejected.

Notes

An earlier version of this chapter appeared in *Hypatia: A Journal of Feminist Philosophy* 13(1): 118–137. Excerpts from Catharine Macaulay's *Letters on Education* are reprinted with permission from Garland Publishing, Inc.

1. Previously, biographical material on Macaulay was either hard to find or of questionable accuracy. However Bridget Hill (1992) has now produced a fascinating account of Macaulay's life, works, and role in the political life of England, from which the account in this section is drawn.

2. The *Letters* were first published in 1787, reprinted in 1790, and then again in 1974.

3. It should be noted that Eileen O'Neill does treat Macaulay's work as forming a whole, however, O'Neill sees the *Letters* as focused on a theory of education in the Lockean tradition (see O'Neill 1998, 26).

4. Even if one allows that West is a moderate feminist exposing the burdens of marriage—as Alison Sulloway contends—this hardly places in her the same league as Wollstonecraft or, I hold, Macaulay (see Sulloway 1989, 69–72).

5. This would appear to connect with Macaulay's political views. Lynne Withey contends, "the republic vs monarchy issue was not so important to her as insuring the existence of democracy, whatever the form of government" (Withey 1976, 65–66).

6. Macaulay's views here have been criticized as unoriginal. The discussion of religious matters in part 3 does, however, have the merit of being an impressive display of learning.

7. It is interesting to note that Macaulay believes that God intends the perfection and happiness of all his creatures. Macaulay speculates on the possibility of an afterlife for animals, but finds it a little hard to imagine this afterlife being ex-

tended to insects. She decides that if it is not, then their earthly life must instead be a truly happy one (see Macaulay 1974, 358).

8. The claims in this paragraph are based on the work of Lynne E. Withey (1976). Bridget Hill also believes that a claim of postmillennialism as central to Macaulay's ethicoreligious beliefs is valid (Hill 1992, 154).

9. For specific comments on this see Macaulay (1790).

3

Allegory and Moral Philosophy in Christine de Pisan's
The Book of the City of Ladies

An examination and interpretation of *The Book of the City of Ladies*, a work by the medieval French writer Christine de Pisan, can demonstrate the way the form a work takes can be vital to the interpretation of the philosophical content of that work. In *The Book of the City of Ladies*, her best known work, Christine argues against misogynist theological and popular literature. To counter these written works she builds an allegorical city from stories of virtuous women, in the process rewriting the history of women. It is not just that a neglect of this allegorical form of Christine's work means that we shall lose part of its content or meaning, nor that study of its form is simply an aid to meaning; rather the relationship cuts far deeper. As we shall see, its particular form—the allegory of a city—*is* in a sense part of its philosophical meaning, that is to say it is part of the moral argument *itself*.

There are three interconnected aspects of the form of *The Book of the City of Ladies* which are central to a rich and complex interpretation of the moral defense of women it offers: her argumentative technique, its presentation of moral truths, and the way it requires reader involvement. Central to Christine's "defense" of women is her critique of the misogynist images and ideals of the literary and religious traditions. Yet Christine is not simply critiquing these images and ideals in order to dismiss them, instead she transforms and controls them through her allegory of the city so that, ultimately, these images are transformed from being oppressive to being a liberation for women.

The use of the allegorical form brings with it a specific notion of the appropriate presentation of the (philosophical) truths of a text. Essentially the idea is that truth is a complex matter that cannot be expressed through a simple prescriptive or descriptive presentation; rather it must be expressed metaphorically through layers of meaning.

In the case of *The Book of the City of Ladies*, its moral truths are hidden among the foundations, buildings, and inhabitants of an allegorical city. What is crucial to recognize here is that whatever truths the allegorical author intends to express in the text will ultimately be dependent on the literary skills of that author; while the moral truths that are found in the text are in some sense relative to the reader.[1] These elements of the notion of moral truth for *The Book of the City of Ladies* are clearly antithetical to the ideal of impersonal, reductive moral truth of the dominant model of moral philosophy.

The process of uncovering those layers of meaning will then require a particular response from the reader. Indeed I also found that my interpretive account Christine's moral thought reflected this layering to an extent, a fact that has meant that my argument is often a little more unwieldy than I would have liked. One of the aims of presenting truths in an allegorical form is to provoke a self-reflective reading of those truths. As we shall see in Christine's case, reader involvement is not merely necessary for comprehension, but for the moral development that her book can offer the reader. Metaphorically speaking, the self-reflective reader of *The Book of the City of Ladies* is the reader who can gain entrance to the allegorical city. More literally, the reader gains an understanding of the importance of virtue and what constitutes virtuous behavior for women.

Moreover, there is a sense in which the reader also plays a role in the actual philosophical argument or content of the text. In the case of *The Book of the City of Ladies*, the female reader is not only required to be conscious of herself as reader, but also as a woman; she is required to feel angry at unfounded criticisms of women and to empathize with their sufferings. Most importantly, in working out the different levels of moral meaning in the work, the female reader demonstrates both to herself and others the intellectual and moral capacities of women. Thus the (proper) reading of the book is in itself part of Christine's defense of women.

This way of the reader, and the act of reading, actually playing an active role *in* the philosophical arguments and content of a text conflicts with the way that many of us—as products of Anglo-American graduate departments—have been taught to read philosophical texts. On this latter view the reader does read actively in the sense that he or she adopts a critical attitude to the text, but this critical attitude requires a distanced, objective attitude: one in which emotional reactions to the text are controlled. This reader is still required to be self-conscious of him or herself as a reader, but this consciousness is limited to an awareness of the presence of potential preconceptions or prejudices, as well as emotional reactions. In this way we can see how the ideals of the normative subject on the dominant model of moral philosophy get played out in ways of reading a text that are deemed "philosophical," and thus—by implication—what texts are deemed "philosophical" because of the ways that they are, or can be, read. In this current chapter, I shall just raise questions about this notion of the objective, controlled reader. In a later chapter which examines the different kind of reader involvement required by the novels of George Eliot, I shall explore this problematic notion further.

My claim that attention to the allegorical form of *The Book of the City of Ladies* is crucial for its interpretation may seem overly reliant on literary conventions to provide what I am claiming is—after all—a *philosophical* interpretation. Yet this emphasis on literary conventions may not seem so problematic after a careful examination of the type of defense of women Christine is offering in *The Book of the City of Ladies*. Christine is not writing a political polemic, nor should we expect to find this in her work just because of its general subject matter. Once we lose any expectations we may have that Christine's arguments on behalf of women will be aimed at changing their social or political situation, then we shall be able to recognize that Christine's defense of women offers two central things. It is a demonstration of the fact that—despite claims to the contrary—they perform their allotted roles and duties virtuously, as well as a call for the recognition of the moral worth of women both by others and by themselves.

Christine may appear to agree with the detractors of women that wifely care of husband and household is properly the sphere of women's lives and duties, but in order to defend women she shows how these duties, performed correctly, become the source of the virtue of women. Yet this need not mean that the potential for change offered by Christine's defense risks making women accomplices in their own oppression. What we shall find is that the allegory of the city provides a way for women to develop the moral agency they are denied and thus in this way provides a defense of women. Christine is not simply presenting arguments for the moral capacities of women, she is also inviting her readers into the allegory of the city in order that they too can develop their capacity for morality. In short, to read the book is to be aided in the way that the inhabitants are aided by the protective walls of the city; for the literary defense is also a literal defense.

Christine de Pisan

There is little doubt that Christine de Pisan, sometimes credited with being the first professional writer, is an outstanding figure in the history of women's scholarship. Much of the information we have about her life is provided by Christine herself in her *"Avision"* written in 1405 (see Christine de Pisan 1995) in which she talks about her life and fortunes with three allegorical women.[2] Born in 1365, it seems Christine grew up in a bookish household and that her father encouraged her intellectual growth, although ultimately she was trained in conventional feminine arts according to her mother's wishes. Christine probably started writing society verse about 1394, four years after the death of her much cherished husband, as a way of distracting herself from her personal sorrow and the financial troubles created by her widowhood. Christine herself described these early poems as "pretty things, rather light at first" (Willard 1984, 91). She also appears to have started a program of self-education at that time, and in her *Avision* she acknowledges that her life of study was what gave her the most pleasure in life, a pleasure that she recognizes she would not have had if her husband had been alive.

Christine was involved in the literary debate over *The Romance of the Rose*, and according to Charity Willard's biography of Christine, this involvement marked a turning point towards the more serious form of writing Christine employed throughout the rest of her literary career; indeed Willard claims that Christine's criticism of the hypocritical treatment of women by advocates of courtly love contains the "germ" of her later 1405 work: *The Book of the City of Ladies* (Willard 1984, 81). This later work is part of a prolific period of writing that included work on military ethics, government, and the oppression of women.[3] *The Book of the City of Ladies* is perhaps her most famous work, describing an allegorical construction of a walled city to protect virtuous women; its writing simultaneously inspired by Augustine's *City of God*, and provoked by the misogynist literature of Christine's contemporaries.[4]

Yet despite the fact that *The Book of the City of Ladies*, once neglected, is now being assessed from a variety of perspectives: as a work of literature, as a revision of the history of women, or as a work of proto-feminism, there is comparatively little work being done on Christine's moral thought. Rather unfortunately, it may be the very fact that Christine's work crosses disciplinary boundaries in this way that is one reason for her relative neglect by philosophers. It would appear that one of the reasons Christine's political and moral thought has often not been taken seriously is that she was "also" a poet (see Hicks 1992, 8). For example, Mary Ellen Waithe comments in her introduction to the first volume of *A History of Women Philosophers* that Christine "has usually been characterized as a literary rather than a philosophical writer. This means that most secondary literature focuses on discussions of her style, language and thematic representations. [Yet its] philosophic merits are equally worthy of discussion" (Waithe 1; xvi).

The Book of the City of Ladies

The Book of the City of Ladies begins with a character called Christine in a deep despair brought on by contemplation of the criticism of women by learned male authors.[5] Sitting in her study, she has idly opened *Les lamentations de Mathéolas* as a way of amusing herself after her serious literary studies. This book is a satirical account of the misery suffered in marriage by a cleric, Mathieu. While Christine apparently did not find Mathéolas important as an author,[6] he represents the hostility not only towards marriage, but towards women themselves that is prevalent in the work of male authors. The character Christine wonders "how it happened that so many different men—and learned men among them—have been and are so inclined to express both in speaking and in their treatises and writings so many wicked insults about women and their behavior . . . judging from the treatises of all the philosophers and poets and from all the orators . . . it seems that they all speak from one and the same mouth. They all concur in one conclusion: that the behavior of women is inclined to and full of every vice" (Christine 1982, I.1.1).

Three ladies: Reason, Rectitude, and Justice, then appear to Christine and tell her that with their help she will be able to construct a walled city that will protect women from the harms, both physical and moral, that they suffer at the hands of men. Reason, the first lady to help Christine, aids her—both literally and metaphorically—in excavating misogynist prejudices and slanders which serve to maintain the oppression of women. Christine and the Lady Reason dig up and discard a wide range of both secular and religious misconceptions about women; at one stage answering claims that women are gluttonous, and at another denying that the creation of Eve from Adam's rib signifies that women were formed to serve men. In her denial of the latter, Christine argues that Eve's formation surely means that women should be at the *side* of men, not under their feet!

Such replies are usually models of careful argument; for in arguing that women are capable of intelligent thought, Christine as author must show that she herself is an accomplished reasoner. But Christine does not merely reason away prejudice, she also aims to promote a positive conception of women's nature and abilities. A frequent argumentative move that Christine makes is to turn a misogynist slander into a previously undervalued quality. For example, faced with the claims of an (anonymous) author who writes that women by nature have a servile heart and are childlike in their emotions and understanding, Christine does not attempt to dispute any empirical evidence for these behaviors; instead the Lady Reason reminds us that children love tenderness and gentleness, surely a desirable characteristic in women. Furthermore, Reason asks us to recall that Christ told the apostles that those who have a childlike humility and innocence will be the most rewarded.

> [Reason's reply] "They are evil, diabolical people who wish to twist the good as well as the virtue of kindness naturally found in women into evil and reproach . . . if women resemble infants in kindness, they are superbly well advised to be so, for as the Gospel recalls, did not our Lord tell His Apostles, when they were arguing among themselves who was the greatest among them and He called a child and placed His hand on the child's head, 'I tell you that whoever humbles himself like this child shall be the most rewarded, for whoever humbles himself is raised up and whoever raises himself up is humbled.'" (I.10.2)

In replying to the criticisms made against women, Christine draws on examples from both contemporary Europe and the Classical world to demonstrate the contributions women have made to civilization; indeed as Willard states, these examples "provide the cement to hold the city's foundations together"(Willard 1984, 139). Thus in response to the criticism that—due to the weakness of women's minds—they do not have the capacity for government, Reason cites the wise and successful rule of the Ethiopian Empress Nicaula and the just government of the countess of La Marche, a contemporary of Christine's. It is important to notice that Christine is not aiming to produce some sort of chronological record of the achievements of women, rather she deliberately intertwines classical and contemporary examples in order to emphasize the universality of the virtue of women. It is both this universality, and Christine's focus on the goodness of women, that distinguish *The Book of the City of Ladies* from its main literary model, Boccaccio's *De mulieribus claris* (*Concerning Famous Women*) (see Christine 1982, xxx–xxxviii).

Once the foundations and outer walls of the city are in place, Christine builds, with the help of the lady Rectitude, the palaces and streets of the city; for it is not enough to show that women are capable of thinking intelligently, it must also be demonstrated that they are able to think and act morally. Thus in part two of the book, Christine introduces examples (again both pagan and Christian, classical and contemporary) that refute common misconceptions about the virtue of women. The discussion of Rectitude and Christine concerning women's moral behavior goes beyond the obvious sphere of women's sexual virtue (or lack thereof) which often was the focus of contemporary writers. This section of the book is important not only because it allows us a picture of the prevalent view at that time of the vices of women, but because it indicates the differences between Christine's view of the actual virtues of women and the virtues assigned to women by misogynist theological and popular literature. The first examples of virtuous women introduced by Rectitude are examples of women prophets chosen by God as vehicles for the revelation of miraculous or divine events. The importance of such women should not be underestimated for they are chosen by God because of their wisdom and understanding, not because of their chastity. Indeed Antonia—having seen in a vision that Justinian will become emperor of Constantinople—has the foresight to offer to become his mistress if he promises to marry her when he is emperor. The presence of these women combined with the fact that the majority of the examples given by Rectitude focus on marital devotion seems to indicate Christine's intentions to subvert a traditional moral classification of women. Although Christine does appear to keep the traditional classification of women into the triad of virgin, widow, wife, she does not appear to accept its accompanying moral hierarchy—based solely on chastity—that placed virgins on level with queens, and wives on the lowest rung of the ladder.[7] The inhabitants of the city are "ladies" due to a wide range of virtues, and—as we shall see—when there is a central virtue identified for women to become "ladies" it is not chastity, but prudence.

Rectitude helps Christine not only build the city, but to begin the search for women worthy enough to become its inhabitants. At this point the character Christine asks Rectitude about the truth of the claims that women make married life miserable for their husbands due to their faults, bad temper, and lack of care; indeed, she says, some writers claim that men would be better off with a loyal servant to take care of them (II.13.1). Moreover, Christine adds, people claim that men cannot trust women to remain loyal to them, or to be discreet about their business and political affairs, and any man who listens to his wife's advice is rightly despised. Rectitude denies these claims and gives a multitude of counterexamples of women who show their love and loyalty to their husbands.

The accusations levied against wives produce a disturbing picture for the modern reader, not just of the general disparagement of women, but of the popular and religious opinion of their role in married life. From Christine's comments it seems that wives are seen as essentially the unpaid servants for their husbands, yet—unlike good servants—they do not appear to know their place, nor—like bad servants—can their employment be terminated. It is, however, important for the modern reader to notice at this point, that while Christine is critical of the actual treatment of wives within marriage, and of the way that this is reinforced or encouraged by misogynist writings, she appears to hold that most women should become wives.

The remaining examples in section two are devoted mainly to a discussion of sexual virtue. Rectitude argues that most women are not (as men claim) unchaste, inconstant, unfaithful in their love lives, or coquettish. Moreover, Rectitude charges men with maintaining a double standard for sexual behavior; chastity should be a virtue of men also.

> When a few women lapse (and when these men themselves, through their own strivings and their own power, are the cause), then as far as these men are concerned, it is completely a matter of fragility and inconstancy. It seems to me right, nevertheless, to conclude—since they claim women are so fragile—that these men should be somewhat more tolerant of women's weaknesses and not hold something to be a crime for women which they consider only a peccadillo for themselves. For the law does not maintain, nor can any such written opinion be found that permits them and not women to sin, that their vice is more excusable. In fact these men allow themselves liberties which they are unwilling to tolerate in women and thus they—and they are many—perpetrate many insults and outrages in word and deed. Nor do they deign to repute women strong and constant for having endured such men's harsh outrages. In this way men try in every question to have the right on their side—they want to have it both ways! (II.47.1)

With the slanders of men against the virtue of women refuted by Rectitude, the city is completed, it is now time for the third lady, Justice, to come forward and finish the city. She is depicted as the embodiment of divine justice.

> "I am Justice, the most singular daughter of God, and my nature proceeds purely from His person. . . . My duty is only to judge, to decide, and to dispense according to each man's just deserts. I sustain all things in their condition, nothing could be stable without me. I am in God and God is in me, and we are as one and the same. Who follows me cannot fail, and my way is sure. I teach men and women of sound mind who want to believe in me to chastise, know, and correct themselves, and to do to others what they wish to have done to themselves, to distribute wealth without favor, to speak the truth, to flee and hate lies, to reject all viciousness." (I.6.1)

Her central task is to bring a Queen—the Virgin Mary—to reign over the city and to provide the measure, or the basis, for inclusion in the city. The women chosen to inhabit Christine's city are "ladies" through the nobility of their souls, rather than through lineage. It is Christine's recognition of the way the suffering and oppression of women cuts across barriers of time, culture, and class that prompts her to reinvent the category of the noble lady, making it neither class restrictive nor restricted to the context of medieval society, but applicable to any woman who has a nobility of heart.

Thus in this way, Christine offers her own moral hierarchy of women. Justice states that the most noble of the city's inhabitants will be holy women. Even though they are holy virgins, and some of them have their chastity threatened, what most of these women seem to have in common is their strength and constancy in their often long drawn out martyrdom. This again reaffirms the notion in *The Book of the City of Ladies* that chastity is not the sole basis for a woman's virtue. In the final part of the book, with the city completed, the character Christine addresses the three ladies and women everywhere. The city, she declares, will be a protection for virtuous women, indeed their virtue *is* their protection: "[The city] can be not only the refuge for you all, that is, for virtuous women, but also the defense and guard against your enemies and assailants, if you guard it well. For you can see that the substance with which it is made is entirely of virtue, so resplendent that you may see yourselves mirrored in it" (III.19.1).

The Situation of Women

Apart from the city of ladies constructed to protect women, there are two other distinct places described in Christine's work: the home and the marketplace or public domain. Christine makes it clear that the marketplace or public domain is the province of men and that she believes that it is inappropriate for women to enter this domain. The home is the province of women, yet while they are mistresses of the household, their husbands are their masters. Christine explicitly holds that each sex has been assigned particular occupations and tasks for the fulfillment of God's service and that each sex has been given the appropriate nature (both mental and physical) for carrying out those occupations. Thus, Christine argues, women are kind and gentle, and best suited to raising children and to staying quietly at home, while men are physically equipped to withstand the rigors of argument in the law courts and to enforce those laws when necessary: "God gives men strong and hardy bodies for coming and going as well as for speaking boldly. And for this reason, men with this nature learn the laws—and must do so—in order to keep the world under the rule of justice and, in case anyone does not wish to obey the statutes which have been ordained and established by reason of law, are required to make them obey with physical constraint and force of arms, a task which women could never accomplish" (I.11.1).

However this division of labor is not seen by Christine as implying that one occupation is inferior to another, she holds that both household management and law making are equally pleasing to God and are equally part of human service to God. Moreover, Christine makes it clear that women are not kept from law making by reason of their inability to understand law or politics. Christine gives a list of cases of Empresses and Queens who were widowed and left to rule (that is to say, cases where there were not men to do the work) and shows that these women were truly able rulers. The reason, for Christine, that women are to be excluded from the domain of government and law is simply a question of efficiency. Why, she asks, send women when there are already enough men to do the work?

However, while Christine believes that the home is the rightful place for women, she does recognize that this means that many women will be consigned to a lifetime of oppression and misery.

> How many women are there . . . who because of their husbands' harshness spend their weary lives in the bond of marriage in greater suffering than if they were slaves among the Saracens? My God! How many harsh beatings—without cause and without reason—how many injuries, how many cruelties, insults, humiliations, and outrages have so many upright women suffered, none of whom cried out for help? And consider all the women who die of hunger and grief with a home full of children, while their husbands carouse dissolutely or go on binges in every tavern all over town, and still the poor women are beaten by their husbands when they return, and *that* is their supper! (II.13.1)

Christine further recognizes that even when a woman's life is not one of direct abuse, it is still one of restraints and discomfort. In particular, the woman is responsible for maintaining the household, yet she is wholly dependent on her husband for the money necessary for this. Christine urges us to reconsider our condemnation of women who seem to take pleasure in storing up household goods. Rather than think that such behavior is indicative of greed, we must recognize that it is a sign of a woman trying to feed and clothe her family on the little money that she gets from a profligate husband. Furthermore Christine acknowledges that even being *good* at their assigned roles can be problematic for women: "for you will see that all women, or the vast majority, are so very attentive, careful, and diligent in governing their households and in providing everything for them, according to their capacities, that sometimes some of their negligent husbands are annoyed; they think that their wives are pushing and pressuring them too much to do what they are supposed to and they say their wives want to run everything and be smarter than they are" (I.43.2).

Women and Moral Agency

In this way Christine gives a chilling illustration of some of the aspects of oppression suffered by her contemporaries as well as the ways this oppression is reinforced by misogynist literature. Whether their marriage is abusive or merely unpleasant, they are caught between the cruelty of their husbands and public opinion that lays the blame for such cruelty on the women themselves. Caught in a double bind, with no choices for action that do not lead to some sort of unpleasant consequence for them, the women she is addressing are often so restricted that they are rendered, in a sense, immobile. For us as modern readers of Christine's work, it seems clear that the women living in the oppressive environment of the home are denied the freedom of choice and action that we hold to underlie moral agency. Not only do women remain sequestered in the home, but they have little or no control over their lives in the home, even the women who are not treated as slaves by their husbands have their freedom of choice and action severely restrained. Should a woman try to fulfill her allotted role and run her household properly, she encounters treatment by her husband that makes her effort meaningless. In trying to do what she is supposed to do, the poor woman finds that she has somehow transgressed and must not be allowed to behave in this way.

   The lack of moral agency allowed to women comes not only from the conditions of their home life, but from the way that women are not considered to have the necessary *capacities* for moral behavior. This latter claim is something that Christine herself shows throughout the book as one that is explicitly made by the male authors she discusses. These male experts claim, she says, that women are naturally immoral, moreover women—it is said—lack the necessary character to practice virtue, because they are "fickle and inconstant, changeable and flighty, weakhearted, compliant like children, and lacking all stamina" (II.47.1). Indeed there appears to be no sphere in which women have the possibility to behave virtuously. Even in the location of their home, as we saw, the women who run their households well are accused of behaving badly because they are ultimately challenging the supremacy of their husbands. What we find is that this manipulation of reality is so severe that even what we may think of as the stereotypical "feminine" good qualities have become a sign of the baseness of women; one example of this, as we have seen, that Christine brings to our attention is that the affection that women show in their child rearing is seen as symptomatic of their infantile nature. Clearly, this explicit denial by the learned male authors that women have any kind of capacity for morality functions as a crude but effective denial of moral agency to women. Indeed it would seem that the coercive treatment of such weak and base creatures would be justified and even necessary on the part of their husbands.

We find that one of the consequences of this attack on the morality of women is that women are deceived into blaming themselves not only for their own oppression—for clearly such base beings must be properly controlled—but also for the human condition itself. This is brought out ironically, but poignantly, in the opening passages of the book. The character Christine says that because so many books on morals attack women, she cannot help but believe them. Indeed she says that she is lead to conclude that the fact that she cannot actually see these moral faults in either herself or other women must demonstrate the weak intellect ascribed to women by these authors. The more she considers these authorities, she says, the more she is filled with self-loathing: "God formed a vile creature when He made woman, and I wondered how such a worthy artisan could have deigned to make such an abominable work which, from what they say, is the vessel as well as the refuge and abode of every evil and vice. As I was thinking this, a great unhappiness and sadness welled up in my heart, for I detested myself and the entire feminine sex, as though we were monstrosities in nature" (I.1.1).

Yet despite the fact that women's moral capacities are denied and restricted in this way, Christine clearly wishes to maintain that (most) women are virtuous; it is for this reason that she creates—through the character Christine and the three allegorical ladies—a city in which all these virtuous women can live. But given the restrictions under which these women live, the modern reader may want to ask—if I may use Claudia Card's general question about the intelligibility of moral agency under oppression in this way—what it would mean for these women to be moral agents, for them to develop morally. (see Card 1991, 25)

The Question of Marriage

This question becomes even more troubling when we remember Christine's belief that women's rightful place is in the home performing the duties of marriage: housekeeping, child rearing, looking after her husband, etc. Thus Christine appears to reaffirm the very institution that plays such a major role in the restrictions of women's moral agency. Moreover on an initial examination of Christine's view of marriage, it even seems to echo the prevailing prescriptive views of her age on the roles and behavior of women and the moral ideals set forth in pastoral and literary works. This is not to say that married life actually *was* how it was prescribed or described in these works, rather my interest here is to see how Christine used for her own purposes the literature on marriage and the images of ideal wives that were available to her audience.[8]

It should be noted that these pictures of the ideal virtues of wives do not in fact conflict with the criticisms of the morality of women I have just given, they in fact compliment them. For the central virtue of a wife was obedience to her husband. If followed to the letter, this would mean that the wife abdicated all moral responsibility. And indeed, this would be the result of following the so-called *Ménagier de Paris* (1393), a treatise written by a husband for his young wife arguing for her obedience.

The notion that women should obey their husbands was predominant in prescriptive texts both prior to and during Christine de Pisan's time. Even those moralists who saw marriage as a partnership which was good for both husband and wife, or who promoted the "Christian ideal" of marriage as a sacrament and a union based on mutual affection and consensus, did not argue for equality between the partners. Two inter-mingled strands of thought appear to have underpinned this ideal of obedience. The first comes from neo-Aristotelian thought on the rela-tionship between the sexes, and it should be noted here that this type of thought—albeit at a different level of sophistication—had moved out-side of academia to the pulpit and even to popular literature.[9] Typical to this type of thought was the view that the cohesion of the couple was produced—not through a commonality of aims and work—but through the different roles played by each member. The husband was to make the decisions and to move in the public sphere, while the wife was to obey and to administer to her husband's needs within the domestic sphere.

The other strand was the hierarchical nature of medieval society itself in which the wife had duties to her husband because he was her superior. As Karen Green states in *The Woman of Reason*, "people at all levels of so-ciety were taken to have duties to those either above or below them, which were similar to the duties of children to parents or of parents to children. Though women were subject to their husbands, as the people were subject to the monarch, women were also subject to certain women above them in the social hierarchy" (Green 1995, 36–7). The existence of the husband-wife hierarchy, and a social hierarchy among women in general, and within a household, is something that comes out very clearly in Christine's *The Treasure of the City of Ladies*. One way of defend-ing such hierarchical ordering within marriage for Christine's contempo-raries would have been by reference to the divine plan for humanity: "But I would have you know that the head of every man is Christ; and the head of the woman is the man; and the head of Christ is God" (I Cor. 2: 3); "Wives, submit yourselves unto your own husbands, as unto the lord. For the husband is the head of the wife, even as Christ is the head of the Church" (Ephesians 5: 22–23).

As we have already seen, Christine does not hold that women are vicious or intellectually incapable, nor does she believe that a woman's role in the household is inferior to the man's. However, not only does she concur with the prevailing view of the duties of women, but—and even more seriously—she appears to agree with her contemporaries on the need for women to submit to their husbands. Little doubt can remain about this when we hear the final speech of *The Book of the City of Ladies* in which the character Christine addresses the ordinary women of the city and states that "those women who have husbands neither completely good nor completely bad should still praise God for not having the worst and should strive to moderate their vices and pacify them, according to their conditions. And those women who have husbands who are cruel, mean, and savage should strive to endure them while trying to overcome their vices and lead them back, if they can, to a reasonable and seemly life. And if they are so obstinate that their wives are unable to do anything, at least they will acquire great merit for their souls through the virtue of patience" (III.19.2).

While the moralists of Christine's time did not always agree as to what the specific duties of the wife were, for example, whether she should have a role in the education of her children, there was widespread agreement that she should be a good housekeeper patterned after such models as the woman from Proverbs 31. Indeed this notion had been further developed by earlier writers into a claim that women's domestic service could be understood as service to God. For example, Gilbert de Tournai, writing some time prior to Christine, held that in order for a woman to be a good Christian, she could quite simply be a good wife. This equation of good woman with good wife/housekeeper certainly appears to be echoed by Christine when she clearly equates the virtuous woman with the prudent woman from the Book of Proverbs, quoting directly from the Bible.

> Who can find a virtuous, a prudent woman? Her husband will never lack anything. She is renowned throughout the whole land, and her husband is proud of her because she always gives him every good and rich thing. She seeks out and buys woolens, which should be understood as work to occupy her household in profitable activity, and she fits out her household and lends a hand to the tasks. She is like the merchant's ship which brings all kinds of goods and which supplies bread. And there is plenty of meat, even for her servants. She considers the value of a manor before buying it, and thanks to her own common sense, she has planted the vineyard which provides for her household. She girds her loins with the strength of her constant

solicitude, and her arms are hardened in continual good works. No matter how dark it is, the light from her labor will never go out. She occupies herself even with difficult tasks and does not despise feminine chores but applies herself to them. (I.44.1)[10]

It is important to notice that while Christine's contemporaries held one of the duties of the good wife would be taking care of the children, they gave obedience to a husband moral priority over maternal duties. This may be because maternal love had problematic elements; it was seen as a more intense, less rational, physical love, and thus not the sort of love that could be a virtuous or Christian love.[11] It could also be tied into the hierarchical ordering of the household, for the wife's obligation to her husband, her superior, would override her obligations to inferiors (see Newman 1995, 101). Whatever the reason behind this moral ordering, it was reinforced in both educational tracts and romantic literature. A popular image that reinforced the virtue of a woman's unquestioning obedience to her husband, was "the maternal martyr." This woman is portrayed as "good" because she sacrifices her children—not for God's sake—but for his intermediate in the hierarchy: the husband. While this image originated in early Christianity, by the time Christine was writing it had become a well-known convention in secular romances (see Newman 1995).

The trial of Griselda is one of the best known of these tales. It appeared in Boccaccio's *Decamaron*, and was translated by Petrarch into Latin (apparently he thought it the only part of this text worthy of translation), and into French by Philippe de Mézières. Griselda's story takes maternal martyrdom to its ultimate level, for she was tested by her husband simply for the sake of testing her obedience. Griselda was asked to hand over their children to be killed, which she did without complaint. She was then publicly humiliated and returned to her father's home so that her husband could marry another woman. Finally, she was called upon by her husband to arrange this new marriage and to welcome his new bride. Only then did her husband feel he had sufficiently tested her loyalty, love, obedience, and humility.

What is initially surprising is that Griselda also appears in *The Book of the City of Ladies* among a group of women who enter the city due to their virtuous behavior towards their husbands. As modern readers we may not be particularly struck by the story, especially as some of the other stories of these women are equally bizarre. For example, we are told of how Artemisia demonstrated her love for her dead husband by drinking his ashes mixed in wine. However once we are aware of the sort of significance this story would have had for Christine's audience, its inclusion is surprising. Furthermore, Christine also includes the type of story that provided the pattern for these secular maternal martyrs when she tells the tales of three early Christian women who sacrificed their children to their faith. It would seem then that—through her approving use of these images—Christine affirms the virtue of a woman so obedient to her husband/her superior that she is prepared even to sacrifice her own children.

These similarities have not been explored by commentators of Christine's work, yet it is initially quite astonishing how closely Christine's views of the virtuous wife in *The Book of the City of Ladies* mirror those of the male moralists, theologians, and romance writers of her time. She apparently equates the "good" woman with the good housekeeper/wife. Moreover this identification, on further examination, can be seen to provide the moral foundation for her view of the moral importance of the woman's commitment to her marriage, as well as her apparent belief in the moral priority of husband over children.

However, once we look below the surface, we can see that while Christine is using these stock images and opinions of women, she uses them for her own purpose of developing a notion of virtue that can aid women in developing moral agency. Christine is not saying—as the male writers do—that the woman's virtue lies in merely doing what she is supposed to do, rather Christine locates the virtue of the good housekeeper in the attitude with which she undertakes her household tasks. Christine shows that a woman's virtue lies in her moral attitude, not just in a mechanical performance of certain tasks. Moreover, she can show how this attitude is present in other groups of virtuous women who are not (house)wives. We shall see that while Christine—like her contemporaries—does hold that the ideally virtuous wife would be committed to her marriage and husband, for Christine this is a moral commitment on the part of the woman which ties in with her personal morality and thus her ultimate salvation, as well as with the woman's own responsibility for them.[12]

The Prudent Woman

In the first section of the book, Reason and the character Christine discuss whether women have "prudence" or "natural sense" (I.43.1). And it is here that Christine makes the equation of the good woman with good wife/housekeeper explicit with her identification of the virtuous woman with the prudent woman of the Book of Proverbs. Having introduced the notion of prudence, Reason gives proof of the prudence of both pagan and Christian women. However in following Reason's arguments, we begin to see that Christine is bringing out the significance of the prudent woman as the strong accomplished housekeeper of Proverbs. For Christine the prudent woman is not virtuous simply because she is has diligence, foresight, etc., but because these virtues are the result of prudence, not prudence itself.

Christine contrasts the moral knowledge acquired through learning with the knowledge that comes from prudence.[13] Prudence is a type of practical moral knowledge that teaches us to reflect on what it is best to do and to learn from past events (see I. 43. 1). It is a natural sense, given by God, that all men and women possess to varying degrees; thus, even though Christine's focus is on prudence in women, she makes it quite clear that it is not a "feminine" or "female" virtue. While the virtue of prudence is a complex one, Christine makes it clear that there is one central aspect that is important for her by defining prudence in this way: "prudence means taking pains to be able to finish those tasks which one wishes to undertake" (I.46.1). While Christine allows for aristocratic women to demonstrate their prudence in weathering the vagaries of their positions of power, it is evident from Christine's view of the division of tasks of the sexes that the household tasks of women are their allotted role in life, and that the typical woman who has prudence will shoulder this responsibility and see these tasks through to completion.

Even the female saints and martyrs (described in the third section of *The Book of the City of Ladies*) who gain entrance to the city through their torture and martyrdom (at the hands of men), rather than through their virtuous endurance of married life, can be seen to possess this virtue of prudence. The list given by Justice of these most outstanding inhabitants of the city is a gruesome litany of female saints and martyrs; these martyred women bear their tortures without complaint or calling for punishment for those who have wronged them. They remain unswayed from the path of righteousness that they have chosen; indeed this often seems to be their only qualification for entry into Christine's city. In this constancy under torture we see a rather grim playing out of the virtue of prudence, in that they finish what they started. In the case of these particular women, the reason for their martyrdom—their religious belief— and its moral significance for themselves—salvation—is clear.

In this way, prudence appears to be connected to the *manner* of the performance of one's duties, or one's attitude towards them. The ordinary prudent woman is then one who resigns herself to her allotted role in life and performs its duties with a kind heart. The good woman is not simply the woman who performs her tasks well, she is the woman who performs them in the right way for the right reasons. The right reason is not to better her life, such behavior—as we saw earlier—need not produce any material advantage for women; indeed it may even annoy lazy or neglectful husbands. The right reason is her recognition of the moral significance of her tasks. And, as we shall see, what is crucial about this moral significance is the way it parallels the moral significance of the "tasks" of the martyrs in that it leads to their ultimate salvation.

It would then seem that the consequence of possessing the virtue of prudence for the ordinary woman is that she must take on the responsibility for maintaining her marriage and all that this entails; once the marriage has begun, the prudent woman is morally committed to its continuance. As we shall see later, the prudent woman not only understands the moral commitment of marriage, but she also understands how her role within marriage has moral significance for *herself*. The importance of Christian marriage for Christine should not be underestimated. It is evident throughout her writings, especially in her poems and discussions on courtly love which contrast the ideal of a happy marriage with the illicit love affairs sanctioned by the model of courtly love.[14] The moral significance of Christian marriage for Christine is evident when we recognize that its model was the image of the "marriage" between the church—as the Bride of Christ—and Christ. On this model, therefore, marriage between a man and a woman entailed complete personal moral commitment.[15]

My claim that the central ethical responsibility of the prudent woman is the continuance of her marriage can be supported in a number of different ways. In the second part of *The Book of the City of Ladies* Rectitude finishes building the city and announces that it is now ready to be populated by virtuous women. What is significant is that women who have behaved virtuously towards their husbands are not only among the first virtuous women described by Rectitude to enter the city, but form the majority of those who enter. The virtuous behavior of these women ranges from saving their husbands from death to simple constancy in love. This prioritizing and celebrating of women who have fulfilled their marriage vows—in spirit as well as letter—would seem to suggest that the ordinary prudent woman will exercise her virtue of prudence towards the continuance of her marriage and thus that this is her central ethical responsibility.

What is perhaps most significant here is how, now that we see these stories through the lens of Christine's concept of prudence, our perspective of Griselda, who is included among these women, changes. While Christine's version seems similar to Mézières's translation of Petrarch, she emphasizes the *virtue* of Griselda's constancy: "In her revision . . . the suffering of wives becomes a more general phenomenon, with [Griselda] the first wife actively achieving something of value, while Mézières's Griselda simply suffered" (Quilligan 1991, 166). A similar shift also seems to occur with the stories of the three martyred mothers who allowed their children to be martyred for their faith; women who are the most celebrated of the city. It is still hard for the modern reader to understand why tales of mothers who put love for God over their maternal love, to the point where they comforted their suffering children with joy, would have captured the popular imagination during the time Christine was writing.[16] However we can now see how the true virtue of these women is not located in an unreflective obedience to God, but in their continuing to do what they *know* is the right thing.

The centrality of this moral commitment for Christine can also be seen in her retelling of the story of the Sabine women. In Christine's version of the story the Sabine women have been carried off by force by the Roman men and forced into marriage. The Sabine men wage war against the Romans in an attempt to avenge themselves and have their women returned. The Sabine women bring about peace by throwing themselves on the battle lines, as they do not want their husbands or their kinfolk to die. What is notable about this story is the sense of loyalty to their husbands that Christine attributes to the Sabine women, despite the initial brutal circumstances of their marriages. The leader of the Sabine women in urging the others to plead for peace states that "if our husbands are conquered, what a terrible grief and desolation it will be for us, who rightfully love them and who have already had children by them" (II.33.1). The Sabine women here seem to be saying that now that they are married, they have become committed to loving and protecting their husbands and to producing their heirs.

The ethical centrality of the marital relationship in *The Book of the City of Ladies* explains the content of its 'sequel': *The Treasure of the City of Ladies*. In the prologue of *The Treasure*, we return to Christine in a state of exhaustion after building the city, yet she is still charged by the three ladies to continue her work, this time by writing the lessons of wisdom for women in all ranks of society so that they may join the inhabitants of the city. The three ladies introduce the figure of Worldly Prudence who offers teachings for a moral and well-ordered life. Central to these teachings for all women whatever their rank in society is virtuous conduct towards their husbands. As in *The Book of the City of Ladies*, Christine recognizes that there are some women who are so restricted that they might not be allowed the freedom to follow these teachings, for them she offers the advice "to endure patiently, always to do good so far as it is in their power, and to obey in order to have peace" (Christine 1985, 80).

The Treasure is a practical guide for prudent women not only instructing them how to deal with their husbands and households, but as Willard suggests, encouraging them "to stand on their own feet, to make some sort of contribution to society, to dominate the conditions of their lives that make or break them" (Willard 1984, 146). It appears to be of a different character from *The Book of the City of Ladies* with its focus on etiquette and rules for behavior; it is certainly more pragmatic. For example, Christine says continual good conduct towards a cruel husband has been known to cause him to repent on his death bed and to leave his wife financially rewarded. However at least one commentator has suggested that Christine's advice to women to commit themselves to their husband's every need involves spiritual as well as physical care, and thus that the code of behavior set out in *The Treasure* is ultimately designed to help their husbands achieve salvation.

From these examples, it would appear the prudent woman is one who will devote herself to the responsibilities of her marriage. Christine shifts the meaning of the concept of a "good wife" from the woman who simply obeys her husband, to the woman who understands and commits herself to the moral responsibilities of marriage. In order to make this commitment, and to perform its accompanying duties properly, the wife needs the central virtue of prudence. The crucial difference is not really one of action, but one of attitude. While it may be hard to see *The Book of the City of Ladies* as promoting nothing more than an "ethics of service" for women, it is important to notice that this service is not for the convenience of the husband *per se*; rather it is something closer to the Christian ideal of service. Returning to the final speech in which the character Christine addresses all women and tells them to bear with their husbands, we can now see that her emphasis is not on obedient behavior for its own sake but rather on the virtue of prudence and a commitment to finishing what they started.

The Problem

But these changes for the lives of women that Christine is offering in their defense seem at best, deeply unsatisfactory. Even with this rereading of the final speech through this new conceptual lens, it seems that Christine's notion of the prudent woman is fraught with difficulties. If the prudent woman is one who is committed to finishing what she started—which in the case of the ordinary woman is to commit herself to the moral responsibilities of marriage—then it seems that instead of the ordinary virtuous woman saving herself from oppression, she has instead condemned herself to a life of brutality *through her desire for her own virtue.* Indeed religious martyrdom may at this point seem—due to its comparative brevity—the soft option for virtue.

What further complicates matters is that, even for a personal virtue like prudence, there must be a context within which it can have meaning. Yet, as we saw earlier, Christine makes clear that the situation in which many of her contemporaries live denies them this context. Without some sort of accessible standard by which to judge their behavior, it is not evident how women can properly develop the virtue of prudence. Yet Christine does not initially appear to be arguing for any kind of change in context that would allow the development of prudence to have meaning. Even though Christine recognizes the sufferings of women, the only political or social change she appears to demand in her "defense" of women is the recognition of this injustice.

Sheila Delany in "Mothers to Think Back Through" argues that we cannot excuse Pisan's reaffirming of the social status quo as a result of the social context within which she was writing. Delany claims plausibly that this social context was being transformed. Fifteenth-century Europe was a time of great social and political change, radical ideas were acceptable currency, and women were becoming an integral part of economic and social life. Furthermore, Delany argues, we should not attempt to argue that the special oppression that Pisan was under writing as a woman should mitigate the questionable nature of Pisan's conclusions for women's societal roles. Delany finds this type of apology condescending "because it implies that we should exempt women from moral and political polemic because of their gender," and irresponsible "because although any opinion surely has both personal and social determinants, these do not . . . justify the denial or abdication of choice" (Delany 1987, 196).

Taken in the context of the time within which Christine was writing, Delany may well be correct to argue that Christine's problematic conclusions on the submission of women cannot be excused because of the way Christine, as a woman, was oppressed; although her claims about the radicalism of Christine's period have been criticized for their accuracy (see for example, Quilligan 1991). But the accuracy of Delany's historical data is not the central issue here. What is important for my account is the way Delany has constructed—a construction apparently also accepted by her critics—the problem in terms of two choices for Christine: a "nonfeminist" acceptance of the status quo, or a "feminist" call for justice or social change. If Christine's work falls into the former category, then her interest for the feminist philosopher will most likely only be in terms of her early place in the history of women writing.

But I think that to hold that Christine has only two choices is to assume that any defense of women can only be categorized in these terms. We can certainly claim that Christine could have called for an end to the injustice suffered by women, and we certainly cannot hold that she was unable to make such a call. But it is surely clear that such a call would not help her contemporaries or provide the defense she claims the allegorical city can offer. What we should resist is any temptation to oversimplify, or to create easy categories for the work of women philosophers from the history of philosophy. As we have already seen with Catharine Macaulay's *Letters on Education*, an argument for the equality of women need not be framed in terms of an argument for social and political change. Similarly, we must recognize that not all defenses of women are necessarily political or moral polemics.

To demand that Christine write this kind of polemical defense is to assume implicitly that the form of *The Book of the City of Ladies* is incidental to its content. We need to recognize that the allegorical form of the work, and specifically the allegory of the city, are central to an understanding of the sort of defense that Christine offers women. Moreover, an understanding of the allegory can allow us to resolve the problem of the prudent women apparently embracing her own oppression. I believe that we should take seriously Christine's claim at the end of the book that the allegorical city will provide protection for its virtuous inhabitants. Clearly the city cannot *literally* provide protection. It cannot prevent the actual mental and physical suffering of individual women in the home, or protect them from it. It may seem that the protection the allegory of the city offers is the way it works as an image enhancing the reputation of women. This would mean that the image of the walled city offers an active demonstration of the virtue of women (in other words gaining entrance to the city) and can help them against slanders and attacks on their moral character (as their previously unrecognized virtue is now demonstrated). But the allegorical city also works on another, more significant, level. Christine uses the construction of an allegorical walled city as a way of helping her contemporaries develop moral agency: it defends them through showing them how to take charge of and develop their personal morality, and thus to be responsible for their ultimate salvation. In this way we can see how moral agency and moral meaning can be created within oppression.

The Allegorical City

While the conversation of an author with allegorical figures was a popular medieval convention, we must recognize that Christine would still have deliberately chosen this form and would have had specific reasons for so doing. As Christine used other forms besides the allegory to express her moral and political views, we must assume that she believed that the conventional form of the allegory suited the subject matter of *The Book of the City of Ladies*. The most obvious reason for her choice would be that this was a familiar form that would have had the most appeal for the audience Christine had in mind for her work: educated women from the upper classes.[17] But the relationship between form and content in *The Book of the City of Ladies* goes beyond mere audience appeal. For the allegorical city functions not simply as a description of possibilities for women, it also draws the reader herself into the city. To put it simply, reading *The Book of the City of Ladies* in the manner in which it is intended can literally aid the female reader in the way the allegorical city aids its fictional inhabitants. In focusing on the female reader this is not meant to imply that the allegory can only be understood by women, for, like all allegories, there are layers of meaning in *The Book of the City of Ladies*. However, the meaning of the city as a defense of women is of particular interest to the feminist philosopher.

In order to show this, I want first to begin by showing how we can understand that the allegorical city can protect its inhabitants. And here we must not forget that the city is not just offering protection to its fictional inhabitants, but to prospective inhabitants among its readers. I intend to claim that the role the city plays is not merely as a symbol of community or shared grievances; instead it provides a context within which the actions and lives of the women can take on moral meaning. I hold that the city is able to perform this task because it provides standards of conduct, a recognition of the acts of its inhabitants, and an appropriate system of justice.

Outside the city if and when there are standards for the behavior of women, more often than not these standards are set by men with the intention of preventing women from causing the harm that is (supposedly) in their nature to do.[18] Entrance into the city provides women with a positive set of standards: they have clear standards for virtuous behavior as well as an understanding of their potential for virtue. Moreover, the fact that it is the role of the lady Justice to choose women worthy enough to live in the city indicates to us that these standards are set for women by God.

As we saw, outside the city the life of the prudent woman may have no outwardly distinguishing signs, her lot may be as brutal as that of any other woman. While kinder treatment from her husband *may* be a result of prudent behavior, there is no guarantee of this; nor is an amelioration of her domestic life the motivation of the prudent woman. No matter how the prudent woman is treated by her husband, her virtue is recognized, in the first place, by entrance into the city—that is, her virtue will be its own reward. And in the second place, as Christine makes clear, her reward will be ultimately to move from the kingdom of femininity to the kingdom of God. Thus the women who have taken on their marital responsibilities as a moral choice are distinguished by their membership of the city of ladies, and by their future rewards.

The role of the lady Justice, therefore, not only offers the promise of a reward for the suffering of women, it also allows the distinction to be made between the women who perform their household tasks well out of fear of their husbands or some kind of mechanical obedience, and women who perform their tasks well from a desire for virtue.[19] The city

of ladies will provide its inhabitants with a system of justice and government, but it is clear from the presence of the lady Justice, and the role of
the Virgin Mary as the queen of the city, that justice for women will be divine not earthly justice. Justice is not an image of secular justice with the
law courts, rights, etc.; *that* is something that Christine has made clear is
the province of men. The justice of the city of ladies described by Christine is closer to divine justice. It is impartial and rewards constancy and
faith; and it teaches us moral self-examination so that we can provide the
necessary checks on our behavior and deeds by ourselves.

Thus when we examine the differences between the life of the prudent
woman living within the city, that is to say the woman who commits herself to the moral responsibility of maintaining her marriage, and the life
of a woman who has not gained entrance to the city, there may appear to
be no outward difference in their circumstances. There is, however, an
important difference between their lives: the prudent woman can be seen
as having made a choice to take responsibility for her personal morality
(and thus her ultimate salvation). It is true that women seem to have
been denied the sort of freedom of choice and action that the modern
reader will see as underlying moral agency. But we need to recognize
here that the moral agency of the prudent woman is more a question of
the attitude she adopts than the actions she takes.

Through the city Christine allows women (and most importantly, the
woman reader of the book) a way to refuse to be brutalized by their circumstances. These women cannot change their circumstances, but they
can develop virtues that enable them to live morally within their confined indoor world, rather than the virtues such as courage, needed for
the outside male-dominated world. The women addressed in Christine's work are shown that they can choose to make sense of their situation and that they can choose to develop those virtues that will allow
them to do this. They cannot leave or change her situation, but they can
choose to take responsibility for that situation and thus for their personal morality and ultimate salvation. In making such a choice they are
exercising moral agency, creating a moral meaning within their circumstances.[20]

In this way, we can see that even though Christine—like many of the
moralists among her contemporaries—advocates the good housekeeper
of the book of Proverbs as the paradigm of virtue for women and claims
that women should resign themselves to the oppressions of married life,
she has appropriated these ideas for use by women themselves. Through
the use of allegory, Christine transforms these ideals and images drawn
from misogynist culture, and by entering in the allegorical city, women
create a moral meaning for *themselves* from these images and ideals.
Christine does not envisage the possibility that women can rebel against

their divinely ordained roles, but she does show how within the proper (virtuous) performance of these roles, women can develop virtue and thus play an active role in their own salvation.

Christine creates this ideal of virtue and virtuous behavior for women in response to the type of misogynist stereotype she criticizes throughout *The Book of the City of Ladies*. Misogynist writers claim, for example, that women are incapable of moral behavior, that they are weak willed and childish, perhaps even evil. As we have seen, Christine often combats such criticism by turning it into a compliment. What we now find is that Christine is not simply rebutting individual stereotypes and misreprensations of women, but that, ultimately, she makes the whole work a rereading of the ideals and images of the misogynist religious and literary traditions. What we find is that these images and ideals from pastoral and literary works—instead of being a way to restrict or suppress these problematic creatures—become a way to liberate them, and even to ensure their ultimate salvation.

The Need for Allegory

However it might not be, as yet, obvious to the modern reader *why* Christine employs allegory for her defense of women. If we want to understand whether Christine's employment of this particular form of writing has a *philosophical* significance and is not simply due to convention or audience appeal, then we need to learn how to read the allegory of the city.[21] Whereas we saw with Macaulay that the form of a text need not be a hindrance to our understanding of the argument of the text, in the case of *The Book of the City of Ladies* its allegorical form is an integral part of its arguments in the moral defense of women. The initial problem here, for the modern reader, is to understand how an allegory can function as more than an explanatory image. As C. S. Lewis states, "the art of reading allegory is a dead as the art of writing it, and more urgently in need of revival if we wish to do justice to the Middle Ages" (Lewis 1953, 116).

As modern readers the sorts of images to which we are more accustomed are examples of people seeds and the ubiquitous Smith and Jones. These images are employed to support or elucidate arguments, and we know how to judge them: in terms of their success or failure in their representation and amplification of particular arguments or concepts. However these examples are not part of the philosophical argument itself, for if they fail then they can always be replaced with a better image. The most crucial point to recognize is that we cannot treat Christine's allegorical city as we do these modern philosophers' examples. It is not simply a means to an end which, once we have grasped the meaning of the work, can then be cast aside. This is not how allegories are read; instead when we read them we must keep both the literal sense and the allegorical sense firmly in view. If understanding the allegorical sense of a text is important to our understanding of its philosophical content in this way, then this means that the judgment of the philosophical reader regarding the relative success or failure of Christine's arguments will also—directly or indirectly—include a judgment of the literary success of the work.

While it can be argued that the reading of all literature is allegorical in the sense that the reader searches for meaning, allegory as a form specifically controls the meanings which the reader will find within the text; and thus the reader is more aware of themselves as reader and what is expected of them as reader. Indeed it even seems possible that in *The Book of the City of Ladies* Christine is employing a specific convention to produce self-awareness in her reader. This convention is summarized by Maureen Quilligan in *The Language of Allegory* in the following way: "Another favorite technique [of the allegorist] for producing self-consciousness in readers is to make the action of the narrative parallel the process of reading, so that as readers read the action, they are, in reality, reading about their own reading experience" (Quilligan 1979, 254). In this way when the reader of *The Book of the City of Ladies* reads about the existence of virtuous women and their entrance into the city of virtue, she is also reading about her own experience of gaining a sense of moral worth and agency.

Certainly in becoming aware of herself as reader, the female reader of *The Book of the City of Ladies* simultaneously becomes aware of the falsity of the notion that the only role women play in written discourse is as the object (of contempt) of a written text. This is important because it then implies that the notion that the only role that women can play in morality is as the passive object of moral injunctions is equally false. This implication can be drawn because the city is both a literary city composed of the (re)writing of women's history, and of stories and anecdotes about the virtue of women, and an allegorical city of virtue and of the moral agency of women. Moreover, and more importantly, in reading the allegory of the city the reader gains an understanding of the moral agency of women, and thus becomes aware of her own potential to develop this agency. Christine is not simply presenting arguments for the moral capacities of women, she is also inviting her readers into the allegory of the city in order that they too can develop their capacity for morality. In short, to read the book is to be aided in the way that the inhabitants are aided by the protective walls of the city.

The allegorical city, like all allegories, works on different levels. On a representative level it shows the possibility of virtuous behavior for women, and it provides advice to women by showing them the virtues and skills they need in order to perform their tasks properly and to achieve ultimate salvation. Yet the allegorical city is neither merely an argument for the moral agency of women, nor simply a picture of their potential for moral agency, it also provides the medieval woman reader with the moral community—necessary for moral development—which she has been denied. The city can perform this role in the development of the moral agency of women because it functions as a place in which women can separate from men, and thus establish a place in which they can make sense of their situation, and develop the virtues necessary to carry out the tasks of that situation. The city allows women to withdraw in some sense from the world dominated by men.

This withdrawal allows the possibility of an alternative understanding of the nature and virtue of women and their importance in this world; an understanding that is made impossible by the oppression of the male-dominated world outside the city. Entrance into the city also allows its inhabitants to see themselves as part of a community. The development of the moral agency of these women does not happen in isolation, but as part of a community with a shared form of life; indeed it would seem that the city provides a moral community within which the values of its inhabitants are created and maintained. Thus as a symbol in an allegory the city means something both literally and as a trope (Honig 1960, 113), it is both a city or community and it signifies the possibility of women's moral agency.

Often allegory persuades the reader of the crucial truth or truths of the work through the retelling of old or authoritative stories. This central truth in the work supports the parabolic mode of recounting a story, and the reason for that recounting, thus this truth connects all three aspects together, and the successful allegory creates a completely new work (see Honig 1960, 12–13). Christine uses classical and Biblical stories to support the possibility of new patterns of women's behavior, and these are both connected by and serve to reinforce the central truth of her work: the (near) universal virtue of women. Thus Christine's use of stories of past virtuous women is not merely the (re)writing of women's history, it is an inseparable component of the allegorical form of her work and its underlying truth: the stories are the bricks and mortar of the city.

The significance of allegory for Christine herself can be drawn out from the recently recovered "Phillipps preface" to the *Avision*, in which Christine discusses her view of poetry. It is clear that she equates the form of allegory with "its subtle covers and beautiful material hidden under pleasant and moral fictions" with literature itself (Reno 1992, 209). Christine claims that this form of writing contains "much secret knowledge and pure truths" hidden under "the figure of metaphor or veiled speech" (Reno 1992, 209). It is also evident that Christine connects the possibility of multiple meanings in allegory with its aesthetic value: "What is put in poetic language can have several meanings, and poetry becomes beautiful and subtle when it can be understood in different ways" (Reno 1992, 209). These notions are later reiterated in *Le Livre des faits et bonnes meurs du sage roy Charles V* (see Solente 1936–1941) where we find that, for Christine, "The word poetry is taken to mean either some fiction used for the narration as a whole, or the introduction of something which signifies one thing on the surface, but has one or more hidden meanings, or, one might better say, poetry's object is truth and its technique is doctrine clothed in ornamental words and suitable nuances" (Willard 1984, 93).

This belief that the complexity of the truth requires metaphorical expression, rather than simple prescription or description is shared by other writers of allegory (see Clifford 1974, 53). This is a significantly different notion of truth and its appropriate presentation to that which most philosophers—including myself—are accustomed. It certainly conflicts with the way that the dominant model of moral philosophy conceives of moral truth as open, impersonal, and precise, as well as with the way that this model conceives of the whole point of the philosophical enterprise being to remove ambiguities, not to reinforce them. While the "truth" that the walled city stands for is clear—the virtue of women—to say that the meaning of the work is simply that Christine is presenting an argument defending women's reputation against misogynist attacks is to miss how its meaning functions on many different levels. I have only brought out one level of meaning—one that is of potential interest to feminist ethics—with my claim that the walled city also "means" that women can develop moral agency. Many possible paths of meaning in the city—paths that are clearly intended by Christine—are still unexplored, for example the significance of the deliberate allusion to Augustine's city.

Thus to ignore the relationship between the (allegorical) form of *The Book of the City of Ladies* and its content is to neglect important aspects of its moral thought, specifically we shall not see the role the allegorical city plays in women's moral agency. The use of the allegory of the city allows the book to function on many different levels, from providing arguments for the moral capacities of women, to providing a way that the reader can develop such capacities herself. In short, the allegorical form of *The Book of the City of Ladies* is central to its actual philosophical content, moreover the latter cannot be properly grasped without an understanding of the former. To ignore this relationship is also to fail to acknowledge the philosophical significance of the form of the work *itself*, for Christine deliberately chose to write in an allegorical style because of her belief in the way it complemented the moral truths expressed in her work.[22] Indeed, as we can see from Christine's own comments on allegory, the form is not incidental to the content of her work, for she explicitly held that poetry is an essential cover for truth. And it is here that we find the roots of the problem with the form of *The Book of the City of Ladies* for the dominant model, for integrated into this allegorical form is a notion of moral truth that conflicts with the ideals of the precision and clarity of moral truth of this model.

Problems with the City

Interestingly enough, the real philosophical problems for the *modern* reader of Christine's moral defense of women ultimately should come not so much from its metaphorical presentation, but from the sense in which this defense is *only* a moral defense. What we find is that although Christine argues throughout the book that women have equal understanding to men, and she herself clearly values education, she holds that women do not need to be educated. For she believes that education is not necessary for the fulfillment of the their allotted task of maintaining their marriage and home:

> [Reason] "If it were customary to send daughters to school like sons, and if they were then taught the natural sciences, they would learn as thoroughly and understand the subtleties of all the arts and sciences as well as sons . . . "
>
> [Christine] "My lady, since they have minds skilled in conceptualizing and learning, just like men, why don't women learn more?"
>
> She replied, "Because, my daughter, the public does not require them to get involved in the affairs which men are commissioned to execute . . . It is enough for women to perform the usual duties to which they are ordained." (I.27.1)

The modern reader of *The Book of the City of Ladies* should ultimately feel frustrated at the price that women will pay for their "protection" by the city. Although the city leads to the kingdom of heaven, which for Christine is the supreme good for humans, modern readers may find that the city does not in the end contribute towards the good of women on this earth. For while the city is the locus of moral agency and moral development, this will come at the expense of the intellectual and personal development of women. In order to carry out her ethical responsibilities, the virtuous woman will need to focus on developing the skills and characteristics that will enable her to perform her God-given tasks prudently. While these skills and characteristics are essential, her personal virtue, and her ultimate salvation, they will exclude the possibility of other skills or characteristics that we, as modern readers, may find vital for personal fulfillment.

Conclusion

I believe that any analysis of Christine's moral thought in *The Book of the City of Ladies* that does not take into account the existence of the allegorical city cannot give a full picture of her moral thought, for to ignore the allegorical city is to ignore what is distinctive about Christine's account of the virtue of women. But it is not simply that the allegorical city has a role to play in our understanding of the central meaning of this work, the city is part of this meaning or content *itself*. By this I mean that it is through the allegorical city that its fictional inhabitants find their moral agency, and it is through the reader's metaphorical entrance into the allegorical city that she finds the central (but not necessarily the only) meaning of the work: recovery of female moral agency, particularly her own.

In this way, it seems evident that the form *itself* of *The Book of the City of Ladies* has philosophical significance. Moreover, Christine makes it clear that she is conscious of the relationship between the presentation of a work and its philosophical content. The multiple meanings of the allegory both hide and expose the truth expressed in the work and thus require an active, reflective search on the part of the reader. In this way there is a sense that the moral truth in a work is not impersonal, but relative to the reader. This has the further implication that if such a work is not written by an author with sufficient literary skills, then the philosophical content itself will suffer. Obviously these notions of the relationships of both author and reader to the text and of the connections between philosophical form and philosophical content are at odds with dominant paradigms of the philosophical form, reader, and author.

On the dominant model of moral philosophy, it is doubtful that *The Book of the City of Ladies* as it stands would count as a work of moral philosophy. Given my claim that the form of the work is part of its philosophical content, it seems certain that it would not. The notions of the allegorical form of the work, the self-reflective reader, the skilled writer, and the need for moral truths to be hidden in poetry are all "non-philosophical" on the standards of this dominant model. But these notions reflect the moral ideals of *The Book of the City of Ladies* and thus are not incidental to the work. For example, moral activity is less about decision-making and more about understanding and coming to terms with one's situation. Or virtue is tied into performing certain tasks well and with the correct attitude—housekeeping for example, and even, by implication, writing. It is these ideals that are incompatible with the set of moral ideals that get played out in the paradigms of the dominant model of moral philosophy: of critical judgments being made by an objective distanced reader, of the rational capacities (not literary skills) of the philosophical writer, and of moral truths as precise, clear and impartial.

In other words, the moral ideals that underpin the designation of the allegorical form of *The Book of the City of Ladies* as "non-philosophical." We must be careful, however, in allowing a claim that the tension between my way of reading Christine's *The Book of the City of Ladies*, and dominant paradigms of philosophical interpretation is caused by the fact that I am merely mistaken in holding that philosophical form, or the roles of reader and author can have any philosophical significance. For the judgment that these aspects of Christine's work fall into the category of the "non-philosophical," or that the presentation of her argument does not have philosophical importance, is not somehow neutral, or independent of particular definitions of moral philosophy: it is the result of moral judgments about what is to constitute moral philosophy. In the same way, the ideal of the critical, objective, emotionally controlled reader is just that: an ideal. It certainly may be the only appropriate way to approach the vast majority of philosophical work, but—as I shall show with my examination of the novels of George Eliot in a later chapter—it is not the *only* way to approach *all* works of philosophy.

Notes

Selections by Christine de Pisan from *The Book of the City of Ladies*, translated by Earl Jeffrey Richards. Copyright © 1998 by Persea Books, Inc. Reprinted by permission of Persea Books, Inc.

1. See the comments by Cora Diamond in my Introduction.

2. My information is also based on Charity Cannon Willard's 1984 biography of Christine, *Christine de Pizan: Her Life and Works* (New York: Persea).

3. For a comprehensive listing of Christine's works, see Earl Jeffrey Richards's introduction to *The Book of the City of Ladies* (New York: Persea, 1982).

4. Not only Augustine, but Aquinas, and Boethius apparently had an influence on Christine's moral thought. Unfortunately I do not have the space to devote to an examination of these influences. I suggest that the interested reader begins with Karen Green's 1995 work *The Woman of Reason* (New York: Continuum).

5. As it is now customary to refer also to the author as "Christine" rather than "de Pisan," I shall make it clear—if necessary—when the "Christine" I refer to is the character of the book.

6. See Joan Kelly, *Women, History and Theory: The Essays of Joan Kelly* (Chicago: Chicago University Press, 1984): 72.

7. This triad appears to feature in her work, however it is unclear how much of a grip on the public imagination it would have had during the time she was writing.

8. It was probably not that uncommon for some women to be in a more equal partnership with their husbands, and even—especially in the case of aristocratic women—to have a certain amount of economic and social privilege acquired through marriage. Moreover some women, at least, were prepared to challenge their treatment by their husbands. For example, records from a Parisian Episcopal court dealing in family matters in the 1300s and 1400s show that most of the cases dealt with wives' complaints of cruelty by their husbands (see Lévy 1965).

9. See Prudence Allen, *The Concept of Woman: The Aristotelian Revolution, 750 BC–AD 1250* (Grand Rapids, MI: W.B. Eerdmans Publishing, 1997): 468–470.

10. It is interesting to note that in *The Treasure of the City of Ladies*, Christine specifically compares the tasks of the wives of barons, knights, and other similar landowners to those of the prudent woman in the book of Solomon 2: 10.

11. See for example, Thomas Aquinas, *Summa Theologica* II, II, q.26, a.10.

12. This is not to ignore Karen Green's 1994 detailed account of a "maternalist" ethic in Christine's work (reprinted in Green 1996). However, it is not certain how committed Green is to this analysis. It is important to notice that Green's account in *The Woman of Reason* of the ethical aspects of Christine's work focuses more on analyzing Christine's notion of virtue and less on finding something akin to contemporary maternalist ethics (see Green 1995).

13. Christine raises the question of which is better: prudence combined with acquired knowledge, or prudence with little acquired knowledge. She declines, however, to answer the question.

14. This is not to say that Christine idealized marriage as something that was good for women *per se*. In *The Treasure of the City of Ladies*, Christine states that, given the typical marriage, it would be foolish for widows to remarry unless it is financially necessary. It may then not seem quite clear why Christine then places so much importance on first marriages, if she so clearly discourages second marriages. The answer to this may be quite simple. The widow would have a household and estate to occupy her time, and—as she is no longer a virgin—she would be less likely to be preyed upon by men. Moreover, she has already performed her ethical commitment by maintaining her marriage for a lifetime (her husband's).

15. Earl Jeffrey Richards discusses this issue more fully in the introduction to his translation of *The Book of the City of Ladies*.

16. Newman (1995) offers some interesting suggestions.

17. At her request a copy of *The Book of the City of Ladies* was sent to Queen Isabeau, and *The Treasure of the City of Ladies* was dedicated and presented to Princess Marguerite of Burgundy.

18. An example of this would be the double standard on chastity—see Christine, 1982, II.47.1.

19. The importance of being able to make this distinction is something I learned from Green 1996.

20. Whereas on Green's (1996) account, Christine's acceptance of the subservience of women is a *consequence* of Christine's central virtues of dependence and care, on the account I have just given caring subservience to one's husband has been *actively included* among the central virtues. The virtue of prudence means that women carry through their duties, specifically the duty of the maintenance of marriage; caring submission appears to be the only way that a marriage can be maintained given Christine's emphasis on humility and resignation.

21. Obviously there is disagreement among literary critics as to the defining characteristics of allegories. For this reason, I have aimed to keep my discussion of how to read allegory based on established and non-controversial ideas.

22. At this point I should acknowledge the work of Maureen Quilligan in *The Allegory of Female Authority* (Ithaca: Cornell University Press, 1991). Quilligan

through a multi-layered reading of *The Book of the City of Ladies* demonstrates the importance of the reading of allegory for its interpretation. However, Quilligan begins from identifying the mother-daughter relationship as central to the book, placing this in a larger analytic framework of psychoanalytic theory. While I am in no position to dispute Quilligan's literary scholarship, her reading, for the purposes of my account of Christine's moral philosophy anyway, raises more questions than it answers. For example, Quilligan sees Christine as offering quasi-Machiavellian advice to women in *The Treasure* in counseling them on the importance of the appearance of virtue. This seems at odds with Christine's emphasis on the importance of personal virtue and salvation throughout both books.

4

Mary Wollstonecraft and the Separation of Poetry and Politics

There is already a preponderance of critical work on Mary Woll-stonecraft, and—given the predominant interest in my work in discussing the writing of lesser known women philosophers—it was with some initial hesitation that I included an account of her moral philosophy. However on a closer examination of Wollstonecraft's work, I found that even though I may be able to offer little in the way of a fresh or innovative interpretation, I would be able to offer an interesting analysis of how exactly *A Vindication of the Rights of Woman* has been—as well as should be—read. An analysis that ultimately, I believe, demonstrates the incredible range of Wollstonecraft's philosophical thought, and in so doing can also demonstrate the narrowness of dominant views of what is to count as philosophical argument.

From our examination of Catharine Macaulay's *Letters on Education*, we have learned to recognize how our expectations and assumptions of the form that the *Vindication* takes will inform our reading of it. While from our examination of Christine de Pisan's *The Book of the City of Ladies*, we have learned how the form it *actually* takes should inform our interpretation of it. In addition, in Wollstonecraft's case, we shall learn that a particular way of writing can be central to the philosophical content of a work. This is something that requires us to not only to consider what is to count as a philosophical "point" in a work, but to continue with the discussion raised in the preceeding chapter of the relationship between literary style and philosophical content. And again, just as in the previous chapter but in a different way, we shall be confronted with the narrowness of the dominant model of moral philosophy.

For on this model, a philosophical point is something that we should be able to understand independent of the way it is made, in this sense it is extractable from the work. Indeed it would even seem that, hypothetically at least, the points of this work should be open to formulations of symbolic logic. Making the way a work is written significant philosophically hinders the central aims of philosophy to clarify and systematize moral data. Moreover it will expose the philosopher to potential errors in judgment, because it would seem to require different—or even oppositional—capacities to those required for philosophical judgment on this model. What I shall show instead with my interpretations of the work of Wollstonecraft, and in particular of George Eliot, is other possibilities of conceptualizing the aims and methods of assessment of philosophy.

In my previous discussion of Macaulay, I indicated that part of the reason Macaulay's thought has remained unrecognized is because Wollstonecraft's *A Vindication of the Rights of Woman* has provided a yardstick for early feminist philosophy. In a similar way, all of Wollstonecraft's works themselves are also typically measured against this second *Vindication* (the first being *A Vindication of the Rights of Men*) and thus have remained—to a great extent—unrecognized. Given the magnitude of this work and the relative weaknesses of her other works, it may appear that Wollstonecraft commentators are justified if they have no interest in her other works, or if their only interest in these other works is in their potential to illuminate either the content of the second *Vindication* or how such a groundbreaking work came to be written. Yet I want to argue that if we do not pay proper attention to the novels (or indeed to any of Wollstonecraft's works other than the second *Vindication*), we shall miss important elements in her moral thought.

There can be little doubt that part of the reason why many of Wollstonecraft's works other than the second *Vindication* have remained neglected is that—unlike the second *Vindication*—they do not appear to fit into the typical forms that are deemed "philosophical" on our dominant moral view. Unlike the second *Vindication*, which apparently takes the form of an Enlightenment treatise, most of her other works are novels, or letters; both of which—as I have claimed—have associations with "feminine" or domestic concerns. However a neglect of Wollstonecraft's works that do not fit the standard philosophical form of a treatise reaffirms the problematic assumption about the form of the second *Vindication* itself: that it is a treatise of Enlightenment rationalism. For we shall miss the elements it shares with her other works, elements that indicate it is something other than an Enlightenment treatise. What is further interesting—as we shall see—is that some of the apparent philosophical failures and weaknesses of the second *Vindication* commented on by critics (and especially feminist critics) are often failures only when it is located within the model of the Enlightenment treatise.

While it is clear that Wollstonecraft invaded the masculine preserve of moral/political writing with the writing of *A Vindication of the Rights of*

Woman (and indeed also with the writing of the first *Vindication*), it is not so clear that she is writing from within a standard Enlightenment rationalist treatise; nor that she has accepted the accompanying reason/passion dichotomy of Enlightenment philosophy. I want to move beyond the assumption that Wollstonecraft was writing an Enlightenment treatise, and also beyond its accompanying assumption that the fiction cannot be legitimately included in a study of her work because it does not fit our parameters for philosophical writing at that time: it is not an Enlightenment treatise. For, correctly or not, this is the genre we associate with philosophy for her era, and there is a tendency—as we saw with Macaulay— to ignore all the other possibilities. I want to claim that while the concepts of rights and equality are the bread and butter of Enlightenment thought, an argument—even an eighteenth century argument—for them can be forcefully made outside of the standard Enlightenment treatise. I want to show—through my interpretation of Wollstonecraft—that this is precisely what Wollstonecraft does through the use of a different notion of philosophical argument, and in so doing forces us outside of the boundaries of the "philosophical" on the dominant model of moral philosophy.

In order to do this I show that, for Wollstonecraft, the expression and form of her work is integrally connected to its moral content. And here we need to understand that, in this instance, form is not so much a specifically identifiable *structure*, but a particular *way* of writing with its own set of criteria for what is to count as having this particular form and what does not. Wollstonecraft holds that the truly moral work is one that not only comes from genuine feelings, but is simply and honestly expressed. She is not writing inspired by "cold" reason (the mainstay of the Enlightenment treatise), instead she writes from the heart. I shall argue that central to Wollstonecraft's view of morality, and thus central to the second *Vindication,* is the notion of a genuine sensibility, a notion that—far from being in opposition to the rights of women—is a part of Wollstonecraft's arguments for such rights. For it is the restrictions placed on the development of a genuine sensibility in women that prevents them from being able to become truly moral beings capable of a benevolent love for mankind and an improving, reflective love of God.

Finally, and most importantly, I shall show that we must be careful how we treat Wollstonecraft's notion of sensibility. It is not simply "a piece" of her argument for the equality of women or of her moral philosophy. Wollstonecraft herself writes "sensibly" in order to persuade the reader of the importance of sensibility. In so doing she intentionally smudges the boundaries between creative or imaginative writing, and reasoned or philosophical writing; and specifically she explicitly smudges the boundaries between poetry and philosophy. If we are to give a responsible and fruitful interpretation of Wollstonecraft's moral thought, we too must follow her lead and not cling to standard disciplinary divisions between poetry and philosophy. Indeed we should be led to consider where the boundaries of moral philosophy lie, specifically those of the dominant model, and to question their narrowness and rigidity.

Rather unfortunately for me I had begun work on the connections between expression and content before I read Virginia Sapiro's fascinating work on Wollstonecraft: *A Vindication of Political Virtue.* Thus a few of my ideas were not so original as I had initially imagined. However after a closer examination of Sapiro's work, I decided to continue my analysis of Wollstonecraft, for I found that it was the differences—not the similarities—between our accounts that were ultimately of significance, specifically the way in which the relationship between language and/or expression, and politics and/or morality, is delineated. My discovery of Sapiro, combined with the fact that—unlike many other women philosophers—there has been a great deal of philosophical commentary on Wollstonecraft's work (particularly on the second *Vindication*), has meant that this chapter is slightly different in its approach from the others in this work. My focus will be not just on offering a particular interpretation of Wollstonecraft's work. I shall also show the development and changes in Wollstonecraft commentary that parallel the increasing inclusion and interest in her works other than the second *Vindication*, as well as the complexity and intertwining of the themes in Wollstonecraft's work.

Wollstonecraft's Corpus

While Wollstonecraft is best known primarily for her *Vindication of the Rights of Woman*, and then, perhaps, secondarily for her *Vindication of the Rights of Men*, she also wrote fiction both for children and for adults, travel letters, reviews, and advice on the education of daughters. As I intend to argue for an account of Wollstonecraft that maintains the importance of a reading of her whole corpus, it is necessary that I begin by giving a brief account of each of her works and by indicating themes central to Wollstonecraft's later works that are also present in her earliest works. The reader who already has an acquaintance with Wollstonecraft's works, or who desires simply to "get to the heart of the matter," is advised to move on to the next section.

Mary Wollstonecraft was born in 1759 and spent her early adult years working in different positions as companion and governess, as well as founding a day school. It was at the suggestion of a friend that she started writing, and she eventually became self-supporting through translation work and reviews, as well as through her own work. Her first published work, *Thoughts on the Education of Daughters: With Reflections on Female Conduct, in the More Important Duties of Life* ([1787], see Todd and Butler 1989), may initially seem of no particular interest, especially as it was apparently inspired by a need for money. The sort of advice for conduct that Wollstonecraft offers seems little different from other female conduct books of the period, indeed Janet Todd and Marilyn Butler, the editors of the collected works of Wollstonecraft, state that as a work of an educationalist it is "immature and essentially derivative" (Wollstonecraft 1989, 1:13). But I think that in this work we can find a key to appreciating the later mature Wollstonecraft of the second *Vindication*.

If we look closely at the *Thoughts*, many of the themes that occupied Wollstonecraft in her later writings (and in particular the second *Vindication*) are already present. Wollstonecraft is critical in the early chapters of neglectful mothers who follow their own pleasures and do not allow reason and duty to govern their behavior towards their children. She is critical of dress and cosmetics because they occupy time and thought and act as a disguise: "truth is not expected to govern the inhabitant of so artificial a form" (Wollstonecraft 1989, 4:17). Here we have an inkling of the idea that runs throughout Wollstonecraft's work that truth and morality are connected as truth is the foundation of virtue (see Wollstonecraft 1989, 4:9). Wollstonecraft discusses the fate of women who are left without money and a proper education. Although at this stage she simply exposes the problems of such women, and does little more than suggest that they be treated more sympathetically, and that their parents pay more careful attention to their education. In her discussion of love, Wollstonecraft comments that it is a natural part of life and therefore we should not avoid it as this is to try to raise ourselves above the level of being human. However she does qualify this comment by claiming that we must also not allow ourselves to be so engrossed by love that we forget our primary duty of universal benevolence (see Wollstonecraft 1989, 4:30).

What is so interesting about all these (and many other) comments throughout the *Thoughts* is that while they are less than original, they ultimately are transformed into the polemical arguments of the *Vindication of the Rights of Woman*. The same arguments, once placed within a context of criticism of the oppression of women, become arguments for the equality of women. Wollstonecraft had come to see how the "failures" in behavior to which female conduct books are addressed are a product of the social system in which these women live. Thus, for example, the humiliating situation of the governess becomes in the second *Vindication* a symbol of the oppression of women, for women are kept out of all other employments in which they could support themselves properly and be respected in society. Similarly, the neglectful mother sometimes addressed in the conduct books of that era is a product of a society that trains women to be an infantile object of pleasure for men, not a responsible adult for the caring of children.[1] The second point to notice about the *Thoughts* is that already elements of Wollstonecraft's moral view (of which I shall give a detailed account later) are in place: the relationship between truth and morality and the importance of Christian principles for the regulation of the mind. (Wollstonecraft 1989, 4:33) Again there seems little that is original in content about these views, yet, as we shall see, it is the use that Wollstonecraft puts them to in her later works as part of her argument for the equality of women that is so extraordinary.

Wollstonecraft's second published work, *Mary*, is a work of fiction. It is an apparently semi-autobiographical portrait of a young woman with too much sensibility, intended to illustrate Wollstonecraft's belief that "a genius will educate itself" (Cameron 1970, 860). While this book has been frequently dismissed or ignored, some commentators such as Virginia Sapiro and Miriam Brody Kramnick have pointed to the presence of themes characteristic to Wollstonecraft's later works, such as the bondage of marriage and the criticism of female propriety. Kramnick states in her introduction to the second *Vindication* that while "Wollstonecraft is no ideologue yet . . . [in] reading *Mary* one meets the incipient female revolutionary" (Wollstonecraft 1983, 13). As we shall see, while I would not claim that Kramnick's statement is incorrect, I believe that it is significant because of its underlying assumption (held by many other commentators also) about the relationship between the second *Vindication* and Wollstonecraft's other works. The assumption, I believe, goes something like this: Wollstonecraft's other works can only be examined in the light of what they can offer for our interpretations of the second *Vindication* or for evidence of her early interest in politics of gender, because—unlike the second Vindication—they are not works of "real" philosophy.

Wollstonecraft next wrote a book of stories aimed at the moral education of children: *Original Stories from Real Life: With Conversations Calculated to Regulate the Affections and Form the Mind to Truth and Goodness* ([1788], see Todd and Butler 1989). It depicts two young girls being taught a series of moral lessons by their teacher, and while its tone and content were not atypical for the period within which she was writing, its "rather dour character" is often surprising to the modern reader (Sapiro 1992, 16). At this time Wollstonecraft was also working on a work of fiction, *Cave of Fancy*, that was never finished. From 1788 to 1797, Wollstonecraft also contribute a large number of reviews to the *Analytical Review*, although, as Sapiro points out, there are some difficulties in identifying Wollstonecraft's work, as the reviews were published anonymously, and it is for this reason that I have chosen not to include an account of them.

In 1788 Wollstonecraft translated Jacques Necker's *De l'importance des opinions religieuses*, and in 1790 she translated both Salzmann's *Elements of Morality* and Madame de Cambon's *Young Grandison*. What is interesting about these works is the changes that Wollstonecraft saw fit to make to the original texts. In the case of *Young Grandison*, she claims that changes and omissions were necessary in order that the book—due to its overzealous attempt to educate—did not produce affectation rather than virtue (1989, 2: 215). In the case of Necker's work, she apparently made stylistic changes, for in a review of the translation that has been attributed to Wollstonecraft she states, "This book is certainly very unequally written; in one passage easy flowing eloquence gives dignity and interest to the diction, in another the thoughts are laboured, and bombast swells the turgid periods. These remarks will account for some liberties occasionally taken, and we think very properly, by the translator" (Wollstonecraft 1989, 7:65–6).

This comment is significant in light of the connection that we shall find exists between Wollstonecraft's interest in the moral effects of the text and its style and form. A connection that can be seen in embryonic stage in the preface to her first work the *Thoughts*: "I am afraid, indeed, the reflections will, by some, be thought too grave; but I could not make them less so without writing affectedly; yet, though they may be insipid to the gay; others may not think them so; and if they should prove useful to one fellow-creature, and beguile any hours, which sorrow has made heavy, I shall think I have not been employed in vain" (Wollstonecraft 1989, 4:5).

In 1789 Wollstonecraft published *The Female Reader* a selection of prose and verse intended for, as it states in its subtitle, the improvement of young women. Although the vast majority of the selections are not her own work, this collection has two points of interest for an understanding of Wollstonecraft's views on morality and women. First, it should be noted that there is little change in the content of many of these comments on manners, modesty, and cultivation of taste in this collection, and the arguments of the second *Vindication*. What changes is the context within which they are understood. Wollstonecraft later realizes that—without the education of their reason—educating women in such things as modesty, manners, and the cultivation of taste, becomes at best like the training of an animal; and thus the woman must be closely guarded (i.e. oppressed) to make sure she does not revert back to her "natural" behavior. At worst, because the training of the women is not based on moral principles/reason, the modesty, manners, and taste they are taught will be corrupt and corrupting.

Second, we again see a reiteration of the importance of stories for moral education for Wollstonecraft (and again these last two points may not appear to us original, until we see their connections to her arguments for the liberty and equality of women). In the Preface to *The Female Reader* she states that, "In this selection many tales and tables will be found, as it seems to be following the simple order of nature, to permit people to peruse works addressed to the imagination, which tend to awaken the affections and fix good habits more firmly in the mind than cold arguments and mere declamation" (Wollstonecraft 1989, 4:56).

The first *Vindication: A Vindication of the Rights of Men* (1790) was a response to Edmund Burke's *Reflections on the Revolution in France*. Wollstonecraft herself admits that it was written spontaneously, and as Sapiro states, "Later writers are nearly universal in their condemnation of this first *Vindication* as a rushed, unscholarly, personal, emotional diatribe against a great political thinker, or at least as a most uneven match for the talents of Burke" (Sapiro 1992, 25). The second *Vindication, A Vindication of the Rights of Woman*, was published in 1792. However, it is important to notice that while Wollstonecraft has been praised for the ideas of this second work, her form of expression—like that of her first—has frequently been a subject for criticism. For example, Moira Ferguson comments that "she could plunge head-first into her material and create striking embellishments within lengthy syntactical structures, laced with hyperbole and high pitched emotion. . . . Everything before 1797. . . reads as if it could have been, in tone if not in form and sometimes in both, a gigantic, complicated, sprawling letter" (Ferguson 1984, 125–6).

Wollstonecraft had two major publications after the second *Vindication*: *An Historical and Moral View of the Origin and Progress of the French Revolution; and the Effect It Has Produced in Europe* ([1794] see Todd and Butler 1989) and *Letters Written during a Short Residence in Sweden, Norway, and Denmark* ([1796] see Todd and Butler 1989). While the former seems to be essentially a political tract disguised as history, it is of interest to a study of Wollstonecraft's moral philosophy because she considers the moral improvement of mankind—not as individuals—but as nations, and the social and political changes that will be necessary for this improvement. As a work of any description, it has inspired little secondary literature. The latter work has sparked more interest, and more controversy; it has been both praised as "the most imaginative English travel book since Sterne's *A Sentimental Journey*" (Holmes 1987, 17) and condemned for overt Romantic sensibility. Wollstonecraft's final major piece of work was another novel: *The Wrongs of Woman, or, Maria*. Due to her death in 1797 it was never completed, but even in its unfinished state it is her most radical work on the subject not only of the oppression of women and the institution of marriage, but also on the social conditions of the poor.

Once we see the two *Vindications*, and especially the *Vindication of the Rights of Woman*, within the context of all the other kinds of work that Wollstonecraft both wrote and published, it may initially appear that the second *Vindication* is rather an anomaly. On the surface a political polemic of this kind does not fit in well with conduct books, novels, and children's stories. And this—coupled with the exclusion of fiction from the dominant view of moral philosophy—may have been why Wollstonecraft's works other than the second *Vindication* have often been neglected. However the apparently anomalous nature of the second *Vindication* should suggest that we reconsider its supposed differences from her other works. Indeed a focus on the second *Vindication* and a neglect of the other works, rather ironically, can create difficulties in its classification.

As Jean Grimshaw argues in "Mary Wollstonecraft and the tensions in feminist philosophy," an exclusive focus (by commentators such as Cora Kaplan or Diana Coole) on the second *Vindication* means that we shall fail "to see the ways in which Wollstonecraft's work *resists* easy classification" (Grimshaw 1989, 12). Such commentators have been led to categorize the second *Vindication* as espousing a rejection of feeling (both sexual and romantic) for women, placing in its stead reason and a life dedicated to maternal/civic duty. Grimshaw claims that, on the contrary, Wollstonecraft did not reject sensibility for women in the *Vindication*, a fact that becomes clearer when we examine Wollstonecraft's views on women's passions throughout *all* her works. Instead Grimshaw claims, based on the fiction, that "Wollstonecraft's work . . . taken as a whole, does not *simply* imprison feminist thinking in a puritanical denial of female pleasure, nor does it *simply* consign ideas of female virtues and strength to the flames," but rather it struggles with the problem of how women can develop their passions while achieving independence and recognition as rational beings (Grimshaw 1989, 16). Moreover, given that fictional work tends to be more closely aligned to the description and evocation of feeling, rather than reason, any neglect of Wollstonecraft's other (fictional) writings will reinforce the description of Wollstonecraft's thought as espousing the dominion of reason over passion. And this, in its turn, will further reinforce the assumption that the second *Vindication* takes the form of an Enlightenment philosophical treatise.

The Second *Vindication* as an Enlightenment Treatise

Yet initially it may seem safe to assume that the best description of the form of the second *Vindication* is that of an Enlightenment treatise. It is clear from the arguments of the second *Vindication* that Wollstonecraft accepted much of the Enlightenment philosophy, the notion of the *tabula rasa* on which experience writes our character underpins the whole argument of the work, and the opening lines contain what Sapiro calls "an

Enlightenment catechism" (Sapiro 1996, 34): "In what does man's pre-eminence over the brute creation consist? The answer is clear as that a half is less than the whole, in Reason" (Wollstonecraft 1983, 91).

Given this, and other examples of Enlightenment thought in her work, it is perhaps unsurprising that the second *Vindication* has often been seen as an Enlightenment treatise *itself*. Jane Martin states in *Reclaiming a Conversation*, for example, that Wollstonecraft is writing a standard Enlightenment rationalist treatise and that the originality of the second *Vindication* is in her discussion of the rights of women (Martin 1985, 75–6). Whereas Moira Gatens in ""The Oppressed State of My Sex": Wollstonecraft on Reason, Feeling and Equality" argues that Wollstonecraft is clearly writing within the Enlightenment tradition: "Reason and feeling is the governing dichotomy and the source of major conflicts in Mary Wollstonecraft's work and in her life. It is her concentration on this dichotomy and her obvious faith in the power of reason to reform sociopolitical life that places her firmly within the Enlightenment tradition" (Gatens 1991, 112).

In saying that Wollstonecraft has been taken to be writing an Enlightenment treatise, I am claiming that we will then have two central expectations about her work. For while there is no specific detailed formula for what constitutes the form of such a treatise, there are certain typical elements connected to the content of a standard Enlightenment treatise; two of which are particularly relevant for the second *Vindication*. The first expectation of Wollstonecraft's work is that she is arguing for the authority of reason over passion, the second is that she is adopting a particular mode of writing: "masculine" rational discourse. These expectations then direct critical commentary on Wollstonecraft's in the second *Vindication* and also serve to justify a neglect of her other work, while this commentary can, in its turn, serve to reinforce the correctness of those original expectations.

Certainly it may often appear in the second *Vindication* that Wollstonecraft holds that virtue is produced by the subordination of passion by reason and at times additionally by what Catriona Mackenzie calls "a kind of self-denying fortitude" (Mackenzie 1996, 189). Wollstonecraft, for example, exclaims against the misery of women who have not been properly educated or encouraged to use their reason. She states that, "Miserable, indeed, must be that being whose cultivation of mind has only tended to inflame its passions! A distinction should be made between inflaming and strengthening them. The passions thus pampered, whilst the judgment is left unformed, what can be expected to ensue? Undoubtedly a mixture of madness and folly!" (Wollstonecraft 1983, 152). Such an impassioned creature who does not have her passions controlled by reason, will neither be "useful to others" nor "content with its own station"

(Wollstonecraft 1983, 152). Here Wollstonecraft also seems to be implying that there is a social cost if passion is cooled or even removed. And indeed in relation to marriage, she claims that "a master and mistress of a family ought not to love each other with passion. I mean to say that they ought not to indulge those emotions which disturb the order of society" (Wollstonecraft 1983, 114).

Yet for a modern feminist critic, Wollstonecraft's apparent approval of the subordination of passion to reason is problematic, not only for the ensuing difficulties it creates for her arguments, but in itself. Martin, having attributed to Wollstonecraft the goal of educating women in order that they can subdue their passion through reason, accuses her of creating a false dilemma in the second *Vindication*. Martin claims that Wollstonecraft mistakenly believes that if the passions are not controlled in this way, then it is they that will subdue reason. Wollstonecraft's apparent devaluation of passion has meant that some commentators have believed that she rejected emotion and sexual feelings altogether, and they have criticized her accordingly. Thus Cora Kaplan argues that Wollstonecraft in the second *Vindication* "turned against feeling, which is seen as reactionary and regressive, almost counter-revolutionary." Indeed "Sexuality and pleasure are narcotic inducements to a life of lubricious slavery," and "Reason is the only human attribute appropriate to the revolutionary character, and women are impeded by their early and corrupt initiation into the sensual, from using theirs" (Kaplan 1986, 35).[2] And indeed Wollstonecraft's rejection of sexual passion after marriage may appear to confirm such a reading.

The second expectation about Wollstonecraft's writing in the second *Vindication*: that she is writing "masculine" rational discourse, surely underpins the criticism of her writing style that we saw in the introduction; for impassioned, apparently uncontrolled, hyperbole has little place in an Enlightenment treatise. More sophisticated criticism of Wollstonecraft's writing style has focused on how the second *Vindication* is an attempt to utilize the authority of male discourse to legitimate her arguments for the rights of women and on the tensions and the possibilities that this creates. Thus Mary Jacobus, for example, claims that Wollstonecraft's attempt to appropriate the language of Enlightenment reason for her own sex produced alienation from her self as a woman. Jacobus further argues that it was only in fictional writing that Wollstonecraft could utilize the language of feeling, that is to say literary language, a language which allowed her to speak for and as a woman. This then produces a tension for Wollstonecraft's work.

[The] crushing opposition between Reason and Imagination is also present in Mary Wollstonecraft's writing. *The Rights of Woman*—directed against the

infantilizing Rousseauistic ideal of feminine "sensibility"—not only advocates the advantages for women of a rational (rather than sentimental) education, but attempts to insert the author herself into the predominantly male
discourse of Enlightenment Reason, or "sense." Yet, paradoxically, it is
within this shaping Rousseauistic sensibility that Mary Wollstonecraft operates as both woman and writer—creating in her two highly autobiographical novels, *Mary* (1788) and, ten years later, *The Wrongs of Woman*, fictions
which, even as they anatomize the constitution of femininity within the confines of "sensibility," cannot escape its informing preoccupations and literary influence. (Jacobus 1986, 59)

Wendy Gunther-Canada, on the other hand, while acknowledging the
potential objection that Wollstonecraft was "seduced and co-opted by the
gendered categories of eighteenth-century discourse," claims that the
second *Vindication* also subverts those categories (Gunther-Canada 1996,
76). She adds that "Wollstonecraft at once opposes and participates in a
debate in which women have been absent as authors as well as citizens.
She attempts to create a literary space to expound her theory of political
rights by confounding the distinctions of sex in discourse" (Gunther-
Canada 1996, 76).

Yet these criticisms by Kaplan, Jacobus, and (to a great extent) Gunther-
Canada only carry weight if the initial interpretation of the second *Vindication* is correct: she is aiming to write an Enlightenment treatise. In order
to show that this was not her intention, I shall begin first by examining recent work—such as that by Catriona Mackenzie and Susan Khin Zaw—in
Wollstonecraft criticism on the relation of reason to passion, work that not
only demonstrates the importance of feeling for Wollstonecraft's philosophical views, but that utilizes the fictions and the other works for this
demonstration. However, as I shall argue, I do not hold that work like that
of Mackenzie or Khin Zaw offers the most complete or final analysis of the
moral philosophy and its relation to feeling in Wollstonecraft's work. I
want to claim that we must move beyond a general textual analysis of
Wollstonecraft's corpus and examine the possibility that there are a set of
principles underlying her works that are principles of style or form; principles that—as we shall see—are ultimately principles of morality as well.

The Second *Vindication*
Is Not a Work of
Enlightenment Philosophy

There appears to have been in recent Wollstonecraft commentary an up-
surge of interest in her other writings and in analyzing the second *Vindication* within the context of these other works. Catriona Mackenzie, for

example, argues that Wollstonecraft's treatment of the distinction between reason and passion is not a clear-cut case of the former controlling or subordinating the latter. Instead, Mackenzie claims, we can find a subtler concept of self-governance which does "not pit women's reason in opposition either to their bodies or to affectivity," that is more fully developed in her travel writings and in *The Wrongs of Woman* (Mackenzie 1996, 183). Although Mackenzie is careful to point out that this does not mean that there are no tensions remaining within Wollstonecraft's account of the autonomy of women. Mackenzie holds that Wollstonecraft's arguments for the ability of women to reason in the second *Vindication* are used to perform the function of responding to claims about women's equality by Enlightenment thinkers such as Rousseau. But this function does not entail that Wollstonecraft accepted without reservation arguments for the foundation of virtue on reason, or that her concept of self-governance is equated with rationality pure and simple. Instead Mackenzie claims that "the role of reason figures more as a necessary part of a virtuous character than as the sole authority in all matters" (Mackenzie 1996, 185).

Mackenzie claims that while in the second *Vindication* Wollstonecraft is often ambiguous as to the control of the passions, in *The Wrongs of Woman* Wollstonecraft states clearly that not only should women be free to express their passions, but that a lack of passion can undermine virtue itself. Looking to the travel letters, Mackenzie offers an explanation for Wollstonecraft's apparent ambivalence. In one of the letters Wollstonecraft expresses her concern that if she allows her daughter to develop her sensibility and cultivate her mind, that this will be to make her vulnerable to the society in which the daughter must make her way. And indeed this is a theme that is also apparent in the later part of *The Wrongs of Woman*. Thus if we examine works other than the second *Vindication* we can see that Wollstonecraft's often ambiguous view of the passions may find its roots not so much in authorial inconsistency, but in a reaction to "a social situation that denied to women the scope for expressing desire and passion and hence gave rise to devastating conflicts between reason and sensibility" (Mackenzie 1996, 191). Moreover, if the development of women's sensibility was encouraged, this social situation was also one that had a tendency to corrupt or debase this sensibility away from virtue and towards the type of excessive emotionalism that contributed to the subordination of women.

While Mackenzie uses Wollstonecraft's later writings to bring out the moral thought, specifically the concept of self-governance, that can be found in the second *Vindication* and also to provide support for Mackenzie's interpretation of the *Vindication*, Susan Khin Zaw focuses on Wollstonecraft's earlier works to demonstrate Wollstonecraft's moral view.

Khin Zaw claims that a focus on the arguments of the two *Vindications* has meant that commentators have not recognized its interest or coherence.

In "The Reasonable Heart," Khin Zaw argues that Wollstonecraft's moral view has remained ignored for three main reasons. First, because it is overshadowed by the feminist polemics of the second *Vindication*, which—while it is based on three foundational principles of Wollstonecraft's moral philosophy—offers little in the way of a discussion of these principles. Indeed Khin Zaw claims that in the two *Vindications*, "Wollstonecraft was less interested in presenting an impregnable philosophical theory than in changing opinions in order to change the world" (Khin Zaw 1998, 80). Second, because commentators have not recognized the coherence of Wollstonecraft's moral system. Third because the relationship between reason and passion discussed in the *Vindication* has often been mistakenly interpreted in terms of the Enlightenment opposition, and—consequently—her moral view has remained obscured.

In contrast, Khin Zaw argues that a study of Wollstonecraft's early fiction and educational works—works which Khin Zaw sees as being both politically and philosophically motivated—demonstrates that Wollstonecraft did in fact have a coherent view of moral psychology, moral education, and moral philosophy. Khin Zaw argues, based primarily on *Mary* and *Original Stories*, that Wollstonecraft believed that virtue in adults required the integration of reason and feeling and that the control of the reason over the passions is to keep them from degenerating into mere animal/bodily appetite. Reason's role is also to transform the passions, thus the love for one individual is redirected from their original object to love for God, the perfect object. Love of God then directs our morality, for we wish to emulate he who our reason tells us is the model of moral perfection. Yet, according to Khin Zaw, reason does not do this alone, it is helped by contemplation and imagination.

Thus the educational strategy of Mrs. Mason towards her charges in *Original Stories* becomes clear. She does not punish them when they do wrong, but teaches them by thought-provoking example and analogy and by drawing them into reasoned dialogues about their own behavior (see Khin Zaw 1998, 97). Whereas, "[The] tragic tales and sublime landscapes are . . . meant to work on the imagination and sensibility, to turn them away from the self and open them to the lofty ideals and wide sympathies that will ensure that the moral principles implanted by Mrs. Mason are not merely committed to memory but will actually motivate" (Khin Zaw 1998, 106). In this way, Mrs. Mason is laying the groundwork for the children to progress towards a reasoned morality based on a love of, and desire to imitate, God. For the stories she tells are aimed at directing the children's sympathies towards others, at producing strong emotions "which will perform the function of ennobling passions," and at encouraging the children to reason and reflect on their experiences and feelings (Khin Zaw 1998, 106).

While we may or may not accept these specific interpretations of Wollstonecraft offered by Mackenzie and Khin Zaw, there are important general points that can be drawn from each commentator, points that I believe are worthy of a more in-depth examination. First we can see that once we look beyond the second *Vindication* to the works of fiction, it becomes evident that feeling does play an important role in Wollstonecraft's moral thought. Moreover if we read the fiction we will have a clearer idea of the moral philosophy that underlies—even if it is not explicitly brought out in—the second *Vindication*. Second, if—as Mackenzie implies—Wollstonecraft was not writing a straightforwardly Enlightenment treatise on the equality of women, and if—as Khin Zaw claims—the second *Vindication* was less a philosophical treatise than an attempt to spark a change in public opinion, then we need to know what exactly is the form (or the intended form) of the second *Vindication*. While both Mackenzie and Khin Zaw (and others) rely on a general textual analysis of Wollstonecraft's corpus, neither pursues the possibility that there are principles of style or form underlying her works, whether literary or "philosophical." However, as we shall see, a clearer understanding of the form of the second *Vindication* will also provide us with a better understanding of the role that the passions play both in her moral thought and in her arguments for the equality of women.

Principles of Form
and Expression

Some works prior to the two *Vindications* do contain themes that are relevant to the discussion of Wollstonecraft's philosophical style and the relation of style to content. In particular, I have already noted that in the *Thoughts* and in her translation of Necker, Wollstonecraft was very conscious of a connection between writing style and sincerity, and of the bad effects that an unsuitable writing style could have on the reader. But it is in *A Vindication of the Rights of Men* that she first explicitly addresses the subject, and it is here that we are provided with the key to understanding the form of the second *Vindication*. The structural and stylistic connections between the two *Vindications* have not gone unnoticed. In "Mary Wollstonecraft's 'wild wish'," for example, Gunther-Canada argues that Wollstonecraft would never have written *A Vindication of the Rights of Woman* if she had not first written her response to Edmund Burke in *A Vindication of the Rights of Men*. Gunther-Canada claims that in the latter *Vindication* Wollstonecraft appropriated the "manly" authority of Enlightenment reason in order to challenge the "effeminate" rhetoric of

Burke's work. Wollstonecraft learned from this, according to Gunther-Canada, that "authority in rights discourse is opposed to femininity," and "that to champion the rights of women one must battle the issue of sexual difference in order to claim that women are rational subjects" (Gunther-Canada 1996, 62–3). And thus in the second *Vindication*, "Wollstonecraft confounds the rhetorical distinctions of sex in political writing by opposing the fragile "flowery diction" of sentiment to the intellectual strength of rational argument," as well as challenging "the ideology that women are naturally less rational than men by exposing the social prejudices and historical conditions that stunt the growth of reason in women" (Gunther-Canada 1996, 62).

I am not sure how far I agree with Gunther-Canada's analysis of the connections between the two *Vindications*. On an examination of the first *Vindication*, it is clear that while criticizing Burke, Wollstonecraft also criticized his style of writing, and it is clear that there are connections between an approach to the expression of ideas and the content of those ideas themselves. Yet I am not sure that to describe the second *Vindication* as purely composed of rational argument captures what is going on in it, a point that clearly ties in with work such as that of Khin Zaw and Mackenzie on Wollstonecraft's moral thought not being merely "rational" and based on a simple opposition of rationality to passion. While it is clear that Wollstonecraft eschews the "flowery diction" of sentiment, indeed especial disgust is reserved for the silly sentimental novel written for women, it is not so clear that this means that her style of writing is free from emotion altogether.

The most immediate point to notice is that the second *Vindication* contains what I shall call Wollstonecraft's "flights of imagination" as well as frequent bursts of dramatic—even apparently rambling—hyperbole. Consider for example the following passage on love: "A shadowy phantom glides before us, obscuring every other object; yet when the soft cloud is grasped, the form melts into common air, leaving a solitary void, or sweet perfume, stolen from the violet, that memory long holds dear. But I have tripped unawares on fairy ground, feeling the balmy gale of spring stealing on me, though November frowns" (Wollstonecraft 1983, 231). This passage, and many others like it, do not seem to belong to a work that is supposed to demonstrate the intellectual strength of rational argument. What appears to be a typical way of dealing with such passages is to see them, therefore, as flaws or weaknesses in Wollstonecraft's writing style, and I have already given an example of the sort of criticism that is targeted towards her apparently digressive hyperbolic flights of fancy.

The question of how to deal with this apparent problem no longer seems to be of particular importance to commentators. It is dismissed either because nothing more could be expected due to Wollstonecraft's education, or because a charge of incoherence can become a way of easily dismissing the (often female) author without having to take her work seriously. Moreover, as Kramnick points out, "Too many have already apologized for the style and lack of coherent organization in the *Vindication*. It doesn't seem important any longer, since what she had to say was clear enough" (Wollstonecraft 1983, 41). Yet I think that if we choose to ignore these apparent problems of the style and form of the second *Vindication*, or if we pick and choose what aspects of its style and form are appropriate for our consideration, we are treating them as accidental to the content of Wollstonecraft's work. We shall be treating her way of writing as unintentional, whether due to being carried away by enthusiasm, or being hindered by a poor education; both of which, in a more indirect way, patronize the woman writer. Moreover, as we shall see, a neglect (no matter how well intentioned) of the stylistic characteristics peculiar to the second *Vindication* would prevent us from a potentially productive lens through which we can analyze Wollstonecraft's work, and in particular her moral thought.

Our key to understanding the style and form of the second *Vindication* can be found in comments Wollstonecraft makes on the connections between writing style and moral content in the first *Vindication*. Thus we need first to examine carefully this latter work. Wollstonecraft's *A Vindication of the Rights of Men* was initially conceived as a letter in response to Edmund Burke's *Reflections on the Revolution in France*; indeed, she says, many of its pages are "the effusions of the moment." Once she realized how it had grown, however, "the idea was suggested of publishing a short vindication of the *Rights of Men*" (Wollstonecraft 1996, 11). Wollstonecraft immediately makes it clear that she will not indulge in what she calls the "flowers of rhetoric," but will write simply and truthfully, as these are the criteria for a work of this (moral/political) content. The way that this will then be done, she says, is to attack the foundational principles upon which Burke has constructed his intellectual "folly" (Wollstonecraft 1996, 16). Unfortunately, however, she says that she cannot find any fixed first principle to refute, and this then supplies her with the basis for her criticism of his work.

Yet while Wollstonecraft admires the voice of reason and truth in a work, it is clear that reason need not be in opposition to the inclusion of feeling, as long as it is genuine. It is a work motivated by false or insincere feelings that Wollstonecraft despises. She expresses concern about the man who would write in order to secure public admiration for his wit and style, for he "can never nourish by reflection any profound, or, if you please, metaphysical passion" (Wollstonecraft 1996, 14). Indeed she suggests that wit will always weaken judgment. Wollstonecraft makes it clear that she holds more respect for the misguided work that is driven by the passions, although not properly directed by reason, than work containing opinions that are "empty rhetorical flourishes," written merely for the sake of saying something well (Wollstonecraft 1996, 48). In the genre of poetry Wollstonecraft argues that passion should be given full reign, indeed not even reason has the right to curtail the imagination of real passion. But this feeling is in contrast to "romantic writing" which expresses artificial feelings; this type of writing, she says, is in opposition to simplicity which "in works of taste, is but a synonymous word for truth" (Wollstonecraft 1996, 47). Unfortunately, she says this romantic style of writing has spread to prose, creating "turgid bombasts" and "dry raptures" of the type that it would appear she is implying can be found in Burke's work (Wollstonecraft 1996, 47).

Sadly, she says, society admires wit and sensibility, even though this is at the cost of true virtue: "Sensibility is the *manie* of the day, and compassion the virtue which is to cover a multitude of vices, whilst justice is left to mourn in sullen silence, and balance truth in vain" (Wollstonecraft 1996, 15). This sensibility that she criticizes is defined as a "kind of mysterious instinct" that "is *supposed* to reside in the soul, that instantaneously discerns truth, without the tedious labour of ratiocination" (Wollstonecraft 1996, 49). It is *supposed* (although she says that it is hard to prove this) "to reign paramount over the other faculties of the mind, and to be an authority from which there is no appeal" (Wollstonecraft 1996, 49). Such an instinct is criticized by Wollstonecraft on many different levels. Clearly, as she states, it is not an infallible instinct. If virtue is indeed instinctive, then there would seem little point in praising moral behavior as this only makes sense when virtue is learned and character perfected through reflection. Furthermore, and for Wollstonecraft most importantly, if virtue is somehow instinctive, then it would appear that immortality is out of our grasp, for she believes that it is our ability to reason about our passions and to gain knowledge through doing so that raises us above animals and allows us to perfect our souls.

While sensibility of the peculiarly Burkean kind may appear to have a pure instinctual source: "the moral constitution of the heart," it is in fact contaminated by the proprieties of society (see Bromwich 1995, 622). The Burkean man of sensibility has had his perceptions and feelings artificially refined, yet this refinement has reached a level where his feelings appear to be spontaneous or natural. As David Bromwich in "Wollstonecraft as a Critic of Burke" shows, Burke holds that certain types of vice will even appear lessened by refinement, "taste" thus being identified with manners. Yet, according to Bromwich, Wollstonecraft shared Burke's view on the coherence between taste and morality, although she developed it in a different direction. He states that "She wants to isolate a truth in his idea of the coherence of taste and morality in order to reverse the direction in which Burke believed his idea necessarily pointed. She will therefore argue, from similar intuitions about the authority of feelings and habits of thought, to a radically different conclusion than any entertained by Burke" (Bromwich 1995, 619). Bromwich claims that both Burke and Wollstonecraft agree that virtue is not an instinct, but a habit, although there are times when Burke does seem to write as if it were the former. However Wollstonecraft "parts company" with Burke "in identifying the kind of acquired power it is" (Bromwich 1995, 626). It does not, Bromwich says, "spring from and does not trace its authority to the conventional life of society. . . . It is rather a habit acquired by the soul in contest with adversity, or the soul struggling in the usual current of unforeseeable questionings" (Bromwich 1995, 626).

The theme of taste and morality is central to Wollstonecraft's early work of fiction: *Mary*. Thus, before we go on to examine the connections between the first *Vindication* and the second, we should look to this novel in order to flesh out Wollstonecraft's view of delicacy of taste or sensibility. At present I do not want to look at any of the works written *after* the first *Vindication*, as I want to examine in a later section how the notion of sensibility is played out in the second *Vindication*, and thus I do not want to prejudge the issue. In *Mary*, Wollstonecraft makes it clear that her (Wollstonecraft's) notion of taste here is a "natural" one, in the sense that natural is understood as not being produced by social mores or attitudes. We are told that Henry's taste was "just" as "it had a standard—*Nature*, which he observed with a critical eye," and Mary "could not help thinking that in his company her mind expanded, as he always went below the surface. She increased her stock of ideas, and her taste was improved" (Wollstonecraft 1976, 27, italics used for emphasis).

Mary herself appears initially inspired by nature, although—unlike Henry—her sensibility is excessive. When Mary was a child, "Sublime ideas filled her young mind—always connected with devotional sentiments; extemporary effusions of gratitude, and rhapsodies of praise would burst often from her, when she listened to the birds, or pursued the deer" (Wollstonecraft 1976, 5). The focus of Mary's sensibility is love, but not romantic love (although we are told that her love for her friend Ann came close to resembling "a passion"), rather a love of humanity that prompts her to help the sick and the unfortunate (Wollstonecraft 1976, 5). Moreover Mary appears to see our ability to love others as proof of our immortality, indeed in a conversation with Henry, Mary claims that she believes that "the great part of our happiness" in the hereafter will be "the society of beings we can love, without the alloy that earthly infirmities mix with our best affections" (Wollstonecraft 1976, 40).

Wollstonecraft, however, makes it clear that Mary's excessive sensibility is problematic, we are told that Mary was "too much the creature of impulse, and the slave of compassion" (Wollstonecraft 1976, 7). Mary's sensibility does become—to an extent—more controlled as she matures, as well as through her relationship with Henry. Wollstonecraft uses Mary herself to describe these changes (on an initial reading, Wollstonecraft's attitude towards Mary may seem ambiguous, and this is why). Mary writes in her journal a rhapsodic account of sensibility: "this quickness, this delicacy of feeling, which enables us to relish the sublime touches of the poet and the painter"; yet Mary values this feeling not simply for the happiness it brings, but for the way it disposes her to morality: "Softened by tenderness, the soul is disposed to be virtuous" (Wollstonecraft 1976, 54). Mary recognizes that this disposition of the soul needs principles— specifically those of Christianity—in order to channel its growth. She understands that "Christianity can only afford just principles to govern the wayward feelings and impulses of the heart: every good disposition runs wild, if not transplanted into this soil; but how hard is it to keep the heart diligently, though convinced that the issues of life depend on it" (Wollstonecraft 1976, 55).

Thus Mary's sensibility is only a force for good when it has become the habit of a principled thinker. When it is purely instinctual, or allowed to run wild, then the "inconsiderate and violent" aspects of her nature—characteristics that are not in accord with the pivotal virtue of love towards others—will show through (Wollstonecraft 1976, 29). Clearly then, as Janet Todd's definition brings out, sensibility is a complex concept: it is "the faculty of feeling, the capacity for extremely refined emotion and a quickness to display compassion for the suffering" (Todd 1986, 63). For Wollstonecraft, this becomes spelled out (using Mary as an example) with her capacity to love and her spontaneous desire to help the needy. But it is also refined through her love of God and her reading of authors "whose works were addressed to the understanding," for such works "taught her to arrange her thoughts, and argue with herself, even when under the influence of the most violent passions" (Wollstonecraft 1976, 13).

Thus far we can see that while Wollstonecraft admires feeling in her early works, it must be both sincere and developed by reason based on principle in order for it to give us moral direction; mere feeling itself is not enough, and she reserves a special contempt for the form of affected "sensibility" that is at the basis of Burke's moral and thus his political argument. (see Bromwich 1995, 619). Moreover it also appears that, for Wollstonecraft, the mode of expression of the moral and/or political writer is in a direct relationship to the content of their views. The writer who has true delicacy of taste will write genuinely and simply, and speak the truth, while the writer of artificial feelings will write empty, self-conscious, rhetoric.

Form and Sensibility

Given this understanding of Wollstonecraft's criticism of Burke, I wish to argue that once we have grasped how Wollstonecraft connects expression or style and morality, we are given a key not only to understanding the apparently digressive form and hyperbolic style of the second *Vindication*, but also to defining the form of the work itself. This understanding, in its turn, will allow us to see the role that passions play in the moral philosophy that is at its foundation; as well as being in a better position to understand Wollstonecraft's view of the passions in women.[3]

In her criticism of Burke in the first *Vindication*, Wollstonecraft makes it clear that a moral/political work must rest on fixed first principles, and she follows her own prescription in the second *Vindication* when, in the first chapter, she clearly sets forth her foundational principles, which are summed up as follows: "The perfection of our nature and capability of happiness must be estimated by the degree of reason, virtue, and knowledge, that distinguish the individual, and direct the laws which bind society: and that which from the exercise of reason, knowledge and virtue naturally flow, is equally undeniable, if mankind be viewed collectively" (Wollstonecraft 1983, 91).

In addition, Wollstonecraft comments in the closing passages of the book that the "sagacious reader" will by now have realized that "the discussion of this subject merely consists in opening a few simple principles, and clearing away the rubbish which obscured them" (Wollstonecraft 1983, 316). Clearly then, although the work may seem superficially digressive, if the reader has understood the full import of its foundational principles, then she will be able not only to imagine the ramifications of the arguments that "rise naturally" from them, but also will be able to see their interconnections. Indeed if we think about these principles and then imagine—especially given the social situation of Wollstonecraft's time—where they would lead, then it is perhaps unsurprising that her arguments range freely over a variety of (connected by these principles) topics.

What then of Wollstonecraft's hyperbolic style? I think that it is problematic because of the framework within which we have placed Wollstonecraft. The traditional dichotomy of reason and passion that has been seen in Wollstonecraft's work is apparently played out stylistically in a dichotomy between (rejected) "feminine" "sentimental writing" or "flowery diction" and (accepted or appropriated) "masculine" rational discourse. But if we turn to the crucial passage from the "author's introduction" that appears to be the central evidence for both Gunther-Canada's and Jacobus's claims about Wollstonecraft's acceptance of this dichotomy (and her subsequent rejection of one half of it) and examine it in the light of her comments in the first *Vindication*, we can see that there is another possible way of classifying the writing of Wollstonecraft.

> I shall disdain to cull my phrases or polish my style. I aim at being useful, and sincerity will render me unaffected; for wishing rather to persuade by the force of my arguments than dazzle by the elegance of my language, I shall not waste my time in rounding periods, or in fabricating the turgid bombast of artificial feelings, which coming from the head, never reach the heart. I shall be employed about things, not words! and, anxious to render my sex more respectable members of society, I shall try to avoid that flowery diction which has slided from essays into novels, and from novels into familiar letters and conversations. (Wollstonecraft 1983, 82)

While this passage can be read—as both Jacobus and Gunther-Canada suggest—as a rejection of "feminine" sentimental writing and an embracing of "masculine" rational discourse, my previous account of Wollstonecraft's criticisms of Burke's writing style should at least call doubt on this interpretation. In both the first *Vindication* and in this passage from the second, Wollstonecraft is criticizing a pseudo elegance in writing that comes from artificial feelings. Indeed she even uses the same expression "turgid bombast" to describe this type of writing. Wollstonecraft is thus claiming for herself a way of writing that comes from the heart, not from the head, and which may then, at times, appear inelegant. But this writing is differentiated from Burkean bombasts and sickly sentimentality not simply on stylistic grounds; it is clear that there is a connection between this way of writing and the morality (or lack thereof) of the author. The author of flowery rhetoric is prevented by his/her very approach to writing from reaching the truth. Instead of looking into his/her heart and reflecting carefully on his/her passions, s/he focuses on the audience and how s/he appears to them; aiming to persuade that audience and to draw their admiration.

It also seems clear that it is not just the connection between expression and content that is of importance to Wollstonecraft, but the effect that such writing will have on the reader; something that I have suggested is indicated even in her very earliest writings. In the "advertisement" to *Mary*, we are told that the author who writes honestly from the heart, and does not attempt to reproduce the thoughts and emotions of others, will be the author who is not only the most creative, but will also have the effect of producing corresponding emotions in the reader: "Those compositions only have power to delight, and carry us willing captives, where the soul of the author is exhibited, and animates the hidden springs" (Wollstonecraft, 1976).

Whereas in the second *Vindication*, Wollstonecraft claims that the overly elaborate rhetoric which has slipped from essays to novels to everyday discourse can corrupt the natural sentiments and thus prevent moral development. She claims that "These pretty superlatives, dropping glibly from the tongue, vitiate the taste, and create a kind of sickly delicacy that turns away from simple unadorned truth; and a deluge of false sentiments and overstretched feelings, stifling the natural emotions of the heart, render the domestic pleasures insipid, that ought to sweeten the exercise of those severe duties, which educate a rational and immortal being for a nobler field of action" (Wollstonecraft 1983, 82). Wollstonecraft is saying here that the "flowery diction" of essays and novels dulls the potential for natural taste in their readers, replacing it with a "sickly delicacy." The undiscriminating reader then turns away from the natural or true emotions towards false sentiments. Having rejected natural or true emotions the reader is uninclined to pursue his or her human duties, duties which are central to human moral development.

Yet it is also important to notice that even though Wollstonecraft is offering up a moral condemnation of the writing of "flowery diction," she does not wish to ban these works completely. Wollstonecraft says in the final chapter of *A Vindication of the Rights of Woman*, "when I exclaim against [silly] novels [written for women], I mean when contrasted with those works which exercise the understanding and regulate the imagination. For any kind of reading, I think better than leaving a blank still a blank, because the mind must receive a degree of enlargement and obtain a little strength by a slight excertion of its thinking powers; besides, even the productions that are only addressed to the imagination, raise the reader a little above the gross gratification of appetites, to which the mind has not given a shade of delicacy" (Wollstonecraft 1983, 306–7).

Wollstonecraft even considers the possibility that a fondness for novels could at least provide some kind of foundation for moral education. If the woman or girl could be persuaded to see the flaws in the romantic sentimentality in the events and characters of these novels, she may thus simultaneously develop her reading taste and moral taste.

While I agree that Wollstonecraft is avoiding "flowery sentiment," I believe that we need to understand what exactly she means by this. Wollstonecraft clearly wishes to avoid not only this style of expression, she also wishes to reject the moral view that is both interconnected with, and (according to her) the cause of, this style. Yet we see that in the works that are not specifically political or moral works, such as the novels, while Wollstonecraft is still highly critical of sentimental writing, she does not wish to ban it outright because in these cases it may still have a moral use as it will at least stimulate the taste of the reader.

Thus it would appear that Wollstonecraft is not rejecting writing based on sentiment *per se* and thereby simply entering (successfully or unsuccessfully) into the masculine arena of rational discourse; she is rejecting writing based on *false* sentiment. Wollstonecraft appears to be aiming at a writing that comes from the heart that will persuade her audience because of its emotional honesty and force. If this is correct, then her occasional bursts of hyperbole will make sense, moreover—as they are no longer to be understood as part of a traditional rational discourse—they would appear to be perfectly appropriate to this other way of writing. While this writing will come from her sensibility, it is clear that it is channeled by (reasoned) moral principles, specifically Christian principles; and thus, in this way, her writing will be able to express through its form or style the moral view she espouses.

But it then becomes clear from all the works that we have examined so far that not only does Wollstonecraft claim that she is writing "from the heart" directed by Christian principles, but that these are the foundations of her view of morality. Yet this must then mean that sensibility or delicacy of taste plays an important role in the moral arguments for social and political reform, and specifically for the reform of the position of women. And it is to this that I turn next. Wollstonecraft's use of Christian principles is usually seen as unproblematic, but the role of sensibility for Wollstonecraft's moral view is a thorny issue, whether due to the sorts of assumptions about her Enlightenment views I have been discussing, or simply because the notion of sensibility was so intertwined with the oppression of women in the eighteenth century. Even when commentators allow that sensibility plays a role in the arguments of the second *Vindication*, they are uncertain how much weight to place on that role. Mackenzie, for example, claims that Wollstonecraft is ambivalent about the role of sensibility for virtue in the second *Vindication*, while Jacobus says that Wollstonecraft's interest in sensibility is restricted by the treatise form of the work. Despite these apparent barriers to giving an account of the role that sensibility plays in Wollstonecraft's thought, I wish to show that—even though it may not always be perfectly straightforward and simple—Wollstonecraft's notion of sensibility is far from unclear and that it plays a fundamental role in her moral thought.

True Sensibility

It is true that it may initially appear that Wollstonecraft is often ambivalent in her account of the sensibility. Wollstonecraft is explicit in the second *Vindication* about the naturalness of love, for this feeling is given to us by God, and a love for God is connected to our desire for self-perfection and happiness (Wollstonecraft 1983, 94). And this would seem to be in keeping with Wollstonecraft's views in *Mary*. Yet, on the other hand, we are told that "*reason*" must "teach passion to submit to necessity" (Wollstonecraft 1983, 115). Or that "To endeavour to reason love out of the world would be to out-Quixote Cervantes, and equally offend against common sense; but an endeavour to restrain this tumultuous passion, and to prove that it should not be allowed to dethrone superior powers, or to usurp the sceptre which the understanding should ever cooly wield, appears less wild" (Wollstonecraft 1983, 110).

This emphasis on the control of feeling by reason would appear to signal a change in Wollstonecraft's thinking from *Mary*. Yet, as Mackenzie points out, Wollstonecraft often appears ambivalent about the relationship between reason and feeling. Mackenzie states that "On the one hand, especially in her insistence in women's capacity to reason and in her scathing condemnation of the "manners" of contemporary women, she seems to regard the control of the passions by reason as essential to self-governance. On the other hand, she also seems to be moving toward the view that in a well-balanced, virtuous character, reason and sensibility should mutually strengthen and support each other rather than either dominating the other" (Mackenzie 1996, 190–1).

But how ambivalent is Wollstonecraft being here, and how much has her view of sensibility changed? I think the answer to these questions can be found by considering the specific focus of her writing (a change from the focus of *Mary*) in the second *Vindication*: arguments for the rights of women. Central to the whole book is the fact that women have been denied the exercise of their capacities to reason and thus have had their education neglected. But this is only half the cause of women's oppression, for Wollstonecraft also makes it clear that women are also kept subordinate by the encouragement of their development of an excess of sensibility. This is an important point, it is not just that women are being denied the education necessary for reason and are left with a void, artificial "feminine" sensibility is explicitly encouraged in the place of reason, and Wollstonecraft gives a scathing portrait of the results of such social conditioning.

> I once knew a weak woman of fashion, who was more than commonly proud of her delicacy and sensibility. She thought a distinguishing taste and puny appetite the height of all human perfection, and acted accordingly. I have seen this weak sophisticated being neglect all duties of life, yet recline with self-complacency on a sofa, and boast of her want of appetite as a proof of delicacy that extended to, or, perhaps, arose from, her exquisite sensibility; for it is difficult to render intelligible such ridiculous jargon. Yet, at the moment, I have seen her insult a worthy old gentlewoman, whom unexpected misfortunes had made dependent on her ostentatious bounty, and who, in better days, had claims on her gratitude. (Wollstonecraft 1983, 130)

Thus the sensibility of the "weak woman of fashion" is criticized because it is affected, vain, and self-involved: it is turned upon herself and prevents her from being benevolent to the deserving.

Wollstonecraft speaks positively of sensibility *itself* in the second *Vindication*, that is when it is not being used as an instrument of oppression or it has not turned into mere gross sensualism. For example, she again reiterates her comments from the first *Vindication* about the connection of sensibility to artistic creativity. This time she comments that men channel their sensibility into artistic compositions: "to amalgamate the gross materials; and moulding them with passion, give to the inert body a soul," but in the case of the imagination of women "love alone concentrates these ethereal beams" (Wollstonecraft 1983, 156). In this way it would seem that sensibility becomes an object of criticism or praise relative to its object. Thus we see in *Mary* that Wollstonecraft's attitude towards her heroine's intense sensibility depends on the actions it leads her to perform and the attitudes it leads her to have. Indeed, whatever differences there may appear to be between Wollstonecraft's treatment of sensibility in *Mary* and in the second *Vindication* can be explained in terms of the difference in subject content between the two works, rather than any differences in her notion of sensibility itself.

While it is made clear that romantic love as an object of women's sensibility is a problem, it is not because the feeling of love in itself is problematic, but because love has become misidentified with the sort of romantic fantasies found in women's novels. Wollstonecraft claims we should recognize that romantic love is only a part of the universal love, "which, after encircling humanity, mounts in grateful incense to God," that is part of being a moral being (Wollstonecraft 1983, 160). Thus love between the sexes is important in that it is natural and part of divine love, and this explains Wollstonecraft's surprisingly critical picture of the widow who devotes herself to her children and represses her natural passions, "and in the bloom of life forgets her sex" (Wollstonecraft 1983, 138). This would also then explain why Wollstonecraft believes that it is important for love in marriage to develop into friendship and respect; indeed she says that it can be helpful if there is something, such as a previous disappointment, which will put a damper on the passions. In this way, it would seem, the partners will realize that sexual love on its own does not suffice to produce a true relationship. For—as she states—the move from sexual love to friendship "seems perfectly to harmonize with the system of government which prevails in the moral world" (Wollstonecraft 1983, 114).[4]

The problem comes, for Wollstonecraft, when love in itself is seen (mistakenly) to be the supreme good, which "shall refine the soul, and not expire when it has served as a 'scale to the heavenly'," and it can "absorb every meaner affection and desire" (Wollstonecraft 1983, 168–9). This has meant that women have become the instrument of this good: they are "polished" and educated to inspire it in others, and they in their turn focus on finding an object to love. When the initial intensity of love has died down, the woman—through her arts—must strive to maintain the passion in her male partner, even though this will probably require the dumbing down of her own feelings (Wollstonecraft 1983, 173). In order to be able to achieve these things truth and sincerity then become secondary, indeed she says that the female character "so prettily drawn by poets and novelists" demands this, with the consequence that "virtue becomes a relative idea" (Wollstonecraft 1983, 139). We can understand the seriousness of this situation of women when we remember the connection that Wollstonecraft makes between truth and sincerity, and morality.

Thus it would seem that Wollstonecraft is reasonably clear in her account of sensibility in the second *Vindication*. The praiseworthiness of someone's sensibility is relative to the direction in which their sensibility is turned. If it is turned towards vanity or a life of sensualism, then it should be subject to criticism. Even worse, is when a false or misdirected sensibility is encouraged in women in order to make them more pleasurable companions for men and to make them better fit the eighteenth-century model of femininity. While in men—according to Wollstonecraft—their capacity for sensibility is shown through their creative endeavor, in women their capacity for sensibility is shown through love. Yet this greater propensity for love in women is either manipulated for the convenience of men, or it is prevented (through their lack of education and experience) from becoming part of a more universal feeling. In this way, the stunting and corrupting of the feeling of women not only directly contributes to their oppression, but it also indirectly contributes to their oppression by limiting their capacity for virtue.

An understanding of Wollstonecraft's concept of sensibility is pivotal to a comprehension of her arguments for both the rights and the virtue of women. These arguments reappear in *The Wrongs of Woman or Maria*, and again Wollstonecraft clearly connects them to the issue of women's sensibility, this time specifically the way that this sensibility is crushed and corrupted by the social institution of marriage. Although this is not to say that the book is narrow in its scope as the criticism of marriage, and other social institutions that oppress women, lead to a grim condemnation of the laws and conditions that serve to oppress both women and the poor. In the preface to the novel, Wollstonecraft states that she rather intends "to pourtray passions than manners." (Wollstonecraft 1976, 73) While in a letter to a friend discussing the manuscript, she states that "I cannot suppose any situation more distressing than for a woman of sensibility, with an improving mind, to be bound to such a man as I have described for life; obliged to renounce all humanizing affections, and to avoid cultivating her taste, lest her perception of grace and refinement of sentiment, should sharpen to agony the pangs of disappointment. Love, in which the imagination mingles its bewitching colouring, must be fostered by delicacy. I should despise, or rather call her an ordinary woman, who could endure such a husband as I have sketched" (Wollstonecraft 1976, 74).

Wollstonecraft is clear that such a situation will repulse the woman who has the sort of natural sensibility I have been endeavoring to describe. The more such a woman develops her "taste" and her capacity for human (not romantic/sentimental) love, the more she will become frustrated by her situation. Wollstonecraft does not appear here to be talking simply of some kind of platonic love, sexual love (where appropriate) is also included and is subject to the same restraints of taste and delicacy. After Maria finds out what sort of man her husband is, she retires from his apartment in the house and keeps to her own. In writing of this situation to her daughter, she says that "I was glad, I own, to escape from his; for personal intimacy without affection, seemed, to me the most degrading, as well as the most painful state in which a woman of any taste, not to speak of the peculiar delicacy of fostered sensibility, could be placed" (Wollstonecraft 1976, 146).

In *Mary*, the excessive sensibility and its ensuing need for love and to love of the central character was both her strength and her weakness. Wollstonecraft's lack of critical analysis of this sensibility and this need, and the often ambivalent way they are treated contributes to the weakness of the novel itself. In contrast, sensibility and love—platonic, maternal, sexual, etc.—play a more positive and carefully analyzed role in Maria's life. While Maria is clearly very "sensible" she is not passive or weak; indeed when she first meets Jemima and is trying to get her help, Jemima is cautious because "the very energy of Maria's character" made her suspect that Maria truly is mad (Wollstonecraft 1976, 83). The sort of sensibility that Maria has is the sort of capability for creative love that poets have, creative in that it awakens virtue in others and is inspired itself by grace and virtue: "What a creative power has an affectionate heart! There are beings who cannot live without loving, as poets love; and who feel the electric spark of genius, wherever it awakens sentiment or grace" (Wollstonecraft 1976, 86).

However, Wollstonecraft makes it clear that even such sensibility as Maria's can still be problematic. Maria herself claims if her home life had been more comfortable and if she had been better educated and more experienced, she would have been less likely to believe she was in love with George Venables, or to believe that she could obtain her freedom by marrying him. Locked in the madhouse, Maria starts to develop sentimental or romantic (in the pejorative sense) feelings towards the—as yet—unknown Darnford.

Fortunately Maria is able to exercise control over her feelings, although we are told that she "like a large proportion of her sex" is "only born to feel" (Wollstonecraft 1976, 98).[5] And she reflects on "how difficult it was for women to avoid growing romantic, who have no active duties or pursuits" (Wollstonecraft 1976, 87).[6] When Maria begins genuinely to fall in love with Darnford, Wollstonecraft addresses the reader on the subject of women and love. We are told not to be surprised that Maria begins to feel romantically towards Darnford, indeed it would seem that having romantic ideals of love and friendship is part of the maturing process. It is only when they become the focus of our life (as for many women), or when we continue to maintain them at the expense of personal development and maturity, that such ideals become problematic.

It is the women who marry without love, or when they love another, that Wollstonecraft criticizes through Maria's written advice to her daughter. She says that such women "may possess tenderness," but "they want that fire of the imagination, which produces *active* sensibility, and *positive* virtue" (Wollstonecraft 1976, 153). These women cannot be virtuous, because they are not true to their feelings: "Truth is the only basis of virtue," the woman who aims to please a lover or husband who disgusts her is truly depraved (Wollstonecraft, 1976, 153). The woman who attempts to care for and reform her brutish husband "is required to moralize, sentimentalize herself to stone, and pine her life away" (Wollstonecraft 1976, 154). Yet there is little doubt that this is—in effect—the role that the woman would be expected to play, something that is made chillingly clear in the judge's summary at the end of *Maria*. He criticizes Maria's behavior and her arguments for her divorce as fallaciously based on her feelings, for he says that virtuous women do not think of their own feelings. Thus there is a tension between societal expectations of women and their freedom to feel honestly and behave morally, for they are forced into a false morality and false feelings.

It is here that we can start to see the connections between Wollstonecraft's discussion of sensibility, virtue, and the oppression of marriage. Wollstonecraft claims in her preface that her aim is to exhibit "the misery and oppression, peculiar to women, that arise out of the partial laws and customs of society" (Wollstonecraft 1976, 73). Wollstonecraft offers in *Maria* a critique of the laws that essentially make women and children the property of their husbands, and of the way adultery laws are biased against women.[7] But the oppression that Wollstonecraft demonstrates in *Maria* is not merely legal, social, or physical, it is also an oppression of women's capacities for virtue and for love. Indeed Wollstonecraft claims that "matrimonial despotism of heart and conduct," when a woman stifles her true delicacy in order to be with a husband she does not love, appears to her "to be the peculiar Wrongs of Woman, because they degrade the mind" (Wollstonecraft 1976, 74). The virtue of women is crushed in other ways by the institution of marriage, for the husband will make decisions as to what is right for both, the woman will not be allowed to exercise her own conscience. Instead the virtue of women is bound in with their subordinate role to men, creating "a false morality . . . which makes all the virtue of women consist in charity, submission, and the forgiveness of injuries" (Wollstonecraft 1976, 196–7).

Both novels—with *Mary* providing some preliminary work, and *Maria* providing a more fully worked out account—not only claim the importance of a genuine sensibility, but they demonstrate how, for Wollstonecraft, a genuine sensibility underpins true morality. In both novels, we learn how important it is for women to love and while this love can be romantic and/or sexual, it is made clear that this love is "creative" in that it can inspire others to feelings of benevolence or to awaken in them the desire for virtue. Wollstonecraft also appears to claim that women have a greater capacity for feeling than men. Such a claim for modern feminism is clearly problematic, but taken within the context of Wollstonecraft's arguments it is significant. For it would then seem that women must be allowed the freedom to feel genuinely, and for their feelings—guided by Christian principles—to direct them towards virtue. The social institution of marriage forces women to betray or stifle these genuine feelings, while the social expectations of women in general condition them to admire and develop false feelings leading ultimately to a false morality. [8]

This is not to say, of course, that Wollstonecraft is not aware of the way that sensibility is a double-edged sword for women. Mackenzie argues that Wollstonecraft recognizes that the cultivation of sensibility in women will conflict with the imperfect society in which they live. In a letter about her daughter, Wollstonecraft wrote, "With trembling hand I shall cultivate her sensibility, and cherish delicacy of sentiment, lest, while I bring fresh blushes to the rose, I sharpen the thorns that will wound the breast I would fain guard—I dread to unfold her mind, lest it should render her unfit for the world she is to inhabit—Hapless woman! what a fate is thine" (Wollstonecraft 1977, 56).

Once we focus on the issues of sensibility—in particular the oppression of women's sensibility and thus their virtue—that come out in both the novels and in the second *Vindication*, we can see that genuine sensibility (and the capacity for sensibility) need not be at odds with a call for the education and rights of women. For when Wollstonecraft calls for the education of women, and the recognition of their capacity to reason, it is not simply that these things are important in themselves, but that they are important for the development of the morality of women; for without such things women will more than likely develop a false morality that grows out of unprincipled sensibility. Indeed this point can be extended further, the (correct) development of sensibility in women is not merely compatible with the recognition of their rights, and the development of their reason, it is a necessary part of Wollstonecraft's arguments for women in both the second *Vindication* and in the *Wrongs of Woman*. If this is so, then attempting to place the second *Vindication* into a conceptual framework that upholds the oppositional binary of reason/feeling would appear to be incorrect. Finally we are able to wrest away the second *Vindication* from its cultural role as an Enlightenment treatise on the rights of women, and allow it to be integrated more fully with Wollstonecraft's other more "literary" works.

The Philosophical
Role of Sensibility

But, once we have recognized the centrality of the notion of sensibility for Wollstonecraft's works, we must then consider how it is to be treated. Is it simply one argument or philosophical viewpoint among others in her moral view, or is it primarily a tool of political argument? On one level the answer is both of these options, but on another level these options may not fully cover the role that sensibility plays in Wollstonecraft's work; a role that has strong connections with its literary aspects. While other commentators are clearly aware of the importance of sensibility, and the importance of seeing connections between the fiction and the two *Vindications*, their accounts still typically reinforce (implicitly or explicitly) the disciplinary divisions between philosophy and literature. When there has been philosophical examination of the two novels, it has usually remained focused on identifying their "arguments," which can then be extracted and compared and contrasted to the arguments of Wollstonecraft's more straightforwardly "philosophical" work.

Even though Mackenzie, for example, does see important connections between the second *Vindication* and *The Wrongs of Woman*, she still has a tendency to treat the latter as a fictionalized working out of the ideas of the second *Vindication*. This results in Mackenzie's giving philosophical priority to the second *Vindication* and ultimately ignoring the literary form of the *The Wrongs of Woman*. Mackenzie's similar use of the *Letters* may initially appear to be unproblematic, but again she focuses on their philosophical content and does not acknowledge the possibility that their literary form may also have importance. This approach ultimately serves to reaffirm the philosophical authority of treatises and the lack of, or lesser amount of, authority of works of literature. Moreover, the lack of acknowledgment of the form of the *Letters* and the fictions means that the significance of the form of the second *Vindication*—which I have been arguing is central for its analysis—will be lost.

It is vital at this juncture to give an account of Sapiro's work on the politics of language in Wollstonecraft's work. Given my arguments thus far, it was with a mixture of both pleasure and disappointment that I read Sapiro's work, pleasure because much of what she says supports my ideas, disappointment because I found that my ideas were not as original as I had hoped. Yet I am including a discussion of Sapiro's work not merely for the sake of responsible scholarship, but also to examine, as we shall see, the significance of the differences between our views. While Sapiro recognizes the importance of the notion of sensibility—and its relation to morality—for Wollstonecraft's moral and political thought, she focuses on Wollstonecraft's letters and reviews. This again is to imply that legitimate discussion of philosophical theory—moral or otherwise— is confined to treatises or direct explicit accounts such as a review or a letter. In order to draw out the significance of the concept of sensibility for Wollstonecraft's political theory, Sapiro relies on John Barrell's account of the politicized art theory that was current during the time that Wollstonecraft was writing and aims to show that Wollstonecraft could have been both acquainted with, and influenced by, such a theory.[9] As we shall see, Sapiro's reliance on contemporary art theory and the letters and reviews ultimately produces an account of Wollstonecraft's moral thought that is both too narrow in its scope and too limited in the works that it emphasizes.

Sapiro bemoans the fact that sensibility is now only the subject of interest for literary criticism. She claims that this is unfortunate, because an understanding of the concept of sensibility is pivotal to an understanding of Wollstonecraft's moral psychology, as well as contributing to a discussion of her politics (see Sapiro 1992, 63). Moreover, "an important implication of accepting the importance of sensibility" for Sapiro, is "the rejection of the radical dichotomy between mind and body that Enlightenment and liberal thinkers are often credited with fostering" (Sapiro 1992, 67). While Sapiro notes that Wollstonecraft's views are sometimes ambiguous, and appear to change over the course of her writing, she defines sensibility for Wollstonecraft as "an elevated mode of feeling because it is governed by reason where sensualism is not. At the same time, part of its glory is that is spontaneous. Sensibility is a not a cold calculation of what is right; it is a spontaneous warmth of virtuous emotion" (Sapiro 1992, 65). Sapiro claims that sensibility can be both simultaneously governed and spontaneous because it is trained: When principles learned through reason take deep root in the mind they shape the emotions and feeling. They become habits of mind, an immediate sense perception of good and evil (Sapiro 1992, 66).

Sapiro says that it is mistaken to read the first *Vindication* as a badly written, overly emotional attack, or as having no interest beyond being the precursor to the second *Vindication*. Instead she offers an alternative reading (one that is perhaps more complex and carefully conceived than I am able to do full justice to here) that shows that Wollstonecraft—despite the haste and anger in her writing of the first *Vindication*—is aware of the politics of language. Sapiro claims, citing the same passages as I have used and other similar ones, that the first *Vindication* is "largely a text about writing, expression, and argument," and that Wollstonecraft is responding not only to what Burke wrote, but how he wrote (Sapiro 1992, 197). Sapiro makes three points in particular to support this conclusion: that Wollstonecraft recognized that "rhetorical style could be a weapon, and that Burke's manner of reaching for emotional reactions was very powerful" (Sapiro 1992, 199); that she "understood the substantive importance of form;" and that her argument is addressed as much to Burke's *Sublime and the Beautiful* as it is to the *Reflections*.[10]

Sapiro argues that we need to understand Wollstonecraft's reaction to Burke "as part of a developing sense of a unified theory of art, society, and nature that was inextricably linked to political questions" (Sapiro 1992, 208). Sapiro claims that "Wollstonecraft's primary concern in evaluating written works was that they contribute to education of the citizen for virtue" (Sapiro 1992, 206). And that what "Wollstonecraft sought in writing was the natural expression of a virtuous sensibility; that is, emotions and passions trained through reasoned principle and habit to react virtuously" (Sapiro 1992, 207). Sapiro further claims that this same theme reappears in the second *Vindication*. She holds that Wollstonecraft's awareness of political arguments about the arts shows in her reviews, while her social circle contained many people who were interested in discussing art and politics. In order to draw out the type of theory that appears to underlie Wollstonecraft's views, Sapiro relies on John Barrell's account of theories of art that were prevalent during Wollstonecraft's time and points to evidence of such views in Wollstonecraft's reviews for the *Analytical Review*.

Central to such theories is the framework of civic humanism, and it was held that art would be the medium through which free citizens would be educated in public virtues, and the quality of art would be evaluated accordingly. Sapiro identifies the concept of "representation" as pivotal to the languages of both art and politics, and here representation does not mean mere "servile" or "mechanical" imitation but a depiction of human beings and human activity that both expressed and inspired the highest virtue humans could attain. Clearly such representation would also "require contemplation and imagination" on the part of the artist (Sapiro 1992, 209).

Sapiro argues that Wollstonecraft was interested in this issue of the representation of nature as opposed to its "servile" imitation, because her notion of independence—a key virtue for her—is similar to this notion of originality in art and imagination. There are other connections between art and virtue that Sapiro finds in Wollstonecraft's work. Honesty (another important virtue for Wollstonecraft), Sapiro states, can be understood in a similar manner within the framework of the civic humanist theory of art: "In her texts *honesty* referred not just to telling the truth in the conventional sense of not saying what one knows to be false, but also to striving for greater correspondence between nature and self-presentation, especially with regard to feelings and sensibility" (Sapiro 1992, 215). The importance of honesty in self-presentation can be found (as Sapiro shows) throughout Wollstonecraft's works, perhaps most importantly in Wollstonecraft's discussions—and her criticism thereof—of the distinctions between manners and morals: "outward behavior that may only be a sign of servility to one or another authority, and behavior based on principles of virtue" (Sapiro 1992, 218).

While Sapiro does not—as I have tried to do—pursue the way that honesty and sensibility, both in themselves and in their connections to written expression, are bound up with Wollstonecraft's arguments for the rights of women, she does give an account of how the art theory that appears to influence Wollstonecraft is played out in the second *Vindication*. According to Sapiro, Wollstonecraft focused on the relationship between words and representation in the second *Vindication*. Sapiro shows how Wollstonecraft recognized the differences between language used to describe or discuss the two sexes, and how she attempted a political polemic (albeit not very successfully) through an analysis of language, in particular through the use of the terms "masculine" and "feminine." For Wollstonecraft, the word "masculine" was used in such a way as to include capacities such as reason which she saw as central to the attainment of virtue. Aligning women with the "not-masculine" or the "feminine" meant that these terms could be used against them (see Sapiro 1992, 220).

Sapiro's account is interesting, and I would certainly hesitate to try and prove her wrong, but I have concerns not simply with the conclusions she draws about language and expression in Wollstonecraft's work, but about the approach she takes to an examination of Wollstonecraft's work. If we treat the language of the second *Vindication* (or any of the other works) as forming an extractable argument, then I think we have missed part of what Wollstonecraft wants to say with her account of the relationship between expression and content. We cannot extract the "honesty" from what she has written, but we think that we can examine the "language" in isolation. Again this is to treat the second *Vindication*—or any of the other works we approach in this way—solely as a work that is nothing over and above a set of arguments. Essentially this is to remain within the boundaries of "the philosophical" set by the dominant model of moral philosophy. However it would seem that we need to question those boundaries, because a focus on expression solely as a political tool will either create difficulties in approaching Wollstonecraft's fictional work, or—as I believe happens on Sapiro's analysis—this work becomes de-emphasized or even devalued.

We should not, I believe, ignore what can best be described as the literary aspects of Wollstonecraft's work. By literary aspects I do not mean that Wollstonecraft's work should be simply judged in terms of aesthetic success or failure. Accounts by literary critics of the two novels have claimed them aesthetic failures, ruined by their overly philosophical or polemical nature; indeed, especially in the case of *The Wrongs of Woman*, the purpose of the novel has been seen as contributing to its clumsy construction (see for example, Wollstonecraft 1976, xvi). But, given Wollstonecraft's emphasis on sincerity and simplicity, such criticisms should not worry us unduly. Instead I mean by literary aspects that we should consider the way that, for Wollstonecraft, sensibility was not simply tied into morality, but was also—as I have already shown—tied into an imaginative creativity, and thus morality and imagination become connected in an important way. It is this connection that I do not find brought out in any particular way in Sapiro's account.

There is no question that Sapiro's account of Wollstonecraft's notions of poetry and the imagination—which I am about to give—is to a great extent correct, but I wish to question whether it encompasses all the nuances of these notions. Sapiro recognizes that in the same way that science is reason employed in its most sublime form, poetry is to sensibility. Sapiro correctly claims that, for Wollstonecraft, the flight of imagination that is required for poetic writing is the creativity of the human mind which gives a depth to our thought, helping us to both "leap past reason" and to avoid sinking into sensualism (Sapiro 1992, 70). Moreover, as Sapiro points out, imagination is the work of "genius" which Wollstonecraft defines as "only another word for exquisite sensibility," and works of imagination and genius are often inspired by the passion of enthusiasm which Wollstonecraft sometimes uses in the sense of being divinely inspired (Wollstonecraft 1989, 7: 9).[11]

Yet, as Sapiro also makes clear, it appears that the frenzied flight of poetic inspiration will be driven away as the reason develops. In *Mary*, Wollstonecraft claimed that "as judgment improves, genius evaporates" (Wollstonecraft 1976, 31). While in the first *Vindication*, she writes of "the genuine enthusiasm of genius, which, perhaps, seldom appears, but in the infancy of civilization; for as this light becomes more luminous reason clips the wing of fancy—the youth becomes a man" (Wollstonecraft 1996, 47). Sapiro argues that Wollstonecraft's apparent acceptance of the "trade-off" between reason and imagination and genius is not problematic: "She did not regret the loss suffered by the gain of reason. As she noted in a different context [*VW*], 'But the welfare of society is not built on extraordinary exertions, and were it more reasonably organized, there would be still less need of great abilities, or heroic virtues'" (Sapiro 1992, 72).

I think that here Sapiro is missing the nuances of the relationship of the poetic imagination to the progress of society. In *Hints*, Wollstonecraft claims that while reason aims to perfect the understanding in this world, the imagination can offer us a foretaste of the true perfection of the eternal life, indeed Wollstonecraft appears to praise the almost mystical devotional nature of imagination. Whereas in describing the poetic process in "On Poetry," we find that poetry is a form of worship—"a temple not made with the hands"—of God (1989 7: 8). The poet is first moved by his own sensibility and his love of others, while he is made reflective by nature. This love of man leads to a religious love. "Grand and sublime images strike the imagination," and "God is seen in every floating cloud, and comes from the misty mountain to receive the noblest homage of an intelligent creature—praise" (1989, 8). Given Wollstonecraft's religious beliefs, and the interconnections she sees between love of God and morality, it would, initially, seem hard to imagine why she would accept the loss of poetic vision in society.

If, as Sapiro suggests, Wollstonecraft accepts the eventual overriding of the poetic imagination by reason, Wollstonecraft must see them as divisible in some way. Yet I would claim that Wollstonecraft seems to see imagination and reason as somehow inseparable in the true poet. While the poetic flight of fancy leaves reason behind, she says, it does not lose sight of it. The poet will achieve understanding, while the cold reasoner—the philosopher—may not. She states that "Mr Kant has observed, that the understanding is sublime, the imagination beautiful—yet it is evident, that poets, and men who undoubtedly possess the liveliest imagination, are most touched by the sublime, while men who have cold, enquiring minds, have not this exquisite feeling in any degree, and indeed seem to lose it as they cultivate their reason" (1989, 5: 275).

Moreover it is clear that at least in one sense Wollstonecraft is critical of the loss of the poetic imagination as civilization progresses, for the creative spirit of poetry is crushed by the growth of civilization. While the original poets were inspired by nature, poets in this more advanced state of civilization are now inspired by the books they read, and they aim to copy producing an artificial beauty: "The silken wings of fancy are shrivelled by rules; and a desire of attaining elegance of diction, occasions an attention to words, incompatible with sublime, impassioned thoughts" (1989, 7: 9). Moreover, Wollstonecraft claims, the original poets of genius exercised their understanding far more than these imitators. She recognizes that this might sound paradoxical but explains that "they exercised it to discriminate things, whilst their followers were busy to borrow sentiments and arrange words" (1989, 7: 9).

While it is clear that the poet will not lead any revolutions nor precipitate social or political reform, I believe that the creative imagination of the poet is still necessary for the development of society. Wollstonecraft's views on moral self-improvement remain more or less unchanged throughout her works, but her subjects do change. Thus in *Mary*, Wollstonecraft deals solely with the development of the individual, and in the second *Vindication* and *The Wrongs of Woman*, she deals with the development of women both individually and as a group. Whereas in the *French Revolution*, the focus of Wollstonecraft's interests in social justice have changed and she begins to analyze social progress, national character, and the nature of man. Whatever hopes Wollstonecraft may have had for the French Revolution, it is clear that by the time she came to write about it, she did not see it as an end but just one step for the cure of France. Wollstonecraft claims that the social framework can only be changed as individuals improve themselves, indeed it would appear that she holds that the moral character of a nation is nothing over and above the characters of its individual citizens. This moral nation will be one that is held together by "the cement of humanity" unlike the pre-Revolutionary era in France which, according to Wollstonecraft, had reached a state of false refinement which made each person the center of his/her own world.[12] At the very root of this improvement lies a true sensibility which will express itself in an improving self-love, a love of others, and a love of God; and it is this sensibility and the ideals which it inspires that is the province of the poet.

In the *Hints*, Wollstonecraft even goes so far as to say that she is "more and more convinced" that poetry is "the forerunner of civilization" (1989, 5: 274). The flights of fancy of the poet increase the understanding; they are not at odds with reason, but they are incompatible with the artificial civilization of Wollstonecraft's time. While she is not demanding a return to ancient times—for it is clear that she connects scientific progress to moral progress—she is making some sort of demand that society is more natural in its progress towards a state of civilization. Once civilization has begun, it seems that poetry will no longer be its driving force, that will be the job of reason, but Wollstonecraft does not appear to desire the sacrifice of poetry to reason; rather the ideal is that they work together.

Clearly, as Sapiro points out, few people will show true poetic imagination and understanding, but this does not—I think—mean that we should dismiss the role of poetry in the progress of a society. The poet will not lead any revolutions, but he embodies the drive that leads ordinary men (and is kept from women) towards a desire for morality, for self-perfection, and a love of God. Moreover, if we remember that the moral progress of a nation is, for Wollstonecraft, nothing more than the moral progress of its citizens, then it is also possible to argue that the *reading* by citizens of poetry that is inspired by nature, love of man, and God may affect social progress.

What I am trying to do here is to show how intricately bound up poetry is with Wollstonecraft's views of moral progress both for the individual and for a society. If we accept Sapiro's view—which I have questioned—that Wollstonecraft was prepared to allow reason to override imagination for the welfare of society, then we will ultimately also place a division between politics and poetry where one may not have been held by Wollstonecraft. However accepting that Wollstonecraft was not making any rigid distinctions between politics/morality and poetry requires us to include in our discussion of political or moral theory elements that fall into the category of the "non-philosophical" on the dominant model of moral philosophy. Indeed Wollstonecraft's notions of poetic imagination and sensibility are clearly at odds with this model.

We may have to accept that there are strong romantic (or even what Wollstonecraft calls "mystical") elements in her views of the love of mankind and the love of God. This may not be something with which we are comfortable, philosophers do not often tend to be divinely inspired, but it is something that clearly runs throughout Wollstonecraft's thought, both in *what* she writes, and in the *way* she writes. We may even find such things as Wollstonecraft's descriptions of the effects of nature on Mary when she is a child rather embarrassing, especially, perhaps, given the autobiographical nature of the fictional *Mary*. We are told that "Enthusiastic sentiments of devotion . . . actuated her; her Creator was almost apparent to her sense in his works; but they were mostly the grand or solemn features of Nature which she delighted to contemplate. She would stand and behold the waves rolling, and think of the voice that could still the tumultuous deep. . . . Many nights she sat up . . . *conversing* with the Author of Nature, making verses and singing hymns of her own composing" (Wollstonecraft 1976, 10–11).

Yet we cannot deny the existence of this romantic strain of thought and expression in Wollstonecraft's works. We should not forget, for example, there are many "flights of fancy" in the second *Vindication*, which are typically concerned with love, with visions of an improved society, or with God. Nor should we ignore the fact that many of Wollstonecraft's comments on poetry and the imagination can be found in her collection of notes for the sequel to the second *Vindication*. Denying the poetic element in Wollstonecraft's language and ideas is ultimately to deny the source of their power and their grip on our imagination. Surely one of the reasons that the second *Vindication* has not been doomed to obscurity is the visceral effects it has on its reader, rather than the intellectual appeal of conclusive proofs produced by well-turned, logical, arguments. Although this is not to say that the arguments offered by Wollstonecraft are unphilosophical.

Thus while Sapiro's analysis of Wollstonecraft's language politics, and the theory of art that may underlie Wollstonecraft's views, is both important and interesting, it is ultimately too narrow in its focus, and it reinforces disciplinary divisions between Wollstonecraft's "literary" and "non-literary" works. In concentrating on the imagination and creativity only in relation to the political content of Wollstonecraft's work, Sapiro treats them as part of another argument and ignores the multi-layered role they have in Wollstonecraft's works. While Sapiro argues that writing style is important for Wollstonecraft's political works, its importance is only measured insofar as it is part of an overall argument. Ultimately this emphasis on language and/or expression only as a political tool means that Wollstonecraft's fictional work becomes de-emphasized, and indeed we find that Sapiro relies far more heavily on the letters and reviews to produce her account than any other source. To focus on the letters and reviews, and the possible ways that Wollstonecraft may have incorporated contemporary art theory into her own work, may even implicitly devalue Wollstonecraft's work as a whole. It suggests that Wollstonecraft did not write a coherent body of work, either due to the literary forms it includes, or due to a lack of continuity between the content of the works. Given the disciplinary divisions typically made between literature and philosophy, this probably amounts to the same thing.

Conclusion

Thus we can see that—while the second *Vindication* may be Wollstonecraft's central philosophical work—we should not focus exclusively on the it for an understanding of Wollstonecraft's moral thought. For to do so, is to forfeit a grasp of her wide-ranging and complex moral philosophy. If we examine her other works as well, we not only get a more nuanced view of the relationship between reason and emotion in her philosophy, but we gain a clearer idea of the form of the second *Vindication* itself: whether or not it is an Enlightenment treatise. An examination of the first *Vindication* in particular not only tells us about the form of moral writing for Wollstonecraft, it also gives us the key towards understanding Wollstonecraft's attitude towards sensibility throughout her work. In particular, it allows us to understand Wollstonecraft's attitude towards sensibility in the second *Vindication*, which has typically been seen as containing a rejection of feeling. We find that Wollstonecraft is rejecting false sensibility, whether the overblown sentiments of the writer, or the sensibility inculcated in women in order to make them mindless objects of pleasure for men. Yet we also find that "true" sensibility both underpins and is interconnected with morality for Wollstonecraft.

Once we recognize the centrality of sensibility for Wollstonecraft's thought then it becomes far easier to see the connections between the second *Vindication* and her other works (in particular her fictional works), than it is to find such connections when the second *Vindication* is categorized as an Enlightenment treatise with all that this entails. If the second *Vindication* is read as an Enlightenment treatise, then *Mary* or *The Wrongs of Woman* are only of interest insofar as they demonstrate a certain continuity of interest in the themes of the second *Vindication*. If we claim—as Mackenzie does—that *The Wrongs of Woman* is a fictional working out of themes of the second *Vindication*, we are still implicitly using the "philosophical" form of the latter work as part of our justification for its philosophical priority. The temptation to do so is obvious, the eighteenth century novel was typically a "woman's" genre, and tended to focus on love and relationships, especially of the romantic kind. Yet I have argued that central to the second *Vindication* is the question of what is the right kind of love and that sensibility—far from being in opposition to the rights of women—is a part of Wollstonecraft's arguments for such rights: women have a right to love whom they choose, and to love mankind and God in a reasoned and educated manner.

Clearly in order to understand these arguments for the role that sensibility plays in morality for Wollstonecraft, it is necessary to accept a certain approach to her work. We must not treat the complex issue of the sentiment of sensibility and its expression simply as another philosophical point, or as just a tool in political polemic. Rather we must recognize that there are other possibilities for philosophical argument beyond those of the dominant model of moral philosophy. If we do not recognize this then, as I have argued, we run the risk of giving too narrow an interpretation of Wollstonecraft's work—especially the connections between imagination and morality.

In addition, by treating sensibility in this way, we may also de-emphasize or implicitly devalue some of her works, in particular the fictional works. If we do not accept the creativity both *in* Wollstonecraft's work, and *argued for* by her work, and we deny the inherent romanticism of much of her work because it is not "philosophical" enough, then we ultimately are continuing to examine her work—albeit indirectly and subtly—through the lens of the Enlightenment treatise and the expectations that accompany this examination. Indeed it would seem that the forms which are to count as a "philosophical" on the dominant model of moral philosophy are ghosts of the Enlightenment treatise.

In order to interpret Wollstonecraft properly, and to understand the complex role that sensibility plays in her moral and political thought, we must be prepared to smudge the boundaries that have been made between creative or imaginative writing on the one hand, and reasoned or philosophical writing on the other. Any resistance we may have towards this approach to an analysis of Wollstonecraft's work must be recognized for what it is: a need for the comfortable narrowness and rigidity of the boundaries of the dominant model of moral philosophy. Yet we cannot claim that if the boundaries between philosophy and poetry are no longer clear-cut, then confusion will reign. As we have seen, Wollstonecraft herself successfully achieves a crossing of disciplinary boundaries, whereas any confusion in interpreting her work is created by a search for an eighteenth-century Enlightenment treatise, or for its twentieth-century remains.

Once we have recognized that not only is it possible to question the rigidity of the boundaries of traditional moral philosophy, and, indeed, that this may be necessary in order to provide a fruitful interpretation of works such as those of Wollstonecraft, then we are ready to take the next step. If we are prepared to question what is to count as philosophical argument in a text, then we shall need to consider typical expectations of what is to count as philosophical investigation of a text. And it is an examination of these expectations about philosophical investigation that will form the focus of the following chapter, in particular of the way that they curtail our abilities to read certain texts of philosophy. This is an important point, for what we take moral philosophy itself to be is intimately bound up with what we take to be an appropriate model (or models) of philosophical investigation; and it is to this I turn next with my interpretation of the moral philosophy in the novels of George Eliot.[13]

Notes

1. Indeed I think it would be interesting to trace other similarities in argument from the *Thoughts* to the second *Vindication*.

2. See also Diana Coole, *Women in Political Theory*, New York: Wheatsheaf, 1988.

3. Having done this, I shall then be in a position to get clear how much of what I am saying has been dealt with already by Sapiro, and to explore the significant differences between our accounts.

4. Carol Poston (1996) suggests in "Mary Wollstonecraft and 'The Body Politic'" that there may be psychological reasons for Wollstonecraft's view of marriage: she was an adult survivor of childhood abuse.

5. See also *Mary* p. 7, fn. 1.

6. See also *Mary* p. 52, fn. 1.

7. See for example, the tale of Maria's landlady.

8. It is interesting to note that in the address to Talleyrand at the beginning of *A Vindication of the Rights of Woman*, Wollstonecraft says that her aim is to show how contemporary views regarding women subvert morality.

9. John Barrell, *The Political Theory of Painting from Reynolds to Hazlitt: "The Body of the Public"* (New Haven: Yale University Press, 1986).

10. Sapiro claims that one's mode of expression during Wollstonecraft's time was an important indicator of character, thus Burke's style became part of the political debate. Sapiro notes that Paine also engaged with Burke's style.

11. This view of poetic inspiration was typical for Wollstonecraft's era.

12. *An Historical and Moral View of the Origin and Progress of the French Revolution; and the Effect It Has Produced in Europe.* In Wollstonecraft 1989, 6: 62.

13. I think it is clear that my thinking at this point has been greatly influenced by the work of Cora Diamond. In particular I found her article "Anything but Argument" (Diamond 1995) to have been very helpful for my understanding of the connection between philosophical assessment and an understanding of what philosophy is.

5

George Eliot and How to Read Novels as Philosophy

George Eliot, the nineteenth-century British novelist, has often been described as a philosopher-novelist; indeed Mary Ellen Waithe in *A History of Women Philosophers* states that Eliot is sometimes described as "a philosopher whose *genre* was fiction" (Waithe 1991, 3: 255). Moreover Eliot is one of the few women philosophers to be accorded an entry in *The Encyclopedia of Philosophy*. What is significant for my investigation is how such a description has been understood. But I am not so much interested in the different ways that commentators have discussed this description, rather in the assumptions underlying their work about how this description is to be taken. Specifically, I am interested in the assumption that a search for the philosophical content of a novel must follow the model of philosophical assessment typical for the contemporary dominant model of moral philosophy.

This investigation of Eliot's novels builds on themes that I raised in the previous two chapters. In the case of Christine de Pisan's *The Book of the City of Ladies* we saw that an understanding of written form can be pivotal to an understanding of philosophical content. Eliot can show us why *not* taking account of the form of a work (when appropriate) can be problematic, for it is not simply about the potential loss of interpretation of a particular work, it is also about what position it commits us to philosophically. Whereas in Christine's case we could see how the form of her work reflects some of her philosophical ideals and concepts, Eliot explicitly spells out and argues for a philosophical position that demands the form of a novel.

In the case of the work of Mary Wollstonecraft, we saw that central to an understanding of her moral philosophy was the recognition that she does not hold a clear distinction between creative or poetic writing and

philosophical writing. An examination of Eliot's work shows us the type
of account of moral philosophy that—unlike that of the dominant moral
view—would be able to accommodate this type of understanding. Wollstonecraft's work also showed us the narrowness and rigidity of the
boundaries of the "philosophical" on the dominant model of moral philosophy. A reading of Eliot's novels now makes us challenge those
boundaries themselves. Furthermore, an investigation of Wollstonecraft's
work showed that there are other possibilities for what is to count as
philosophical argument beyond those of the dominant model. Yet if we
allow for these different possibilities, this means that method of philosophical investigation of a text must change accordingly. And it is this
method or model of philosophical investigation that I challenge using an
interpretation of the moral philosophical thought Eliot's novels.

I hold that this method is inappropriate for the examination of novels
(in Eliot's case at least), for it ultimately requires us to separate the philosophical content of the novel from its form, yet the form is—for Eliot—
part of that very philosophical content. Yet this does not mean we should
reject the possibility of analyzing the philosophical content of Eliot's
novels, rather we should recognize that what we take to be the appropriate method or model of philosophical assessment—indeed what is often
taken to be the only model—is bound up with what we take moral philosophy to be. I shall show through an interpretation of Eliot's work that
a different approach to investigating the philosophy in Eliot's novels, one
generated by a different conception of moral philosophy, can produce an
account of her moral philosophy that is both fruitful and no less rational
or evident.

Eliot's Work

George Eliot was the *non de plume* of Marian (Mary Ann) Evans
(1819–1880). While she had little formal education, she moved in progressive intellectual circles. Her relationship with George Henry Lewes
and her friendship with British Positivists such as Frederic Harrison tes-
tify to the fact that she would have been knowledgeable about contemporary currents in European philosophical thought. Eliot's intellectual
career began by writing for the *Westminster Review* and translating works
of philosophy. She translated Strauss's *Life of Jesus* (1846), Feuerbach's *The
Essence of Christianity* (1854), and Spinoza's *Tractatus Theologico-Politicus*
in 1849 and the *Ethica* in 1856. Thus her philosophical knowledge was not
the passive, sponge-like "knowledge through osmosis" attributed to
some women due to their contact with (male) philosophers. It is clear
that—despite her initial disadvantages—she herself possessed a broad
base of actively sought philosophical knowledge by the time she began

her novel writing career. Her most notable fictional works are *Adam Bede* (1859), *The Mill on the Floss* (1860), *Silas Marner* (1861), *Middlemarch* (1871–2), and *Daniel Deronda* (1876).

Given her intellectual background it is not surprising, therefore, that much of the work done on the philosophical aspects of Eliot's novels has been aimed at drawing out a recognizable philosophical theory from Eliot's fiction; indeed it is frequently claimed that there is a deliberate reproduction on Eliot's part of some or all of the theory of an "established" philosopher such as Spinoza or Comte. Obviously this type of claim—that Eliot's novels are philosophical in virtue of the similarity of their content to that of the work of a recognized philosopher—is problematic in a very simple and obvious way. It clearly serves to suggest that Eliot's philosophical thought lacked originality. If her novels are merely "translations" of the thought of others, then it may be unclear to us why we should have any particular interest in studying and interpreting her work.

While I cannot be sure of the motivations behind such interpretations of Eliot, I am lead to suspect that their origins lie in the apparent difficulty the form of Eliot's work poses for a philosophical investigation. The standard notion that comes from the dominant model of moral philosophy of what constitutes a fully systematized philosophy appears to be at odds with a text that—among other things—offers moral knowledge in terms of the fortunes of particular characters rather than in terms of universal principles; and whose strength can lie in the moral ambiguity of its characters, rather than the soundness of its moral arguments. It is far easier to place Eliot's work within the framework of an extant systematized philosophy, and then use aspects of her novels as evidence for this philosophy, and as arguments supporting it. Yet I wish to argue not only that such an approach—at least in the case of Eliot's work—is doomed to failure, but that the apparent tension between the form of her novels and a systematized philosophy signals the need to reconceive what is to count as a systematized philosophy. Moreover an examination of the way that Eliot's description as a philosopher-novelist has typically been understood sheds light on our expectations of philosophy, the narrow boundaries we draw around the discipline, and the way these curtail our abilities to read the text. These are issues that were raised in the previous chapter, and I now explore them fully.

Given what we have learned from the previous chapter on the work of Wollstonecraft about the importance of, at the very least, considering the complete corpus of a writer, I am careful to use a wide range of Eliot's work, both fiction and non-fiction. Moreover I considered that focusing on one particular novel or a small selection of Eliot's fiction would place restrictions on the sort of general claims that I wish to make about Eliot's moral thought. I have not included Eliot's poetry, simply because it has not received the high critical acclaim of her novels. I realized that I would create unnecessary difficulties for myself if I had to explain the aesthetic value in addition to the philosophical value of my chosen texts. Finally, while I support my interpretation of Eliot's moral thought very specifically, it is at the same time broad enough to allow the possibility of Eliot's creative development.

Comte, Spinoza, and Eliot

My concern about the search for the thought of an established philosopher in Eliot's novels is by no means a merely academic point. There has been no shortage of commentators who wish to claim that Eliot was writing novels that embraced the Positivist philosophy, indeed Martha Vogeler in "George Eliot and the Positivists" comments—somewhat caustically—on the wide range of connections that have been made between the thought of Comte and Eliot in contemporary criticism of Eliot's fiction. The range of these connections extends, as Vogeler recognizes, from specific instances of influence to claims that Eliot's novels were a philosophical testing of Comte's axioms:

> Perhaps emboldened by the massive biographical material generated in this century since George Eliot's death, some of which clearly links her with the English Positivists, recent critics have been detecting concentrations of Positivist ore in her canon. Their Geiger counters have registered, for example, a determinism derived from Comte; . . . an inordinate concern for factual accuracy that marks her attainment of the Positivist stage of mental development; social and political thought in part derived from Comte's; even a reflection of Comte's description of fetishism in Silas Marner's care of his little brown pot. Characters in her works as various as Tyran, Farebrother, Felix Holt, Savonarola, and Deronda have been ordained into the Positivist priesthood, and Dorothea and Romola have been beatified as Comtist heroines. At least two scholars have hypothesized that, far from simply inculcating Positivist ideas, George Eliot was testing Comte's axioms in fictional situations. (Vogeler 1980, 407–8)

Vogeler further points out that the excitement of such discoveries has apparently clouded some commentators' judgments about the apparent relationship between the thought of Comte and Eliot. She states that for such commentators, "whatever contradictions exist between her [Eliot's] teaching and Comte's represent her unwillingness to use Positivist ore unrefined" (Vogeler 1980, 408).

The evidence for Comte's influence on Eliot is most convincing when it is stated in general terms. Eliot does appear to employ the Positivist method in her novels, giving an objective arrangement of social attitudes and historical details for the reader before drawing any conclusions. The descriptions of English country town society, and her detailed psychological treatment of the inhabitants of this society, are indeed the hallmarks of an Eliot novel. Such descriptions have even inspired one commentator to claim that "the method she adopted for sociological and psychological studies in the novels was typical of a social scientist of the class of which Comte was a leading early specimen. It made use of laboratory tactics—collecting data, neglecting nothing, undermining the value of nothing; then formulating hypotheses; testing them; and then formulating laws, passing from particular to general" (Prasad 1968, 78).

Unfortunately, when commentators attempt to connect particular aspects or themes of Comte's and Eliot's thought, they invariably fail to make their claims consistent; yet it is important to notice here that the aim of consistency is central to the type of approach on which such commentators have based their examinations. Eliot's "philosophy" must be extracted from her novels and laid side by side with the systematized philosophy of Comte. The more consistent Eliot's views are with Comte's, the stronger the claim that her novels contain a systematized philosophy and that this philosophy is a reproduction of Comtist Positivism.

The clearest example of failure of consistency is the issue of religion. According to Comte's law of the three stages of moral development, moral maturity is typified by the embracing of Comte's religion of humanity. There are two distinct problems with asserting that Eliot held a Comtist religion of humanity. First, this is to condemn her to holding an artificially constructed and synthesized man-made religion that has been described as "little more than an academic joke, or at best a curiosity" (Sklair 1968, 330–1). Second, it is hard to dovetail Comte's view of religion with Eliot's supposed "religion of humanity," even if it can be shown that she has passed through the necessary previous stages of development. Eliot's rejection of traditional religion is in part due to her belief that its emphasis on the rewards of the afterlife only promoted egoism in this life.[1] On the other hand while Comte is not offering salvation or an afterlife, and his eyes are turned firmly earthward, there is still an emphasis on compensation and rewards for one's belief. The Positivist religion is sold to us as providing all the satisfaction of the Catholic church with none of the drawbacks of wasting love on God.[2] For Eliot, the realization that there is no promise of an afterlife, no supernatural being whose role it is to save and protect us, means that we must attempt to provide this love, protection, and sympathy for each other. It is this be-lief that both drives many of the plots of her novels and lies behind the moral development of her characters.

The real failure here is not the lack of consistency between Eliot's and Comte's work, but that an attempt to demonstrate the Positivist thought in Eliot's work is typically at the expense of what is usually perceived as the artistic and moral value of Eliot's novels. Indeed there appears to be an unfortunate relationship between the amount of the evidence that can be found to support the claim that Eliot incorporated the philosophical thought of Comte (and, as we shall also see, Spinoza) in her novels and the aesthetic appeal of Eliot's novels. Simply put, when Eliot appears to be at her most Comtist, her work loses many of its artistic qualities. In *Romola*, for example, the work considered to be the most 'Positivist' of Eliot's novels, we find that on the one hand we are to applaud Eliot's thorough use of the Positivist method in the historical and social details of the novel; on the other hand we are to deplore the didacticism and life-lessness of the novel as a work of art. Henry James in "The Life of George Eliot" complains of the pedantry and the smell of the lamp in *Romola*; and I suggest that the source of this unpleasant odor is the same as the source for a claim of Positivism in Eliot's work (see James 1984, 1: 1004).

This loss of the aesthetic and moral qualities of Eliot's novels is by no means accidental, nor is it simply a failure of this one particular (Posi-tivist) philosophical system; rather it is a direct outgrowth of the particu-lar approach taken to the search for the presence of Positivist philosophy in the novels. Once we recognize that this approach is, to say the least, not optimal, then we may be in a position to recognize that it need not be the only one. This will become more evident after we have considered claims that Eliot was writing some form of Spinozistic philosophy.

It may seem that a claim that Eliot was influenced instead by Spinoza's thought is not an unreasonable assessment to make. As a result of her translation work on Spinoza, Eliot came to feel the need and importance of interpretative work on his philosophy. In a letter to Charles Bray in 1849, Eliot declared that: "What is wanted in English is not a translation of Spinoza's works, but a true estimate of his life and system. After one has rendered his Latin faithfully into English, one feels that there is an-other yet more difficult process of translation for the reader to effect, and that the only mode of making Spinoza accessible to a larger number is to study his books, then shut them and give an analysis" (Eliot 1954–78, 2: 321). This letter has been the foundation for the various claims that Eliot was attempting this "translation" in her fiction; indeed one commentator notes that the connection between Spinoza and Eliot is immediately ob-vious: "even the student who has not read much of Spinoza and the metaphysicians is bound to be impressed by the 'process of translation' she is able to effect" (Hulme 1967, 119).

The effects on the aesthetic value of Eliot's novels of investigating them for Spinozistic thought, and the inconsistencies of her thought and Spinoza's, are even more serious here than in the case of the search for Comtist thought in Eliot's novels. The creative hallmarks of a George Eliot novel—those aspects that make it distinct from the work of say, Dickens—are many and varied. Focusing just on one to make the point I want to make here: Eliot's detailed descriptions of English country life and small town life, one can see that such descriptions, while morally significant, can have no place in a Spinozistic moral system. The exquisite social, political, and pastoral detail of many of the scenes of Eliot's novels can serve to remind us of how many factors, conscious and unconscious, are present in our moral lives. Eliot offers descriptions of the typical inhabitants of these small towns and villages, descriptions of "a monotonous homely existence" that, like Dutch paintings, are a source "of delicious sympathy".[3]

Yet while Eliot's descriptions of people and places are morally significant to the whole enterprise of her novel, this feature, by its very nature, cannot be a part of Spinoza's "pure" philosophical enterprise. Spinoza's system is "pure" in that it expresses an ideal and is aimed at abstracting morality from the emotions and social influences. Eliot, on the other hand, demands that we do quite the opposite: that we direct our moral consciousness away from moral ideals and towards appropriate emotional reaction. Indeed it is in the recognition of the insignificance of much of humanity and of our falling so far short of the possibilities of human nature, that sympathy is born.

In *The Sad Fortunes of the Reverend Amos Barton* Eliot explains why the novel's characters whose complexions are "more or less muddy," and whose conversation is "more or less disjointed," should be the objects of our interest and sympathy: "Yet these commonplace people—many of them—bear a conscience, and have felt the sublime prompting to do the painful right; they have their unspoken sorrows, and their sacred joys; their hearts have perhaps gone out towards their first-born, and they have mourned over the irreclaimable dead. Nay, is there not a pathos in their very insignificance,—in our comparison of their dim and narrow existence with the glorious possibilities of that human nature which they share?" (Eliot 1985b, 42). If we were to deny this demand of Eliot's, or to try and integrate it somehow into claims about her Spinozistic influences, we would not only lose the richness of Eliot's novels, which is after all the reason why we return to read them again and again even when the plot holds no more surprises for us, but we would quite simply lose sight of her moral view.

Those commentators who make connections between Comtist or Spinozistic philosophy and Eliot's fiction ultimately require that we divide
what a writer says from the *way* that he or she says it, for they will need
to be able to place the content of the two authors' works side by side.
While it may be in practice possible to do this with Eliot's novels, it will
cause them to lose much of what is of moral interest to us. As Eliot herself says, the specific moral reactions that she wants from her reader are
to be produced through the *way* that she portrays her characters; the form
being as important as the content to the moral reaction of the reader: "My
artistic bent is directed not at all to the presentation of eminently irre-
proachable characters, but to the presentation of mixed human beings in
such a way as to call forth tolerant judgment, pity, and sympathy" (Eliot
1954–78, 2: 299).

Even if we allowed the extraction of Eliot's moral thought from her
presentation in such a way as to afford comparisons with Spinoza or
Comte, we still run into serious difficulties. We shall need to know
whether Eliot was consistent in her use of Spinozistic or Comtist philosophy, and whether she was accurate in her "translations" of their work
into her fiction. Indeed what else would be the purpose of extracting
Eliot's thought from its presentation? Yet if we are prepared to judge
whether Eliot's novels are in fact successful translations of Comte's or
Spinoza's work, we make our assessments based on criteria for judging
philosophical arguments that are more appropriate for judging the philosophical theorizing of the dominant model of moral philosophy.

If Eliot's views can be justified and made consistent in this way, it becomes unclear why we would want to read them in a novel rather than
in a philosophical treatise; it also becomes unclear why Eliot chose to express her ideas in the form of a novel. Not only is it unlikely that the fictional "arguments" and "evidence" used to support the novel's theorizing are, by their very nature, able to withstand such an examination, but
this assessment requires that we see Eliot's novels as a series of philosophical cases or examples, a series that has no shape or form of its own
beyond that given by the arguments it aims to establish. It would be possible to dispute the interpretation of each of these cases, but the dispute
would be about the correct interpretation of a case, not about its value,
significance, or presentation.[4]

Thus I would argue that claims that the philosophy found in Eliot's
novels is a reproduction (either wholesale or in part) of the ideas of
Comte or Spinoza (or indeed, any of the other suggested contenders such
as Hume and Mill), while not implausible, are incompatible with her
treatment of those supposed influences: the form of the novel. If we find
the philosophy, then we lose the novel. Moreover the same problems will
surface with other, similar, approaches to Eliot's work that, rather than

search for the influences for a specific philosopher, investigate whether a particular philosophical viewpoint (for example, compatibilism) was worked out coherently in her novels. Thus we find that, for example, George Levine's definitive account of causal determinism and moral responsibility in Eliot's novels views the thought in her work solely in terms of criticizing or justifying her philosophical reasoning, losing sight of them as works of art (see Levine 1962).

This type of investigation of the philosophical content of Eliot's novels may initially seem appropriate because the identification, extraction, and analysis of an argument is a standard method of philosophical investigation. However this is to assume that the philosophical argument under scrutiny fits a certain model, whereas, as we saw with Wollstonecraft, there are other possibilities for what can count as philosophical argument. And, accordingly, these arguments would seem to call for a different approach or even perhaps approaches. The standard approach of the dominant model to the finding of the philosophy in Eliot's novels will fail as it will ultimately devalue Eliot's work both as potential work of philosophy and as a work of literature. This failure stems from a focus on the supposed content of the novels and the neglect of the form in which this content is presented. Thus I want now to turn to a way of reading the novels for their philosophical content that has its origins rooted firmly in their form, a way of reading that I believe allows an interpretation that illuminates the significance of her moral insights.

How to Read Eliot

We do not have to look far for this way of approaching Eliot's novels. It is Eliot's own account of the moral value of literature that provides us with a way to read Eliot's novels for their philosophical aspects, a way of reading that produces a fruitful account of Eliot's moral thought. Despite the differences between this approach to the examination of philosophical aspects of a text, and the more standard approaches we have already encountered, this makes it—at least in this case—no less informative or valuable. Moreover, and perhaps most importantly, these differences do not mean that it cannot be recognized as a philosophical approach, for it is both connected to and generated by Eliot's particular conceptions of morality and moral philosophy.

Eliot offered in her essays and book reviews a specific account of how philosophical ideas should be worked out in fiction, indeed she went so far as to maintain that there is a connection between a work having moral value and its aesthetic qualities. And it should be noted here that the majority of these essays and reviews were written before she began writing fiction. Eliot's comments on the moral function of art were not confined to her non-fictional works, but it is important to notice that the comments she makes in her fiction are rare, and occur in two of her earliest works of fiction: *Amos Barton* and *Adam Bede*. It would seem fair to claim that Eliot had worked out most of her ideas about the theory of art (if not all) before she began writing fiction, and thus that it would be reasonable to assume that her novels are, at least in part, influenced by this theory.[5] Certainly an examination of both her novels and her reviews would appear to bear this out.

Perhaps the most significant characteristic of Eliot's book reviews was her attention to what she saw as the 'arguments' of a work of literature, that is to say what she saw as its moral views. Indeed her attention to the 'arguments' in a work was often at the expense of a thorough discussion of its formal and stylistic qualities! For Eliot, the arguments of the author are central to both the aesthetic and the moral assessment of a novel because of the function that Eliot ascribed to art: art awakens sympathy which is, for Eliot, the moral emotion.[6] She states that "The greatest benefit we owe to the artist, whether painter, poet, or novelist, is the extension of our sympathies. Appeals founded on generalizations and statistics require a sympathy ready-made, a moral sentiment already in activity; but a picture of human life such as a great artist can give, surprises even the trivial and the selfish in that attention to what is apart from themselves, which may be called the raw material of moral sentiment" (Eliot 1970, 21: 198–9).

Yet, according to Eliot, while art is to be prized as the producer of morality, it cannot do this by preaching, but through sympathetic presentation. Attempts to preach will inevitably mislead the reader, or lose the attention that is necessary for the development of her sympathy. As we know from reading stories to children, Eliot says, an attempt to moralize loses the sympathetic attention necessary to learn from the book:

> We question whether the direct exhibition of a moral bias in the writer will make a book really moral in its influence. Try this on the first child that asks you to tell it a story. As long you keep to an apparently impartial narrative of facts you will have earnest eyes fixed on you in rapt attention, but no sooner do you betray symptoms of an intention to moralise or to turn the current of facts towards a personal application, then the interest of your hearer will slacken, his eyes will wander, and the moral dose will be doubly distasteful from the very sweetmeat in which you have attempted to insinuate it. One grand reason of this is that the child is aware that you are talking *for it* instead of *from* yourself, so that instead of carrying it along in a stream of sympathy with your own interest in the story, you give it the impression of contriving coldly and talking artificially. Now the moralising novelist produces the same effect in his mature readers. (Eliot 1970, 22: 306)

Eliot explains how art is to produce morality in the reader by comparing the good writer with the good teacher. The good teacher is one who does not merely dispense knowledge but aims at developing the skills whereby the students find learning easier. In the same way, the most effective writer is one who does not state right and wrong, but "who awakes men from their indifference to the right and the wrong, who nerves their energies to seek for the truth and live up to it at whatever the cost" (Eliot 1970, 22: 310). Faced with such a role the responsibilities of the artist are clear for Eliot, the writer needs to be a committed, and truthful, presenter of the reality of human life. Indeed the author who ignores his or her role as a teacher and writes for money or amusement "carries on authorship on the principle of the gin-palace" (Eliot 1970, 21: 297). It is clear from Eliot's emphasis on truthfulness of the artist in his or her descriptions of human life that realistic imitation was, for her, the literary ideal.[7] In chapter 17 of *Adam Bede*, Eliot discourses in her authorial voice on the importance of realism in art. We need to, she argues, be shown the ordinary lives of common people, for these are the people we encounter day to day; we rarely meet saints and heroes.

It is clear from Eliot's book reviews and essays that the production of sympathy through the realistic portrayal of human life is pivotal to Eliot's view of what gives a novel its moral weight.[8] What is further significant is the connection she makes between a lack of realism in a novel and its *philosophical* failures, that is to say, the failure of the overall moral view or 'argument' of a novel. For Eliot notes that a lack of realistic depiction of human life often goes hand in hand with a tendency to discourse (invariably incorrectly) on abstractions and generalizations. The connection between the author's philosophical comments in the work he or she is writing and the moral and aesthetic value that this work holds for Eliot appears to be dependent on the level of concreteness and particularity in those philosophical comments. Eliot praises Thomas Carlyle for being both an artist and a philosopher, indeed it is this combination that makes Carlyle's work so morally significant: "He glances deep down into human nature, and shows the causes of human actions; he seizes grand generalizations, and traces them in the particular with wonderful acumen; and in all this he is a philosopher" (Eliot 1970, 21: 313).

Thus we can see that while Eliot allows that a novel can have an overall argument or view that it is explaining or exploring, this argument or view will fail if there is no connection between the philosophical content of the novel and its function of developing sympathy. For the philosophical maxims, arguments, and purpose of a novel can become part of its moral influence only if they are tied into the concrete particulars of human life; when the author propounds her beliefs at the expense of realism the novel fails both aesthetically and morally.

If the philosophical content of a novel is to be bound up in this way with its moral purpose and its realistic depiction of human life, then it would appear difficult to isolate this content in order to assess its worth. Although Eliot does not directly address this issue, she does make a variety of statements in her book reviews that would suggest that the philosophical truths of a novel cannot be separated from their presentation and assessed in the same way as is often possible with the truths of a philosophical treatise. For example, in her first review of Charles Kingsley's *Westward Ho!*, Eliot argues that we cannot be *told* how to assess virtuous or villainous actions in a novel, for "Art is art, and tells its own story" (Eliot 1855, 475). While in "Leaves from a Note-book" Eliot suggests that we should be careful of criticizing the thought of an author, for while the novel may contain errors, there is truth in the sincerity of the author's feeling. We should ask whether "even where his thinking was most mixed with the sort of mistake which is obvious to the majority, as well as that which can only be discerned by the instructed, or made manifest by the progress of things, has it that salt of a noble enthusiasm which should rebuke our critical discrimination if its correctness is inspired with a less admirable habit of feeling?" (1970, 22: 300).

Thus it can be seen that, for Eliot, a philosophical novel is one that has an overall 'argument' or view. Such a novel can contain, for instance, philosophical maxims, but Eliot holds that the value and intelligibility of both the arguments of the novels and such things as its philosophical maxims are aspects that are inseparable from their presentation in the novel. Indeed it is interesting to note that Eliot was concerned that the publication of her *Wise, Witty and Tender Sayings* might allow her work to be divided into 'direct' and 'indirect' teaching, and said that "I have always exercised a severe watch against anything that could be called preaching, and if I have ever allowed myself in dissertation or dialogue [anything] which is not part of the *structure* of my books, I have there sinned against my own laws" (Eliot 1954–78, 5: 459). Moreover she holds that while an author is allowed to have preconceived notions that s/he explores in a novel, these notions must be expressed in a sincere realistic depiction of human life. For Eliot, writing a novel is itself a moral undertaking; while to be educated morally, and to develop the central moral virtue of sympathy, requires an indirect method such as reading well-written fiction.

Turning now to Eliot's novels themselves, I shall show that not only do they contain those aspects identified by Eliot as necessary for a morally valuable work of literature, specifically the awakening of sympathy in the reader through a realistic, detailed depiction of ordinary human life, but that they also contain an "argument" for the centrality of sympathy to morality.

The Centrality of Sympathy in Eliot's Novels

In reading Eliot's accounts of the fortunes of her characters, it becomes clear that she held that human life was, in some sense, determined. Maggie in *The Mill on the Floss*, for example, finds that her character and intellect are restricted, and thus to an extent determined, by the social mores of Victorian country-town life. Indeed it is these restrictions that create the conditions for her fall into disgrace. The repression of her character and intellect, and her hunger for affection and beauty, mean that she is easily swept into—what is for her at least—the sophisticated world of Stephen Guest. At times Eliot even goes so far as to suggest that the specific fates of her characters are predetermined. For example we are told that Mr Tulliver in *The Mill on the Floss* "had a destiny as well as Oedipus, and in this case he might plead, like Oedipus, that his deed was inflicted on him rather than committed by him" (Eliot 1985a, 198). Indeed it is not just that character can determine fate, the actions of the characters can become part of the way their lives become determined. Indeed in Eliot's novels actions often take on a life of their own: "Our deeds are like children that are born to us; they live and act apart from our own will. Nay, children may be strangled, but deeds never: they have an indestructible life both in and out of our consciousness" (Eliot 1883, 184).

However Eliot's interest is not in the causal story of the particular destinies of her characters, but rather in the way the characters respond to their fate. It is the moral not the causal inescapability of our deeds that is important to Eliot: we are "caught" in a web of responsibility for our actions and relationships. The characters who do wrong in Eliot's novels can never escape their deeds. Sometimes they are caught easily, like Hetty Sorrel in *Adam Bede*; sometimes they will give themselves away by trying to cover their past, like Bulstrode in *Middlemarch*; occasionally they will even confess to their past wrong actions to make amends, like Godfrey Cass in *Silas Marner*. Yet despite the fact that Eliot makes it clear that such characters should assume moral responsibility for their actions, there is a marked absence of blame and punishment in her works. Even Hetty Sorrell in *Adam Bede* has her sentence for the murder of her child transmuted at the last moment from execution to transportation, a dramatic turn of events that is very much downplayed in the finale of the novel.[9]

Rather than "moralize" for the reader's benefit by showing the repercussions that will befall the wrongdoer, Eliot encourages the reader to feel sympathy for his or her situation. One of the most moving passages in her work is in *Middlemarch* when the distinctly repulsive Bulstrode is comforted by his wife, despite the fact that she suspects his involvement in the death of Raffles. Rather than feel repulsed by his moral flaws, the reader shares with him his pain at the recognition of those flaws and the humiliation of admitting them to his wife.

> It was eight o'clock in the evening before the door opened and his wife en-
> tered. He dared not look up at her. He sat with his eyes bent down, and as
> she went towards him she thought he looked smaller—he seemed so with-
> ered and shrunken. A movement of new compassion and old tenderness
> went through her like a great wave, and putting one hand on his which
> rested on the arm of the chair, and the other on his shoulder, she said
> solemnly but kindly—
>   'Look up, Nicholas.'
>   He raised his eyes with a little start and looked at her half amazed for a
> moment: her pale face, her changed, mourning dress, the trembling about
> her mouth, all said, 'I know'; and her hands and eyes rested gently on him.
> He burst out crying and they cried together, she sitting at his side. (Eliot
> 1999, 832–33)

It would seem from this passage that the reader is also meant to have sympathy for the unappealing Bulstrode, not because his actions were determined for him by the rigors of a causal universe, but because his destiny as a human being is to be weak and thoughtless and to suffer due to these traits. For Eliot the inevitability of the downfall of Bulstrode is not due to the causal chains of events that lead to the public exposure of his past; it is due to Bulstrode's humanity. By tracing the events that lead to Bulstrode's downfall, we can only explain why it happened at that particular time. A causal explanation cannot give us a full explanation of why it had to happen at all.

It should be clear that Eliot's determinism is not to be equated with a concern for, or interest in, philosophical causal determinism. Instead it is in the concept of human fate as suffering that Eliot sees the universe as determined. Eliot rejects religion and its offers of salvation in a future life and the amelioration of the present one. Believing that there is no God to pray to for the relief of our sufferings, Eliot draws the depressing conclusion that all we are left with is our sufferings, and it is these sufferings that then must occupy the central place in our lives.[10] In a letter to Charles Bray, she even goes so far as to suggest that "the worship of suffering is *the* worship for mortals" (Eliot 1954–78, 1: 284). Yet for Eliot, a human life without its sorrows and dreary insignificance would not be a truly beautiful or human life. In another letter to Sara Hennell, Eliot warns that "it would not be well for us to overleap one grade of joy or suffering—our life would lose its completeness and beauty" (Eliot 1954–78, 1: 159).

It is clear from even the most cursory reading of Eliot's work how the inescapability of human suffering affects the way we should live our lives. Eliot's characters, faced with their human destiny, have their responsibilities to themselves and others clearly delineated.[11] They must adopt a stand of noble resignation to the wrongs done against them by others and towards events beyond their control. They must attempt to fight the weakness and vanity that lead them to hurt others, the same weakness and vanity that can also lead to their own misery. And, finally, they must develop a strong sense of sympathy in order to shelter others from the slings and arrows of fortune.

Within Eliot's universe, resignation towards one's fate becomes not only paramount but noble. There are no panaceas for the defects of human existence. Even if we were to believe in divine love, this would not nullify "a past which widens more and more in the consciousness as a wasted good" and a "visibly narrowing future" (Eliot 1954–78, 4: 499). For Eliot, the compensation offered by belief in the Christian religion is dangerous because it encourages us to seek this compensation just for ourselves, while feeling comfortable about ignoring the needs of others. True resignation can never have this kind of personal compensation; we are to develop resignation because Eliot believed that this was "a part of our life task." She held that once we have rejected the false comforts of some kind of divine compensation, "that wretched falsity which makes men quite comfortable about their fellows' troubles"; we shall "be more tender to each other while we live," quite simply because there is no one or nothing else to rely on (Eliot 1954–78, 4: 128).

Resignation to fate in Eliot's novels is frequently a quiet submission to mediocrity. Dorothea Brooke's moral growth in *Middlemarch* is marked by her resignation to an ordinary life as a wife and mother, and Eliot is clear that we are to regard this life as a sacrifice. Yet despite the fact that Dorothea's life has been wasted in the sense that she never carried out the heroic deeds that she was suited for, we are assured by Eliot in the Finale to *Middlemarch* that this ordinary life is of value: "Her finely-touched spirit had still its fine issues, though they were not widely visible. Her full nature, like that river of which Cyrus broke the strength, spent itself in channels which had no great name on earth. But the effect of her being on those around her was incalculably diffusive: for the growing good of the world is partly dependent on unhistoric acts; and that things are not so ill with you and me as they might have been, is half owing to the number who lived faithfully a hidden life, and rest in unvisited tombs" (Eliot 1999, 924). The unhistoric act of living an ordinary life like Dorothea's is valued because her sympathetic understanding of others helps them to live their lives with resignation, perhaps even with happiness.

Eliot's attitude towards heroic acts of resignation can initially appear ambiguous. Romola, in the novel of the same name, leaves her husband, Tito, because he betrays her dead father's trust by selling her father's library. She meets Savonarola and is persuaded by him to return to Tito and to accept the duties and ties of her marriage. Savonarola urges Romola to make her unhappy marriage an offering to God, "Make your marriage-sorrows an offering too, my daughter: an offering to the great work by which sin and sorrow are being made to cease;" such a sacrifice, he assures her, will bring a reward, for "there is rapture in the cup— there is the vision which makes all life below it dross for ever" (Eliot 1993, 367). Yet Romola eventually leaves her husband and loses her faith in Savonarola. The temporary nature of her heroic act of resignation to her fate combined with Eliot's dislike of sacrifice with an eye to the compensations of religion, suggests that Romola's act is not true resignation for Eliot.

Something similar is suggested by Maggie Tulliver's conversion after reading *Thomas a Kempis* in *The Mill on the Floss*. Maggie earnestly begins a life of renunciation and resignation to her life and the duties it contains. She tells Philip that "it makes our mind very free when we give up wishing and only think of bearing what is laid upon us and doing what is given us to do" (Eliot 1985a, 397). Eliot makes it clear that it is wrong for Maggie deliberately to narrow her life to one of monastic self-denial and to starve both her mind and her nature of the beautiful things in which she takes such delight. It is partly due to this starvation that Maggie falls in love with Stephen Guest, for he seems to represent the type of life of beauty and knowledge that she has felt that she must be denied. Eliot seems to suggest that Maggie's self-denial should not be confused with true resignation.

The cases of Romola and Maggie indicate that, for Eliot, true resignation is not trying to make the lack of a full life bearable by compensation with religion, the ascetic pleasures of sacrifice, or by the comfort of feeling that one has chosen one's own fate. There appears to be a degree of passivity and a distinct lack of glamour in Eliot's view that we are not accustomed to see in an ethical account of the virtue of resignation. It is more a submissive acceptance of the pinpricks of misfortune of an unheroic life, than an active resignation to Job-like trials sent to test our mettle. Yet as we can see from the struggle of characters such as Dorothea Brooke in *Middlemarch*, the former need not take any less integrity or strength of character than the latter.

One of the crucial elements necessary for resignation is a clear-eyed unsentimental perception of the world and our place within it. This clear-eyed perception coupled with the self-directed virtue of resignation can enable us to develop the central virtue found in Eliot's work, that of sympathy for others. Yet many of the characters of Eliot's novels lack a clear-eyed perception of themselves and the needs of others. In the "philosopher's parable" in *Middlemarch*, Eliot describes this lack of perception thus:

> Your pier-glass or extensive surface of polished steel made to be rubbed by a housemaid, will be minutely and multitudinously scratched in all directions: but place now against it a lighted candle as a centre of illumination, and lo! the scratches will seem to arrange themselves in a fine series of concentric circles around that little sun. It is demonstrable that the scratches are going everywhere impartially, and it is only your candle that produces the flattering illusion of a concentric arrangement, its light falling with an exclusive optical selection. These things are a parable. The scratches are events, and the candle is the egoism of any person now absent. (Eliot 1999, 294)

Even the "heroes" in Eliot's novels are frequently deceived by their own egos and remain blinkered to their own imperfections and to the real, as opposed to perceived, needs of others. In *Adam Bede*, for example, Adam has to learn not to judge others according to a set of moral standards based on his view of himself. In *Middlemarch*, it is Dorothea Brooke's aspirations to moral greatness that produce her distorted perception of Mr Casaubon as a spiritual teacher. Rosamond Vincy in *Middlemarch* is Eliot's egoist *par excellence*; her candle shines so brightly on events that she is led to believe that she has her own personal providence. This providence not only arranges for the arrival of a handsome eligible doctor to the town, but even plays matchmaker by causing Rosamond's brother to fall ill. In describing Rosamond's egoism and its effects, the narrator's tone is one of wry resignation rather than moral condemnation, which seems to indicate that Eliot sees egoism as a natural trait of the human character.

> She was in such entire disgust with her husband that she wished that she had never seen him. Sir Godwin's rudeness towards her and utter want of feeling ranged him with Dover and all other creditors – disagreeable people who only thought of themselves, and did not mind how annoying they were to her. Even her father was unkind and might have done more for them. In fact there was but one person in Rosamond's world who she did not regard as blameworthy, and that was the graceful creature with blond plaits and little hands crossed before her, who had never expressed herself unbecomingly, and had always acted for the best—the best being naturally what she best liked. (Eliot 1999, 738)

It is important to get clear about Eliot's claims regarding the human ego. Eliot does not want to dismiss the claims of the human ego, or—strictly speaking—to condemn egoistic behavior, indeed she is concerned with the need for her characters to keep a sense of self intact within a fully human world that offers no hope of divine salvation. It is the denial of self-interest and even survival of the self that Christianity can demand: essentially a denial of our humanity, that in part caused Eliot's rejection of Christian beliefs. For Eliot there is nothing wrong in wishing for gratification of one's desires or in following the dictates of one's ego *per se*; in a letter to Maria Lewis, Eliot wrote that "the martyr at the stake seeks [the] gratification [of his ego] as much as the court sycophant" (Eliot 1954–78, 1: 27). The difference between the martyr and the sycophant is not that the martyr denies himself the comfortable life of the sycophant, but lies "in the comparative dignity and beauty of the two egos" (Eliot 1954–78, 1:127).

In Eliot's novels the distinction between the "good" or "beautiful" ego, and the "bad" or "ugly" ego is brought out by whether characters develop the ability to understand themselves and their relationship to others. Dorothea Brooke in *Middlemarch*, for example, never loses her passionate desire to help others, but throughout the novel her acts of kindness lose their self-referential quality, and she learns to develop a genuine sympathy for others. When Dorothea decides to marry Casaubon, she hopes to improve herself while helping him, believing that she deserves the sort of education marriage with an intellectual can give her. As she discovers Casaubon's personal and intellectual limitations, she begins to resent him. But this resentment develops into a sympathy for these very same failures at a crucial moment when she is able to protect him from the knowledge of their sterile, loveless situation, and she feels "something like the thankfulness that might well up in us if we had narrowly escaped hurting a lamed creature" (Eliot 1999, 476). Here we see that Dorothea's self-interest is overridden by her sympathy for Casaubon and has become tempered by resignation and sympathy.

What Dorothea Brooke learns is not only to resign herself to her life, which she does in part by seeing herself and her situation clearly, but to turn this perception towards the misfortunes of others; and to use what she has learned from her own misfortunes to help others. In the world of Eliot's novels this perceptive sympathy must necessarily become the central virtue, for it is this virtue that will allow us to help others deal with the central human task of resignation. In a letter to Mrs Elma Stuart, Eliot writes that the "one good which seems the more worth having, the more our own life is encompassed with shadows" is "the certitude of having helped another to bear some heavy burthen—of having lessened pain and given the sweetness of fellowship in sorrow" (Eliot 1954–78, 6: 327).

This becomes clear when we consider the paradigm case of sympathetic involvement in *Middlemarch* when Dorothea tries to help Rosamond Vincey. Dorothea returns to offer her help to Rosamond despite having found her in a compromising situation with Will Ladislaw. Dorothea realizes that she is not the only one affected by the event, it is "bound up with another woman's life—a woman towards whom she had set out with a longing to carry some clearness and comfort into her beclouded youth" (Eliot 1999, 872). Once Dorothea can see the scene free of the confines of her own self, she is moved to sympathy for Rosamond prompted by the experiences of her own unhappy marriage. Dorothea realizes that we cannot ignore the web of our responsibilities to others: "Far off in the bending sky was the pearly light; and she felt the largeness of the world and the manifold wakings of man to labour and endurance. She was a part of that involuntary, palpitating life, and could neither look out on it from her luxurious shelter as a mere spectator, nor hide her eyes in selfish complaining" (Eliot 1999, 873). In contrast, Rosamond does not change. She recognizes—and admires—the moral superiority of Dorothea, but Rosamond continues to be the center of her own world, and thus she continues to fail to understand her husband and the frustration she causes him. Indeed after Lydgate's premature death, Rosamond marries a wealthy physician and "often spoke of her happiness as 'a reward'—she did not say for what, but probably she meant that it was a reward for her patience with Tertius [Lydgate]" (Eliot 1999, 921).

Adam in *Adam Bede* also undergoes a similar change in his perception of others based on a development of his sympathy. From the very outset of the novel, it is clear that he is a character made of fine moral material. Yet, in one sense, this is what prevents him from being sympathetic, the root of true morality for Eliot. Adam sees his own virtues as the standard by which to judge his family and friends and, unsurprisingly, often finds them wanting. It is only after Adam's recognition of this, and his realization that his virtues untempered by sympathy become flaws, that Adam achieves an understanding of the related duties of sympathy and resignation of Eliotian morality.

Eliot describes this change and the process by which it was brought about for the reader:

For Adam, though you see him quite master of himself, working hard and delighting in his work after his inborn inalienable nature, had not outlived his sorrow—had not felt it slip from him as a temporary burden, and leave him the same man again. Do any of us? God forbid. It would be the poor result of all our anguish and our wrestling, if we won nothing but our old selves at the end of it—if we could return to the same blind loves, the same self-confident blame, the same light thoughts of human suffering, the same

frivolous gossip over blighted human lives, the same feeble sense of that
Unknown toward which we have sent irrepressible cries in our loneliness.
Let us rather be thankful that our sorrow lives in us as an indestructible
force, only changing its form, as forces do, and passing from pain into sympathy—the one poor word which includes all our best insight and our best
love. (Eliot n.d., 438)

We may want to ask why, when Adam is clearly a good man in so
many ways, must he suffer and change? Adam Bede is not without
faults, but they are faults common to many of us: harsh and inconsistent
judgments of the behavior of others. Clearly the answer to this question
is connected to Eliot's view of the restricted nature of human life. Although Eliot's human "determinism" is perhaps not as evident in *Adam
Bede* as her other novels—not unsurprising perhaps, as *Adam Bede* was
Eliot's first novel—the careful reader can still understand why Adam's
faults are so problematic for Eliot. Adam's faults within an Eliotian universe are troublesome, because they rest on assumptions about human
life and character that are inappropriate for this universe. Adam can neither change his father nor protect Hetty Sorrell from the paths their nature and circumstances have set them on. All he can do is to accept that
he cannot change them and forgive them for following the path of their
destiny and character.

I wish to claim then that Eliot's vision of human life emphasizes the restrictions and limitations of our lives, limitations that are frequently the
product of our human nature. The development of moral feelings and
virtues—and specifically the moral feeling of sympathy—to ameliorate
the restrictions of the human condition is, for Eliot, not only a necessary
response, but the only possible response. But it is not just that these
virtues are the necessary virtues for dealing with the restrictions and
frustrations of human life, but also, at least in her later novels, we can see
that Eliot holds that morality is not possible without the limitations of
human life and choices.

This is perhaps best exemplified by the connections between the moral
development of Daniel Deronda in *Daniel Deronda* and his discovery of
his Jewish heritage. During the first part of the novel Deronda lives the
unrestricted life of a wealthy upright Englishman: "a gentleman by inheritance" (Eliot 1984, 143). He is good-natured and thoughtful, but dull.
Moreover Eliot makes it clear that while Deronda would always theoret-
ically support the objects of prejudice, there is no doubt that he is influenced in his thinking about real people by many of the worst racial
stereotypes; indeed he is rather horrified at the idea of having actual contact with Mirah's family as he imagines them to be: "Deronda's thinking
went on in rapid images of what might be: he saw himself guided by

some official scout into a dingy street; he entered through a dim doorway, and saw a hawk-eyed woman, rough-headed, and unwashed, cheapening a hungry girl's last bit of finery; or in some quarter only the more hideous for being smarter, he found himself under the breath of a young Jew talkative and familiar, willing to show his acquaintance with gentlemen's tastes, and not fastidious in any transactions with which they would favour him—and so on through the brief chapter of his experience in this kind" (Eliot 1984, 176–7).

Deronda's attitude begins to change both through his growing fondness for Mirah and through his admiration for Mordecai, Mirah's brother. It is through them that he learns of the suffering and rich spiritual inheritance of the Jewish race. This change in attitude is given the ultimate test when Deronda discovers that he himself is Jewish. Deronda embraces this discovery eagerly, not simply because of his love for Mirah, or due to a romantic attachment to a disenfranchised race, but also because he wants to take on the "bondage" of being Jewish: "He beheld the world changed for him by the certitude of ties that altered the poise of hopes and fears" (Eliot 1984, 585). Indeed Deronda thanks his mother for apprising him of his heritage and remarks that she has saved him "from robbing my people of my service and me of my duty" (Eliot 1984, 567).

Deronda's life no longer has the relative freedoms of wealth, rank, and no family ties. He has found a family and a race and now faces the restrictions that these will bring with them. Yet Deronda's entanglement in a web of human relations and duties also produces an understanding of the connectedness of human life that Deronda previously lacked; and from this point on in the novel there is a marked moral growth in Deronda. This moral development is subtle, since Deronda was introduced to us at the beginning of the novel as possessing a high moral nature, but there are clear developments in his character in the later parts of the novel. In the opening scenes of the novel, Deronda helps Gwendolen Harleth by anonymously returning her necklace from a pawnbroker's shop, yet he helps her as a stranger; there is no sense that our kindness to others can bind us to them as much as they to us.

Later Deronda's kindness and concern for Gwendolen become blended with uncertainty about his ability to help; he is even fearful of the responsibility that her needs place on him: "Deronda's anguish was intolerable. He could not help himself. He seized her outstretched hands and held them together and knelt at her feet. She was the victim of his happiness. "I am cruel too, I am cruel," he repeated, with a sort of groan, looking up at her imploringly" (Eliot 1984, 690). What has occurred is that Deronda has learned that our connections to others do not allow us to maintain an easy abstract sympathy for their suffering, yet it is these connections that are necessary for true sympathy.

The relation of sympathy to human relationships or connections is brought out clearly when Deronda discovers that Mirah's father has stolen his ring. To forgive Mirah's father would be a generous act, yet Deronda's sympathy for Mirah, and for the moral poverty of her father, makes him go further than forgiveness. Deronda claims a relationship to this unworthy man: "Mirah, let me think that he is my father as well as yours—that we can have no sorrow, no disgrace, no joy apart" (Eliot 1984, 679). Deronda's realization of the relationship between human connectedness and sympathetic understanding is further exhibited in Deronda's goal of uniting the Jewish nation. Deronda believes that the lack of human connection produced by the dispersement of the Jewish race has in part contributed to the spiritual and moral poverty of the Jewish people, the very poverty that originally served to fuel Deronda's racial prejudices.

In order for Deronda to gain these insights it is not enough that he should help those for whom he feels sympathy, or even that he should associate with them; he must also take on the restrictions of their lives. The fact that Deronda willingly loses the freedoms of the English aristocrat, and takes on the restrictions that Eliot sees as the destiny of the Jewish race, is certainly a testament to his good nature. Eliot makes it clear, however, that without restrictions on his life and choices that are produced by birth and his web of relationships and responsibilities, Deronda cannot be truly sympathetic, and thus cannot be truly moral.

Philosophy

Even given this admittedly skeletal account of the moral thought in Eliot's novels, it seems clear that the novels not only have a coherent and systematic view of human moral life, but that they contain an overall philosophical "argument" (the phrase Eliot uses herself) which places sympathy firmly at its center. But it is not simply that the plots of the novels, and the fate of the characters, lead us to the conclusion that sympathy is central to morality. Rather we find that the aspects Eliot identifies as characteristic of human life—its determinism and our egoism, as well as the virtues necessary for dealing with them—resignation and perception, entail the need for sympathy as the central virtue for humans.

This argument—located as it is within the story of a novel, and played out through the fortunes of fictional characters—shares little with the standard function of philosophical argument in a text. Eliot does not intend our grasp of her moral thought to be generated by the soundness or irrefutability of her argument. She does not *explain* to us what sympathy, resignation, and perception, etc. *are*, but instead she brings out their meanings and connections throughout the length of the story, specifically against the background that frames these meanings and connections: the restrictions of human life. Yet it is clear that what we learn from the novel follows on from the events portrayed in it no less reasonably or certainly than the conclusion we draw from the premises of a traditionally structured philosophical argument.

But we do not grasp her argument through logical analysis of her points, instead we are intended to grasp her moral thought through the sympathy that has been generated in us as readers. This sympathy can be generated through identification with some of the characters themselves, which is made possible through the depictions of a realistic and detailed human psychology. But it can also be produced by the way that Eliot does not attempt to preach to us. As we have already seen, her novels rarely contain elements of blame and punishment. While Eliot clearly identifies wrong behavior for the reader, the way this behavior is treated encourages sympathy rather than condemnation on the part of the reader. Thus in *Middlemarch*, some of Rosamond Vincy's worst excesses of egoist behavior are treated with humorous irony. While in *The Mill on the Floss*, we are encouraged not to judge Tom Tulliver's deliberate cruelty towards his sister too harshly, for we are shown that this cruelty stems from an unthinking, overly rigid morality, rather than any intentional viciousness on his part.

Yet all these ways of producing sympathy in the reader are not simply aimed at producing some emotive response. It would be a mistake to believe that because our sympathy has been engaged, our reason and intellect are not required as part of our response to the novels. Our sympathetic involvement with the characters means our aim is to understand the individual and the particulars of character and destiny; indeed this involvement *prevents* us from aiming towards an understanding of the novel and its characters that is universal and abstract. This is in sharp contrast to the goals of the theories of the dominant model which are typically those of creating a systematized, abstract theory. While it cannot be said that we make moral judgments about these characters in the sense of assigning praise or blame, it would be a mistake to say that this then means that we do not make a moral judgment of any kind about them, or that we somehow remain morally neutral towards their behavior. Our "judgment" of these characters takes the form of a recognition and understanding of even the tiniest details of their flaws and virtues; a "judgment" that can only come about through our sympathy for them.

Conclusion

If we have a genuine wish to understand the originality of Eliot's moral thought and how such thought can—and should—be taken seriously as philosophical thought, it would appear that we will ultimately be required to reassess our approach to philosophical investigation. This is something that we saw indicated with the potential difficulties of giving an account of Wollstonecraft's notion of sensibility if it is extracted from its presentation. It is clear that Eliot's account of morality also cannot be easily subtracted from its presentation. I have claimed that it is not possible to give an account of the moral centrality of sympathy in Eliot's work without also describing the deterministic web within which the characters act. If we are committed to an examination of Eliot's work for its philosophical aspects, we must then be prepared to allow both for the particular form that her work takes and the connections between the form of her work and its content.

It would appear that Eliot has an overall philosophical "argument" about morality in her novels. But, given the form of the novels, as well as the philosophical content that necessitates this form, her argument does not fit well into what is to count as moral philosophy based on the dominant model. It is equally apparent, however, that the moral content of Eliot's work is no less reasonable or evident due to the form in which it is conveyed. In order to read Eliot's work as moral philosophy we are required to understand her notion of philosophical argument not as something that can necessarily be subtracted from a text and broken down into premises and a conclusion, but nonetheless as constituting a piece of coherent reasoned thought.

However, as we have seen, standard approaches to philosophical assessment fail when applied to Eliot's novels. Such approaches require a separation of the content of the novels from their form, yet, for Eliot, the form in which her moral thought is presented *is* part of that moral thought. Even if we were to allow the extraction of Eliot's moral thought from its presentation, the criteria—validity, supporting evidence, etc.— that we would use in assessing such thought are inappropriate. But this need not mean that her work is not open to philosophical assessment at all. Indeed Eliot is quite specific as to how she believes that a work should be assessed for its moral philosophical content.

Central to such an assessment is whether the work awakens sympathy through its sincere realistic presentation of ordinary human life. If the author fails to do this, and instead wanders into the realm of abstraction, he or she will fail to affect the reader. Clearly this type of assessment differs from the impersonal nature of a search for systematized and justified principles. There is no doubt that the "success" of the overall "argument" of Eliot's work—if I may put it this way and not be misleading—is measured in more subjective and personal terms: the sincerity of the author, the accuracy and realism of the author's perceptions of human life, and the emotional effect produced in the mind and heart of the reader. In this way, the reader's judgment of Eliot's work will depend on different capacities from those required for philosophical judgment on the dominant model, perhaps such things as emotional depth or imaginative involvement. And we should remember here that the claim of the dominant model that reliance on this type of capacity will lead to philosophical error is dependent on *that* particular model's criteria for philosophical success.

But despite the differences between the investigative approach I have taken to reading Eliot's work as moral philosophy, and the more standard approach exemplified by commentators searching for Comtist or Spinozistic philosophy in her work, I have tried to show that the former can be recognized as a philosophical approach. For the approach I have taken to reading Eliot's work as moral philosophy is both connected to and generated by a particular conception—Eliot's—of morality and moral philosophy; it is simply that this conception differs greatly from the dominant conception of moral philosophy. In this way we can also see that ignoring the form of Eliot's work is problematic, not simply because we shall lose much of what is important about her philosophical thought, but because it is to commit ourselves to a particular philosophical position which is contrary to hers.

But in order to acknowledge these points, we must be prepared to question whether the dominant model of philosophical investigation of a text is the only possible model, and if it is not, whether it is the best model.[12] And we must recognize how deeply this questioning will cut, for our model of philosophical assessment is bound up with what we take philosophy to be. Attempts to analyze the moral philosophy in Eliot's novels using the standard approach for assessment are destined to fail. This is not simply because they are unable to deal with the form in which this moral philosophy is presented, but because this approach is generated by a particular view of the way moral philosophy is. This view cannot allow for conceptions of morality like Eliot's, while, in its turn, this approach to investigation reinforces this particular view. Ultimately, therefore, I believe that the interpretation and study of work like Eliot's can be significant not only because of the particular moral insights that her novels might offer, but also—and more importantly—because Eliot's work can contribute to a discussion of the boundaries and definitions of moral philosophy *itself*.

Notes

1. See for example, "Wordliness and Other-Wordliness: The Poet Young," in Eliot 1970.

2. "Positivists then may, more truly than theological believers of whatever creed, regard *life* as a continuous and earnest act of worship." Auguste Comte, *A*

General View of Positivism, trans. J. H. Bridges (New York: Robert Speller and Sons Inc., 1975): 365.

3. George Eliot, *Adam Bede* (New York: Bernard Clarke and Co., n.d.): 162.

4. It should also be noted that a claim that Eliot was writing translations of Spinoza's philosophy would condemn her to a charge of creative and intellectual stagnation. W. J. Harvey argues that if Eliot was indeed writing Spinozistic novels, this would mean that she had finished growing intellectually by the 1850s, as by then she had worked out "a formulated philosophy of life and theory of fiction which she then simply translated to her creative work." W. J. Harvey, *The Art of George Eliot* (New York: Oxford University Press, 1962): 26.

5. It is not abundantly clear whether Eliot's view of the primary importance of realism in art ever changed. In a late essay on the form of art written in 1868, Eliot's views appear to change and she stresses the importance of the artistic 'Form': the organization of relations or groups of relations into a whole that is separate from any direct imitation. However it is uncertain whether Eliot was only referring to form in poetry or to form in novels as well. It would appear that her views are more appropriate for the former than the latter, especially in light of the fact that Eliot was writing on artistic form during a period in which she was writing the poem *The Spanish Gypsy*. This later view, however, can still be reconciled with Eliot's earlier view of the function of art, as for her the form of an artistic work is still determined by, and expresses emotion.

6. Much has been made of Eliot's founding her morality on emotion. On the one hand, this foundation is praised for its contribution to the moral insight of Eliot's novels; on the other hand, there is criticism of the wisdom and consistency of such a foundation. This latter criticism is due, no doubt, to the fact that as Eliot is held to be a "philosophical" writer, it is assumed that she must be immediately embroiled in the contentious debate among moral philosophers of the role of emotion in morality. We have already encountered this assumption in a different version in the discussion of determinism, and again it would prove ultimately to be misleading.

7. This does not mean that Eliot eschewed imaginative literature, she merely stipulated that the criterion of truthfulness be adhered to; in this case the writer needed to be truthful to his or her own inner vision.

8. See, for example, "The Morality of Wilhelm Meister" and "Leaves from a Notebook" in Eliot 1970.

9. Henry James felt that Hetty's eleventh-hour rescue was a sign of Eliot's artistic weakness. See for example, his comments in "The Life of George Eliot," in *Literary Criticism* (New York: Literary Classics of the United States: Viking Press, 1984): 1004.

10. This is clearly different from the view that Nietzsche attributes to Eliot. In *Twilight of the Idols* he claims that she clings to a Christian morality (Nietzsche 1998).

11. See, for example, Eliot's *Letters* vol. 6: 99.

12. See Diamond, "Anything but Argument" in *The Realistic Spirit*: 291–308.

6

Knowing and Speaking
of Divine Love:
Mechthild of Magdeburg

Although the examination of the forms used by the medieval mystic Mechthild of Magdeburg in her work *The Flowing Light of the Godhead* can aid understanding of its philosophical content, the forms of this work raise very different issues from the work of the other philosophers I have considered; and it is these new questions that will form the focus of the interpretation of my last philosopher.[1] This time I shall focus on the particular challenge provided by its *overall* form to interpretation, specifically the ambiguity of its authorship. For the writings of medieval mystics like Mechthild provide an unusual case, since essentially they are not supposed to be the authors of their works; rather they are simply reporting their experiences of God, or God is speaking through them. Thus while their contemporaries allowed these works—even though they were written by women—to have authority, apparently spontaneous outpourings and unanalyzed reports of divine visions are unlikely to be the subject of modern philosophy.

While the issue of establishing who wrote *The Flowing Light* is no longer important in order to establish its authority, the question of the authorship of work is still problematic for the modern philosophical audience, especially in the light of the fact that Mechthild goes as far as to claim that God is *actually* the author. However the work is also a deeply intimate spiritual and moral "autobiography" in which Mechthild depicts the relationship between God and herself as that of two lovers. What can make the work even harder to interpret is the way Mechthild employs a dramatic variety of literary genres and forms, from profane songs to courtly love poetry, from curses to prayers. These are carefully crafted and often very beautiful. With the previous philosophers I discussed, the philosophical forms they employed were recognizable as such, and thus not problematic in themselves. But with Mechthild it is sometimes hard to categorize the forms she uses, or even her purpose or organizing principle for using them at all. For she does not simply reproduce these forms, she also develops or changes them as she uses them. Indeed some commentators are prepared to claim that she has created—or has contributed to the creation of—new forms of writing (see for example, Wainwright-deKadt, 1980).

While I hold that her use of these particular forms, as well as the ways that they are employed, can be of interest for the philosophical content of *The Flowing Light*, I want to go beyond merely reinforcing my previous arguments. My central aim is to understand the overall form of the book: how to understand that it is a message authored by God for all Christians. As we saw with Mary Wollstonecraft, issues of philosophical genre forms need not be restricted to specific literary structures such as allegory, they can also encompass issues of style and ways of writing. In the case of *The Flowing Light*, the issues of authorship and the identification of authorship are paramount to its form, and ultimately to an understanding of its philosophical content. While (obviously) distinctions can be made between the actual author and authorial voice, as I shall show, this type of distinction has little purchase on the true notion of authorship of *The Flowing Light*.

We need to get clear about whether, and if so how, *The Flowing Light* takes the form of a message from God, and what exactly is the form of a divine message. If *The Flowing Light* is supposed quite literally to be a message from God, it is not evident in what way it can also be Mechthild's spiritual autobiography, for it certainly takes this form too. An even greater puzzle is the fact that, as Mechthild tells us, the physical book itself in its parchment and ink is somehow part of God the author, or contains him. Moreover, all of these questions are apparently further complicated by the fact that *The Flowing Light* does not appear to have any organizing principle or overall structure.

An understanding of the form of *The Flowing Light* is crucial in order that we can have an understanding of the interconnected issues of the authority of the author, and what is conceived of as the "moral knowledge" offered to the audience by the work: its message. The former issue would have been central for Mechthild's contemporaries, whereas the latter issue is perhaps more pertinent for a modern audience. At this juncture, it is clear that equating the "message" of the book (and thus in some way the form itself) with "moral knowledge" does not fit too well into modern ways of talking and conceiving of moral knowledge. However, as we shall see, this notion of "moral knowledge" makes sense within the context of Mechthild's view of morality.

If we accept that *God* wrote the book, as her contemporaries seem to have done, then we can have no questions about the authority of the author, or the fact that *The Flowing Light* offers its audience a divine message. However, this means that we must accept that Mechthild is simply a passive channel. Yet if we think that in fact *Mechthild* wrote the book (as I suspect most of a modern audience will do), then this then brings with it Mechthild's confusing claim that the supposedly *general* moral knowledge (whatever this is) offered to the audience is based solely on her privileged personal experiences and emotions. There is, however, a third alternative: abandon the notion that authorship of *The Flowing Light* must be tied in to an individualist concept of the self. This, as we shall see, brings with it a different understanding of what is offered to the audience of *The Flowing Light*.

It is not that these three alternatives are problematic on the dominant model of moral philosophy, rather they simply make little sense. Mechthild as a passive channel for God's word conflicts with the (ideal) normative subject of this model as an individualized autonomous self. Whereas, if it is allowed that she did write the book, then the notion that emotion and/or personal experience can somehow constitute—or be the basis of—some sort of moral knowledge conflicts with the standard picture of moral knowledge on the dominant model. The third alternative again makes little sense, for central to the dominant model is the notion of the individual acting autonomously and independently amongst similar peers. Not only does there need to be an individual writing subject, but there needs to be an individual who is the "knower" of the book, for the typical picture of moral knowledge on the dominant model, to use Margaret Urban Walker's phrase, is one of "individuals standing singly before the impersonal dicta of Morality" (Walker 1989, 20).

Given this, it would be rather pointless to show that the dominant model fails to deal with *The Flowing Light*, as I have shown with the novels of George Eliot. What I want to do instead is to challenge the model by showing that, even though the moral thought of *The Flowing Light*—specifically the "knowledge" or message offered to its audience—makes little sense on the dominant model of moral philosophy, this need not mean it cannot make sense at all. Instead, through a step-by-step analysis of the problems raised by the question of the authorship of *The Flowing Light*, I show possibilities of alternative ways of conceptualizing the normative subject, and of moral understanding, as well as how these possibilities form a cogent view of morality once they are understood within Mechthild's moral world. Indeed my whole interest in *The Flowing Light* is to see the way these conceptions interlock, and what we can learn about our own moral views from this.

Once we have understood that we need not posit an individual self as its author, we shall be able to see how, according to Mechthild, *The Flowing Light* is a work made of love, containing love, and written out of uncontrollable divine love. It is in this way that it is written by God and also contains God in its actual pages; but insofar as Mechthild shares in this divine love, she is also its author. Thus there is a sense in asking "who" wrote the text that is misleading. The answer is "Mechthild," but also "God," and also the all-embracing concept of "God as uncontrollable love." Yet this challenge to the notion that authorship must be tied in to an individualistic concept of the self makes sense within a worldview that does not idealize this type of individualism. From *The Flowing Light* we shall see that the supreme goal of the soul is to merge with divine love itself and that this divine love manifests itself throughout the universe in a myriad of different ways. Indeed, Mechthild shows us that even the *withdrawal* of God's love from her is a manifestation of this love.

This notion that Love is somehow an unconfined or uncontainable flood gets played out in the urge to share knowledge of this love through *The Flowing Light*: it is a message to all Christians. Yet the medium for the knowledge that is offered to the audience of *The Flowing Light* is the emotions and personal experiences of one woman. However we shall see that it is possible for Mechthild to give a coherent account of what is conceived as the "moral knowledge" that comes from her own unique experiences. But in order to understand this account, we shall ultimately be required to recognize the connections between what can be thought of as Mechthild's moral epistemology and the conceptual scheme of her world. Similarly if we find the possibility that Mechthild offers a cogent moral epistemology to be problematic or incoherent, we must recognize that this may be due to a clash of her conceptual scheme with ours, rather than any fundamental incoherence in Mechthild's writing. While it would be nonsensical to try to replace our scheme with hers, an examination of it in relation to her moral thought is useful for it illuminates the contingency of our own definitions of moral philosophy.

Biography

There is little known about the life of Mechthild of Magdeburg. She is considered to have been born in 1207 or perhaps a few years after that date.[2] She appears to have spent most of her life as a Beguine, that is she lived in a small-self-supporting community of women, who devoted themselves to an apostolic life but were not attached to any religious order. Mechthild retired from Beguine life to the Cistercian convent at

Helfta circa 1270, a place of recognized piety and learning, and died probably around 1282. Her divine experiences began, according to her statements in *The Flowing Light*, when she was twelve years old, and later on in life she began to write down these experiences. She appears to have been from a wealthy and cultured family, but her education did not include learning Latin. Thus she wrote in her own tongue—middle low German—and indeed she was apparently the first mystic to write in that particular vernacular. Although it is impossible to date accurately the writing of the sections of *The Flowing Light*, it would seem reasonable to suppose that she wrote the first five sections during the period of approximately 1250 to 1260, and the sixth during the period 1260–70, while the final book was dictated during her retirement at Helfta. It also is likely that some, if not all, of these sections circulated while she was alive (see Tobin 1995, 3).

Mechthild's method of writing has created difficulties in identifying the original structure—if there was one to start with—of *The Flowing Light*. It seems that she wrote her mystic experiences down on loose sheets of paper, which were then collected and arranged by one "Heinrich," who is assumed to be Heinrich of Halle, a well-known Dominican. Mechthild scholars have debated how much the editor of *The Flowing Light* may have changed the order of Mechthild's writings; it is uncertain exactly how closely the organization of the text that we have now resembles its original structure. Hans Neumann, however, claims that it was indeed Heinrich of Halle who edited the first six books, and that he made little alteration to the original. Neumann even suggests that Mechthild herself had some level of involvement in the editing of her work (see Neumann 1964).

To complicate matters further, the work in its original Low German has been lost to us. The complete work has survived in a fourteenth-century middle high German translation by Heinrich of Nördlingen and in a Latin version that may have been made shortly after her death. However it would appear that, despite the fact that the vernacular copy we have is a "translation" of the original work into a different version of medieval German, it is probably very close to the original in both order and style. According to Frank Tobin in his introduction to *The Flowing Light*, Neumann has shown that "great pains were taken to render its source accurately . . . aided . . . by the very nature of Mechthild's language and thought, which transcends dialect and geography. Mechthild's modes of expression are often taken from the knightly-courtly world. The ideals and concepts of this world, drawn from a class culture spread throughout Europe, changed very little when transferred from a north German to a south German dialect" (Mechthild 1998, 9).

Describing a work as "mystical" writing need not mean that its entire contents are specifically mystical, or that it is composed solely of visions. In the case of *The Flowing Light*, for example, Mechthild at times offers practical advice to her religious superiors. *The Flowing Light* is mystical in the sense that it is the immediate presence of God that empowers her to write and that gives the book its authority. Works of mysticism are often not included in the histories of our discipline, as they do not contain—as one commentator has put it—"reasoned argument bearing on a traditional sphere of philosophical enquiry (such as logic, epistemology, or metaphysics)" (Dronke 1988, 6). While it is this type of exclusionary classification that I have been questioning, there is little doubt that this immediacy of God combined with the innovative literary nature of the work makes it problematic to know how even to begin to deal with *The Flowing Light* as a work of philosophy. For, as I have already stated, the immediate presence and authority of God means that the overall form of the book is a "message from God," a form—if it is a definable form—that is unlike the other forms with which I have been dealing. Moreover the particular literary forms that compose *The Flowing Light* are incredibly varied, apparently unsystematic, and often hard to classify because she blends one into another to create new ways of speaking about God's love. Despite these difficulties, however, any interpretation of the moral thought of *The Flowing Light* will need to deal with both of these issues.

The reassessment of such mystics as Hadewijch of Antwerp and Mechthild of Magdeburg is of particular interest to a study of women philosophers. In part because of the prevalence of these women mystical writers, and in part because of the respect—and even veneration—that their work inspired in their audience during a period in which women were actively discouraged from writing. Public opinion—supported by a theological tradition that deemed women unsuitable for teaching and preaching—was against women writing. Even the literary tradition—as Christine de Pisan's *The Book of the City of Ladies* shows—indirectly worked against women writing by the way it reinforced the image of women as morally and intellectually inferior.

Given the differences between our worldview and theirs, it is unlikely that we can simply recapture their thought of these medieval women mystics for our use in modern ethics. Yet we can still uncover what it is about their work that made it so important for their contemporaries, as well as find what interest their work may have for constructions of modern feminist ethics. For in analyzing the overall form of the work, we can discover different possibilities for conceptions of the normative subject, moral understanding, and the relationship of these possibilities to their moral world. And, at the very least, this can help us to reflect on, and be aware of, our own ways of thinking about morality.

Women and Writing

It is likely that many of the contemporaries of these women mystics would have assumed that the reason women and not men were success-ful writers of this type of spiritual literature was due to their (supposed) greater capacity for emotion and their weaker capacity for reason. Such a being would be more receptive to and accepting of the love of God through her more finely tuned, natural capacity for love, and she would be able to give herself more freely to that love without the nagging intru-sions of a "masculine" desire to analyze or to understand this love. This is certainly the conclusion the Franciscan Lamprecht von Regensburg reached in 1250, when he wrote of the amazing understanding of these women: "It seems to me that thus it is/A woman becomes good for God;/In the simplicity of her understanding/Her gentle heart, her frailer mind/Are kindled more quickly within her,/So that in her desire she un-derstands better/The wisdom flowing from Heaven/Than does a hard man/Who is clumsy in these things" (quoted in Zum Brunn & Epiney-Burgard 1989, xiv).

Surprisingly some modern commentators would appear to agree with Lamprecht, for example, he has been commended for his "penetrating analysis" of a woman's constitution (Zum Brunn and Epiney-Burgard 1989, xiv).[3] However even if a modern audience was prepared to accept this problematic explanation, it would seem that—at best—the "woman's psychology" explanation can only account for the prevalence of women mystical writers, and their aptitude for writing this type of work. It cannot explain why—if women are inherently more emotional, imaginative, and hysterical than men—female mysticism of this type did not appear earlier (see Bynum 1982, 172–3). Nor does this type of expla-nation offer the modern audience a clear account of *why* work like Mechthild's was taken so seriously by male clerics and others; indeed it makes the acceptance of *The Flowing Light* even more puzzling.

It would seem that the entrance of these women mystics into the pub-lic sphere of writing was not denied by their contemporaries because their work carried with it the authority of God, an authority that stemmed from the fact that they were taken as reporting their experi-ences of God, or that God was speaking directly through them. In other words, the main author is in some sense God, not the woman mystic. Caroline Bynum argues in *Jesus as Mother* that as mediators of the word of God, women gained what she defines as an alternative authority to the male priest. Even though women could not be priests, they could "be themselves what was crucial about priesthood—mediators, preachers, touchers of God, vessels within which God happened" (Bynum 1982, 258).

When these medieval women speak of their divine inspiration to write, it seems that they are well aware of the literary tradition that emphasized their intellectual inferiority and the theological tradition that restricted women from teaching and preaching. For they frequently emphasize that they are merely a channel through which God speaks directly to others. Thus God says to Hildegard of Bingen, "'Thou art timid, timid in speech, artless in explaining, unlearned in writing, but express and write not according to art but according to natural ability, not under the guidance of human composition, but under the guidance of that which thou seest and hearest in God's heaven above'" (Petroff 1986, 26). While Julian of Norwich warns her audience, "God forbid that you should say or assume that I am a teacher, for that is not and never was my intention; for I am a woman, ignorant weak, and frail. But I know very well that what I am saying I have received at the revelation of him who is the sovereign teacher. . . . But because I am a woman, ought I therefore to believe that I should not tell you of the Goodness of God, when I saw at the same time that it is his will that it be known?" (Petroff 1986, 26–27)

Perhaps even more than the other mystics, Mechthild emphasizes the authorship of God for *The Flowing Light*.[4] Even when the "voice" of the book is neither God's nor Mechthild's, it seems clear that the writing of the work is still under God's direction, for it is only through the permission and love of God that the author has had these experiences. Moreover when Mechthild—saddened by the hostility towards her book— asks God for comfort, as he told her to write the book, God appears to her and explains how the book is his alone: "'The book is threefold/And portrays me alone/The parchment that encloses it indicates my pure, white, just humanity/That for your sake suffered death./The words symbolize my marvelous Godhead./It flows continuously/Into your soul from my divine mouth./The sound of the words is a sign of my living spirit/And through it achieves genuine truth'" (Mechthild 1998, II 26). Thus in Mechthild's case, her work not only carries authority because she is a mediator for the word of God, the physical book itself is God's.

The Problem of Authority

The authority provided by God in this way to the writings and teachings of Mechthild and other women mystics is a double-edged sword. There is no doubt that, as Peter Dronke in *Women Writers of the Middle Ages* shows, these claims of divine authority were important, not simply for whether the work of these women would be taken seriously, but for whether they would be permitted to write at all. He states that as Hildegard of Bingen wrote her prophetic utterances in the name of the *lux vivens*, they "were almost beyond challenge" once the genuineness of her prophesying ability had been established (Dronke 1984, 203). Later women writers such as Hadewijch in the thirteenth century did, according to Dronke, write in their own name, but, as Dronke shows, they wrote not as prophets but of their individual experiences of God. Indeed, he states, "They are not prophets, but passionate, often anguished, minds. The beauty of their writing is bound up with their vulnerability" (Dronke 1984, 203).

Dronke further suggests that with this shift in who the earthly writer is comes a parallel shift in how the writing is perceived. It would seem that the more personal the expression of the experience of divine love, the more threatening that expression was for the church. This explains, according to Dronke, the execution for heresy of the fourteenth-century writer Marguerite Porete: "like Hildegard, Porete castigated those in all ranks of clergy who failed to welcome her unique insights. But where Hildegard did this with a prophet's safe conduct, Marguerite did so of her own accord. She spoke only in the name of the 'simple souls,' the 'free souls'—an invisible ideal community to which she aspired to belong, and which she was certain should guide the 'Little Church' [as opposed to the Great Church of the spirit] that is established on earth" (Dronke 1984, 217).

But while the attribution of authorship to God gave Mechthild's work its authority for her contemporaries, it is problematic for any attempt in the present to recapture her work for the history of our discipline. Quite simply the presence of divine authority appears to take away active authorship from these women, instead they become little more than a receptive channel for the word of God; a conclusion that seems supported when writers such as Mechthild *explicitly* acknowledge their humble role in their "own" work. If we are going to analyze Mechthild's work as a philosophical text, it seems we cannot accept Mechthild's claim about the book's authorship at face value, yet to ignore this claim altogether completely means that most of the book will be lost to us. We would lose— among other things—the context of Mechthild's initial motivation for writing, an explanation for its content, and an account of the purpose for this content. Thus we need a way of allowing for the importance of the notion of God as author for *The Flowing Light*, while at the same time also being able to treat Mechthild as the author of the work.

It is certainly possible to take the authorship of God as a literary trope, and simply treat the work of these medieval women mystical writers in the same way that we treat any secular text. It could also be argued that

Mechthild's denial of authorship may have been—at least in part—prompted by the standard formula of humility, as well as a recognition of the lowly position of women. As a woman, she would have been quite aware of her role as author. Even if she believed she was divinely inspired, the humility *topos* and perhaps a certain pragmatic sense may have prompted her to emphasize the role of God as author.[5] It may even be possible to claim that Mechthild deliberately drew attention to her status as a woman in order to remind her audience of God's use of the humble in the Bible as his messengers, thus reinforcing her own authority.[6]

There is no doubt that the authority given to both work and writer by the "authorship" of God could be useful. For example, Hildegard of Bingen may at times have used her prophet status for political ends, for she criticized both pope and emperor. Elizabeth Gössman in Waithe's *A History of Women Philosophers* states that "by virtue of their prophecy, women could criticize the state and the church, even those in the highest positions of authority," and therefore we should not be surprised to find that Hildegard "portrays herself as an uneducated prophetess who lives and speaks from spiritual illumination" (Waithe 1989, 2: 34). Gössman further claims that Hildegard had a strong subjective element in her interpretation of her visions, which she hid "by portraying the interpretation as the audition of the word of God. In fact, though, she here accommodates her own views and positions" (Waithe 1989, 2: 32). Given this, it may also be possible that Mechthild's emphasis on the authorship of God was motivated in part by its convenience. She certainly appears to have used the authority of God as a way of protecting her work from criticism. As Joan Gibson, also in Waithe, claims: "she always insists that she is God's mouthpiece, and thus criticisms of her writings are inappropriate" (Waithe 1989, 2: 119).

There is no doubt that this type of position is a plausible one to take, but I believe that ultimately it is in tension with one of the most prominent qualities of the writings of such women: their genuiness, their directness, and their sincerity. The power of the work of Mechthild of Magdeburg is her portrayal of God as the lover of her soul. But if we must then accept this lover as a trope allowing Mechthild certain literary freedoms, we miss out on the essential quality of her work—a genuine love for a very real experience. We must recognize just how sincere Mechthild was in her attribution of authorship to God. Even when authorship was credited to God in works similar to *The Flowing Light*, the other human author—in keeping with theological tradition—was typically identified too. Yet in *The Flowing Light*, God is declared to be the sole author (see Palmer 1992).

While at first blush the following claim may sound contradictory, I believe that it is possible to hold that the book is "authored" by God in some way, while acknowledging Mechthild's own moral authority, as well as her literary, philosophical, and theological achievements. It is possible to give an analysis of some of the work of Mechthild, that—even for a modern, secular, audience—can legitimately and coherently rest on the acceptance of the claim that God somehow "wrote" her work. Indeed, the assumption that the book *is* written by God is ultimately vital to our understanding of Mechthild's portrayal in the book of the nature of divine love.

The Authorship of God

On the most immediate level, Mechthild has simply been commanded by God to write the book; a privilege that she repeatedly emphasizes she did not ask for: "God himself is my witness that I never in will or desire asked him to give me these things that are written in this book" (Mechthild 1998, IV 2). However it is evident from Mechthild's comments throughout the book on the writing of the work itself, and its relationship to divine revelation, that this relationship has several different aspects. The most crucial aspect of this relationship is the fact that God does not simply direct the writing of the book, he is also its originator. Mechthild states that she writes "out of God's heart and mouth. And so this book has come lovingly from God and does not have its origins in human thought" (Mechthild 1998, IV 2). This relationship between Mechthild the author and God is commented on in a passage that was apparently added by an editor: "The writing in this book flowed out of the living Godhead into Sister Mechthild's heart and has been as faithfully set down here as it was given by God, out of her heart" (Mechthild 1998, VI 43).[7]

This editorial comment is interesting in that it raises the issue of the actual writing process of *The Flowing Light*. Mechthild can be said to be "writing from the heart" or from love, and indeed she frequently contrasts what she has to say with the more cerebral work of those who have more book learning than her. In VI 20, she says that the book came about through a Threefold favor of God: first tenderness, then intimacy, and finally profound suffering. She prefers, however, to remain in this third state, because the first two "are unfortunately so foreign in this world that all who truly grasp them are not at all able to describe them." But such, she says, is the nature of love, which first "flows in sweetness" then "becomes rich in knowledge" and finally "becomes full of longing in rejection" (Mechthild 1998, VI 20). But this suffering is not simply an experience to be described, it is also somehow part of the writing process. For when Mechthild is about to be "taken up" by God—and thus to learn more to be written down—she offers her suffering in return for this favor.

Indeed as a humble sinner all she has to give is her suffering. Her soul says to God: "Lord, where shall I then put you?/I shall give you what I have./I shall put you in my little bed./This little bed is made completely of suffering" (Mechthild 1998, VII 21).

Yet it is through this suffering that the soul gains authority and power. When the soul speaks directly to the body and its five senses: "I am your master./You shall follow and obey me in all things./If I were not going to my Father,/You would remain as fools," Mechthild appears to be implying that this loving soul can also teach the rest of us who are controlled by our physical lives (Mechthild 1998, III 10). Moreover the book does not simply contain the love of God—through his favors to Mechthild—it also contains his suffering: "'Truly I say to you,' said our Lord, 'in this book my heart's blood is written'" (Mechthild 1998, V 34). It is here that we find our key to understanding the authorship of *The Flowing Light*: God is not simply the catalyst for the work, he is not external to the work, rather God is part of the work itself. The book "contains" God in that it expresses the Trinity through its physical form. In II.26, Mechthild states that the book is threefold and portrays only God. The parchment on which it is written represents humanity, the words represent divinity, while the spirit is in the sound or voice of the words.

More importantly, it also "contains" God in that its content is Love itself, and as such is also both an expression of the love of God and of Mechthild's love for God: "This book was begun in love, it shall also end in love; for nothing is as wise or as holy or as beautiful or as strong or as perfect as love" (Mechthild 1998, IV 28). The soul (Mechthild) and God are lovers, and the book describes all the aspects of this relationship (wooing, intimacy, separation, etc.). Mechthild shows us that God as lover needs the soul as much as she (the soul) needs him. This reciprocal need is paralleled in the writing of the book. Insofar as Mechthild has not chosen freely to write the book, so is God's contribution not freely made. Throughout the work, Mechthild uses images that show the constant flow or outpouring of divine love and how the uncontainable quality of this love is the very nature or essence of divine love. In the opening lines of the work, we are told that God "made" the book, indeed he is unable to restrain himself, due to his gifts, from making the book: "I made it in my powerlessness, for I cannot restrain myself as to my gifts" (Mechthild 1998, Prologue). This summary—which was probably written by Mechthild rather than an editor—of the provenance of the work, shows that uncontainability is one of the characteristics of divine love. It is then in this sense of writing from love that Mechthild cannot help but write the book.[8]

Thus while the content of the book comes from God and its physical form symbolizes God, it would be inaccurate to say that it is simply directed by God, or that Mechthild is merely reporting her experiences. Although her inspiration as a writer does come from God (something clearly indicated by the title of the work), she is not a passive channel for this inspiration. In order to receive this inspiration Mechthild must work actively, but not by studying or learning from her educated superiors, but through the offering up of her suffering love for God. Moreover, as lover, Mechthild actively pursues the object of desire, whether her role is as "a virile vassal in battle" or "an eager bride" in her "bed of love with God" (Mechthild 1998, II 19). Even in the later sections of the book when Mechthild is separated from God, and waits in longing for him, it is important to notice that this separation is portrayed as something she actively embraces.

It is love that brings all these aspects of *The Flowing Light*'s authorship together. It is true that Mechthild is helpless and humble in that she has nothing to offer God but her suffering, and also that she is helpless and humble in that she cannot do anything else—once she has experienced divine love—but love God. Yet there is nothing passive about this type of love; rather her lack of control over the writing of the book is a direct effect of her experience of divine love. Insofar as she shares this love with God, she cannot help but write, just as God—as divine love itself—cannot help but make the book. The book is written in uncontained love out of her experience of uncontainable (divine) love, and it is in this way that it is the work of God as God himself is this unrestrained flood of love. It is in this way that we can see that the "authorship" of *The Flowing Light* need not be tied into an individualistic concept of the self. It is written by, or perhaps more accurately "through," Mechthild, God, and divine love (although for the sake of convenience, I shall continue to refer to Mechthild as the "author"). It is in this way also that we can see how *The Flowing Light* can at the same time take the form of a message from God, an autobiography, and somehow to represent God himself. Moreover, we can see that what is meant by the form of a "message" from God is that it is a book of divine love.

Obviously, a claim that the book is written in uncontained love or through an inexhaustible flood of love, and as such requires an emotive response, is in contrast to the notions of philosophical writing and reading generated by the dominant model of moral philosophy. But it is important to see here that even though a modern audience may have difficulty in understanding this notion of authorship, it is still a coherent notion when it is understood in relation to her worldview. However this notion of authorship, as yet leaves two questions unanswered. First, if the book is a "message" of divine love, then given that we cannot identify an individual author, we need to understand who is the "knower" of this message.

Second, we need to understand the apparent connection between the "message" of the book and the moral knowledge it offers its audience.

In response to the first question it appears that, even though there is no individual "author" or "knower" *per se*, the moral knowledge offered to the audience of *The Flowing Light* is transmitted in the following way. God communicates his message to Christianity through the medium of Mechthild's emotions and experiences, while she communicates this message through her chosen mode of expression of those experiences. From the standpoint of the dominant model of moral philosophy anyway, it seems irrational to base anything on a moral perspective that does not rely on common human experience (see Raphael 1983). But *The Flowing Light* is based on the *idiosyncratic* and *unrepeatable* experiences of one woman. However, given the long—and mistaken—tradition of identifying common human moral experience with bourgeois male experience, we should perhaps reconsider any concerns we may have that moral thought or a moral perspective cannot be of philosophical interest if it is grounded in the experience of just one person.

For what we find when we examine how Mechthild's experience of God's love works in her moral thought is that, while her response to this love is utterly individual and personal, the notion of morality she draws from it is universal because God's love is universal. Indeed it is because Mechthild has this unique relationship with God, and is able to give an account of it, that the audience of *The Flowing Light* can learn of God and his love. Moreover, it is through an understanding of Mechthild's experiences of divine love that we shall be able to see how she is offering what can be seen as a moral epistemology.

Morality and Experience

Even though—as most commentators agree—the books of *The Flowing Light* themselves have no inner structure or ordering principle, nor do they appear to have a particular chronological order, there does seem to be an order to the *experiences* described in them.[9] Emilie Zum Braun and Georgette Epiney-Burgard in *Women Mystics in Medieval Europe* give an overview of the progression of Mechthild's experiences that is both reasonable enough and broad enough to command general agreement, and it is their account that I shall rely on. According to Zum Braun and Epiney-Burgard, the soul begins with intimacy of love and then realizes the possibility that God may withdraw; the soul must learn to bear this as this is what God wills, although this is something that is very hard to learn. Finally the soul comes to desire this withdrawal—"a realization that this possibility corresponds to the most inward will and law of Love, that the soul-in-love will choose precisely this possibility and none other, when God puts it before her" (Zum Brunn & Epiney-Burgard 1989, 49). To suffer in this way is God's plan, and it follows the destiny of Christ, and thus she calls for this suffering and abasement (see Mechthild 1998, VI. 20).

When Mechthild speaks of love for God, it is clear that she is not talking of the human emotion alone; rather it is the love that has an element of the divine in it. Mechthild differentiates between the love of a "bound" and that of the "unbound" soul (see Mechthild 1998, II 24). The love of an "unbound" soul has its source in the senses and is thus still attached to the earth. Human senses are changeable, and thus love that comes from the senses can easily become false love; indeed the soul that is led by her senses and not by humility can easily fall prey to the devil (Mechthild 1998, II 19). The "bound" soul, on the other hand, has transcended the senses and the call of the body and searches only for God. Indeed, this search for God cannot be achieved through knowledge from books or through the intellect. In III 17, for example, Mechthild describes the torment in purgatory of a religious man who had been overly fond of ideas and words, rather than practicing Christian obedience.

However Mechthild never actually *defines* love for her audience.[10] While we do our best to love God in the proper manner, we shall not be able truly to understand love, because that would ultimately be to understand God. This is made clear in a dialogue between the allegorical figures of Lady Knowledge and Lady Soul. Lady Knowledge asks the soul to speak of her intimacies in her lover's bed, and the soul replies that: "Brides may not tell everything they experience/Holy contemplation and precious enjoyment/You shall learn about from me./My privileged experience of God must always be hidden/From you and from all creatures except for myself" (Mechthild 1998, II 19). Instead Mechthild tells the audience of *The Flowing Light* about God's love by giving an account of her own response to it and of her personal relationship with God. She cannot say what it is, she can only describe her personal experiences.

Given Mechthild's apparently unformulated, non-intellectualized notion of love, commentators have tended to hold that Mechthild's response to this love is more instinctual than reflective. Tobin, for example, in a comparison with the more intellectual alienation from God experienced by Meister Eckhart, claims that "Mechthild describes this passage from God to God as being accompanied by existential uncertainty. She is not in control. Something mysterious and incomprehensible is happening to her, and her actions are reactions" (Tobin 1994, 52). Similarly, Edith Scholl states that, "We must not expect theology from her; her piety was of a more popular kind. She accepted the doctrines of the Church with no attempt to see their connections or to penetrate them more deeply. She had little or no use for the theoretical; her own experience of God was the starting-point and impetus of all her writings. When something puzzled or troubled her, she did not reason about it, but turned directly to God for an answer" (Scholl 1987, 225).

It seems evident that those commentators who categorize Mechthild's notion of love as uncontrolled, reactive and simply experiential, as opposed to controlled, active or reasoned, seem to be working—consciously or unconsciously—within the standard reason/passion and intellect/body dichotomies. For example, Tobin claims that—in contrast to the intellectual cravings of Eckhart to *know* God—Mechthild has something akin to a physical hunger "to *see*, *hear*, *taste*, and *touch* God" (Tobin 1994, 45). It is certainly true that Mechthild makes great use of metaphors of the body and its appetites, especially with her use of the bridal metaphor for intimacy with God, and her imagery of the "taste" or "savoring" of the flow of God's love. But these are just metaphors for an experience of the soul that transcends *both* body and intellect and *both* reason and the passion connected to the senses.

If we look more carefully at Mechthild's descriptions of her experience of this love, we can see that her response to it is not merely reactive or unreflective; rather this love requires a different kind of capacity.[11] Mechthild is clear that the loving "bound" soul has a particular capacity for what can best be described as a "loving" perception. We cannot truly see what it is we wish to know and understand, for our eyes have physical limitations (Mechthild 1988, VI 31). Our intellect is equally limited, for even though it can allow us to understand non-physical things, we can understand them only through faith, so that we become like blind men in darkness. However the loving soul has had one eye illuminated by God and thus can truly "see". But what is it that Mechthild's loving soul "sees" in her experiences, what particular results are produced by this peculiar perceptive capacity? Nothing less than knowledge of God. Thus love becomes knowledge; indeed in I 20 Mechthild comments on the blind saints who have not received God's love and thus do not know God.

Mechthild does not—and cannot—inform us of the actual content or truths of this divine knowledge. As the soul says, she cannot tell of the intimacies of the bridal bed. The reason why the "bound" soul can find knowledge in her intimate moments with God but cannot return with that knowledge becomes clear in V 29. Here Mechthild tells us that if a person were to behave righteously after being with God, s/he would be so filled with ecstatic knowledge that it would be beyond human capacities to hold it in their heart; instead they would become more like an angel in a union of love with God. But, unfortunately, the soul returns to the body of the weak sinner and thus does not receive this knowledge. However even though the soul cannot return with specific knowledge of

God, the loving soul can "see" the connection between knowledge of God and love of God, for it is only when the soul has been "awakened in the light of open love . . . does she see truly and understand" (Mechthild 1998, II 19).

Thus, the relationship of Mechthild's experiences to her moral thought is a somewhat complex one. Mechthild's response to her experiences is not one of pure reaction, instead her "bound" soul "sees" with its one illuminated eye, and thus understands, the love of God present in her visions and experiences of God. In this way her moral understanding comes through the capacity produced by her particular experience of God's love. It is because she has had these privileged experiences, and thus can now "see" that she is able to communicate love/knowledge of God to her audience. Because of the nature of God, we cannot "know" in any real sense, instead we can only learn about it indirectly through experiences such as hers. But, in a similar way to the non-individualistic notion of the authorship of *The Flowing Light*, we need not think of Mechthild's experiences of divine love only in terms of experiences of an individualistic self. While they are without a doubt hers, they are also ours in that they are given to us from God as a message; furthermore they are in a sense God's in that God is Love itself. In this way we can see how Mechthild's personal experiences can provide the universal moral knowledge offered by *The Flowing Light*. Moreover we can now see the connection between this knowledge and the "message" of the book: they are both *about* and *are* divine love.

The spiritual teachings of *The Flowing Light* are intended to produce this "bound" (humble) love of God in others. Mechthild cannot offer the knowledge that her bound soul has seen, nor does she offer the type of instruction typically found in works of theology; teachings that presumably speak more to the intellect, rather than to the heart. Indeed in VII 21, Mechthild tells the sisters of Helfta—an order known for its learning— that she cannot offer them the sort of instruction they desire, *that* is something they will find far better in their books. Immediately following this statement (and perhaps in a rather pointed manner), Mechthild then describes how she puts herself into a state of complete humility in preparation for being taken up by God. It is this type of instruction that she can offer: how to love God truly, and thus how to be in a position to receive love from/knowledge of God. Or, in other words, how to be in a position to experience proper love for God, and how to be in a position to experience God's love.

What we, as the audience of *The Flowing Light*, can know of God's love is dependent on a particular response—Mechthild's—to her experiences of a unique individual relationship with God. On one level, Mechthild is describing her unique, idiosyncratic experience, but on another level—

because of what she shares with God in this relationship—she is describing God's love itself. But if Mechthild cannot offer any standard sort of theological instruction, how then can she communicate what she has "perceived" and understood? For, as I have said, these experiences are in a sense ours to share: we are all able to love God. While instruction of how to conduct oneself on a daily basis, of suitable prayers, of the moral responsibilities of clerics and abbesses, can be communicated in a more prosaic manner, the understanding of God's love which Mechthild's soul has gained through her loving perception of her experiences and visions of God requires a different type of writing. For Mechthild not only needs to bring out the special nature of this love, but—as much as she can—to communicate to her audience how her soul "sees" and what it "sees." It is at this point that we need to understand the appropriateness of Mechthild's use of courtly love literature for the expression of her knowledge of divine love. For what she knows *is* what she feels and experiences, something that is perhaps best expressed through love poetry.

The Forms in the Flowing Light

Even though there is no central organizing principle in *The Flowing Light*, and neither the books nor the chapters within each book appear to admit of a clearly defined order, the forms with which Mechthild describes her experiences do not appear to be randomly employed or to lack a careful articulation. Even though Mechthild claims to be uneducated, it would seem that she is referring to knowledge of theology and Latin, for her writing demonstrates an in-depth knowledge of the forms and subject matter of the German courtly love literature of her time.

Commentators have questioned just how conscious Mechthild's use was of these literary forms in *The Flowing Light*. Those who wish to commend Mechthild's poetic achievements praise her conscious artistry; for example William Seaton comments on how Mechthild uses contemporary literary conventions "in a way carefully calculated and artfully appropriate" (Seaton 1984, 64). On the other hand, Tobin is critical of the presence of such conscious artistry. He claims that in the early books "she is conscious of being literary in her creation. She is able to turn mysticism into aesthetic experience. She both is and poses as a literary artist. In the final book, the pose is largely gone" (Tobin 1994, 60–61).

While it is obvious that Mechthild was clearly conscious of her exploration of literary genres and forms—and thoroughly enjoyed using them—we should not assume that the wide variety of literary forms in *The Flowing Light* are present merely for their own sake. This becomes clear when we ask ourselves to what end did Mechthild employ these forms. We can certainly agree with Tobin's claim in his introduction to

The Flowing Light that even though the presence of such a variety of forms is not accidental, it would be presumptive to assume that each chapter signifies an attempt to use a different form (see Mechthild 1998, 10). But it would also be presumptive to assume that the only way to evaluate these forms is in terms of their purely literary qualities. We can instead examine the forms that Mechthild uses in terms of their relation to the content they express (her experiences), and also to the overall aim or form of the book as a message from God to all Christians; for it is central to *The Flowing Light* that Mechthild has been charged to share her experience and knowledge of God with others.

Mechthild explores a multitude of different forms in *The Flowing Light*, including—but not limited to—prayer, spiritual instruction, letter, autobiography, and drama (see Mohr 1963).[12] She also uses the exegetical tradition of The Song of Songs to speak of divine love in worldly terms, as well as images and forms from popular love songs and dating rituals and from the more cultivated conventions of *Minnesang*. While it is true that these latter conventions are not the most commonly used in *The Flowing Light*, they are both the most striking and the most central to its content. William Seaton comments that, "She was, however, a devotional rather than an intellectual poet, and she found in *Minnesang* qualities useful to the expression of her themes. The language of hyperbole which has always ornamented love poetry, the emotional similarities between spiritual and non-spiritual giving of oneself in rapturous attachment, the suffering of the pains of separation, and the emphasis on a dedicated self-development to make oneself worthy of the beloved all are closely congruent areas that, in her work as well as in others, made direct borrowing possible" (Seaton 1984, 65). Moreover, these courtly love forms are easier to categorize. Indeed Wolfgang Mohr claims that many of the forms she uses are in a stage of germination; they are often intertwined, or collapse one into the other. He states that only occasionally, and then only briefly, do the classifications of "the lyric," "the epic," "the dramatic," or "the didactic" remain stable (see Mohr 1963, 382).

Given the multitude of forms and their uses in *The Flowing Light*, it would be impossible to deal with more than a few representative examples, so I shall just focus on the forms that are used for Mechthild's portrayal of the union of the soul with the Trinity; a concept that is absolutely central to *The Flowing Light*. Tobin states that this concept is portrayed both as a "visionary and ecstatic personal experience, and as a spiritual doctrine" (Tobin 1994, 55). We may then expect Mechthild to bring out this difference through the use of prose—perhaps even didactic—forms for the latter and poetic or lyrical forms for the former. Yet Mechthild surprises us. In III 9, her personal experience of being taken into the Trinity is described in a prose dialogue between its three personae. Mechthild, is simply an observer, indeed the only part she plays is in the opening prayer where she thanks God for such visions. While often beautifully expressed, it is the least intimate part of the descriptions of the union of the soul with the Trinity. Similarly in IV 14, when Mechthild describes her vision of how man had his nature formed in the Trinity, she places herself in it purely as an observer; even though this vision is clearly personal.

In terms of her spiritual doctrine, however, Mechthild not only plays an "active" role in the discovery of the doctrine, but her discoveries are lyrically described and typically use the conventions of courtly love literature. Mechthild tells us that the souls who know divine love become part of the Holy Trinity, and as such they cannot sin (see Mechthild 1998, IV 16). Mechthild uses the form of a question and answer dialogue between God and the soul to bring out this part of her doctrine, with the soul repeating the simple question "why ?" in order to elicit an explanation from God. In I 22, we are told how the soul was made: "The sweet dew of the eternal Trinity gushed forth from the fountain of the everlasting Godhead into the flower of the chosen maid;" the text then bursts into what appears to be a *Hügeliet* (song of joy) describing the ecstasy of the union between bride and bridegroom: "Under this immense force she loses herself/In this most dazzling light she becomes blind in herself. . . " (Mechthild 1998, I 22).

The meaning of God as bridegroom is then explained in question and answer form, first between an unnamed speaker and the soul, and then between the speaker and the Virgin Mary. We are told that it is in the Holy Trinity that God became the "Bridegroom," and that is because the soul is made of love that enables her to be at the same time to be whole and yet part of the Holy Trinity. Moreover we are also given the reason why the soul is made of love, for she was made in the jubilus of the Holy Trinity itself, when "God could no longer contain himself, he created the soul and, in his immense love, gave himself to her as her own" (Mechthild 1998, I 22). This relationship between the soul and the Trinity is further brought out in a play on the traditional dawn song (the *Tagelied*) when the lovers must part after a night together. The soul is portrayed as the bride resting in the locked treasury of the Trinity, she suddenly realizes that her lover has left her, and she sends away all the creatures of the world because they cannot console her. In another question and answer dialogue, the creatures ask the bride what it would take to console her and in a poem the soul replies that her only consolation can be "the playful flood flowing in the Holy Trinity from which alone the soul lives" (Mechthild 1998, IV 12).

Based on these differences of form, it would then seem that Mechthild differentiates between her visionary experiences and her experiences of

God as lover. While it would be a mistake to draw too rigid a classification or to make too broad a generalization about *The Flowing Light*, it would appear that this difference between the more prosaic forms expressing her visions and the more literary forms expressing her intimate experience of divine love is common throughout *The Flowing Light*. For example, the people described in her visions are typically real people or biblical figures, and Mechthild often presents herself as simply an observer of a narrative. In contrast, her presentation of her experiences of God as lover often draws on the forms and conventions, such as allegory, dialogue, and poetry, that come from the courtly love literary tradition.[13] For example, as we have seen, the account of the estrangement of the soul from God in IV 12 draws on the tradition of the dawn song. When the lovers speak about their love, Mechthild often employs the *Wechsel*, an exchange where they speak of what they share rather than directly to each other. It is not a dialogue, but rather alternating thoughts which create a thinking in unison. This device brings out both the intimacy of God's love, as well as the distance of the love of an infinite unknowable being. In the later books which focus more on the soul's estrangement from God, we find—not surprisingly—little use of the courtly love forms. When Mechthild does employ one of these forms it is—rather significantly—the *Botenlied*: the messenger's song in which the lover speaks of love, but because the lovers are separated s/he must speak through a third party.

The consistency of these types of forms in giving an account of Mechthild's intimate experiences of divine love and the spiritual doctrine of the soul that she draws from them seems to indicate that they were deliberately chosen for this purpose. But why poetry and dialogue, both of which seem in tension with doctrinal content? The answer to this question can be found through an understanding of Mechthild's use of the courtly love tradition and its relationship to her concept of divine love or knowledge. While it is typical for commentators to see the connection between the courtly love tradition and *The Flowing Light* in terms of its rituals and conventions, I believe that the artificial and game-playing qualities that can be part of the courtly love tradition are at odds with the sincerity and spontaneity of Mechthild's writing in *The Flowing Light*. Moreover, in contrast to the Provençal poets, German poems tend to be more naturalistic and less a vehicle for intellectual display (see O'-Donoghue 1982, 213). The forms Mechthild chooses are a means to a particular end, not an end in themselves. It is for these reasons that I focus on Mechthild's use of the different notions of what it is to love, or the feelings of love, that are inherent in this tradition.

This love can be one sided when the lover loves a lady of too high a rank, or who is too aloof. While he devotes himself to her service, he suffers because she is unattainable. He sings songs of praise for her and laments that he cannot win her love. In the other scenario the love is returned, but the lovers can rarely be together, and thus they speak of their longing and the pain of separation. The love experienced in these two scenarios is sometimes differentiated between high love (*Hohe Minne*) and low love (*Niedere Minne*). Both types of love are extreme, they can never be completely fulfilled, nor will they ultimately bring peace. Low love is physical love, which—both through its nature and through such *Minnesang* conventions as the Dawn Song—does not remain. When it has gone, the pain can be even more intense than the desire was before it was fulfilled. High love is the love which reaches beyond the lover and thus—by definition—cannot be satisfied, this then produces the pain of unfulfilled desires.

Mechthild employs *all* these notions of human love in *The Flowing Light* to bring out her experience of divine love. In the early books of *The Flowing Light*, she integrates bridal mysticism with the secular conventions of an intense physical union that can only last for a brief time. In the later books the notions of the pain of separation and the bliss of reunion become far less dominant, and instead Mechthild now stresses her growing sense of humility and the suffering of longing and estrangement. In this way, Mechthild can combine these two extremes of human love to try and indicate the all-encompassing, overwhelming nature of uncontrolled divine love. For human love, there is a tension between high and low love and between the identification of love with consummation and the identification of love with unrequited desire. Yet this tension does not exist in the final level of love that the soul feels for God, a level that has moved beyond the two types of human love. In this third and final level, the soul not only accepts, but calls for, the separation and longing. The soul must suffer for love of God as Christ did for his love of humanity. So it is only in a desire for unrequited desire that the soul can fully achieve consummation. In this final state of estrangement, the soul is now earthbound. Thus the fact that Mechthild rarely uses courtly love forms in the later books and uses more humble, less consciously literary forms instead would seem all the more appropriate.[14]

Thus it is through Mechthild's use of literary forms, and in particular those of the courtly love tradition, to give an account of her experiences that *we* come to an understanding of both love *for* and *of* God and the spiritual doctrine that Mechthild draws from it. In terms of spiritual doctrine, Mechthild's knowledge of the unity of the soul with the Trinity comes—more than anything else—from her intimate experiences as the lover of Christ. Although I want to stress here that I am not making any claims about the work being doctrinal in general; rather the main thrust of her work is about divine love itself. In terms of understanding divine love, as humans we cannot say what this love is exactly, or describe it directly; instead, as Mechthild shows, we can only say how it feels. We cannot hold anything of ourselves back, yet we are humbled by the object of our love. The object of our love is both close enough for us to be completely absorbed and overwhelmed by this love, yet we cannot possess this object for it is out of our reach. Yet we also love this object precisely because of the way that it is. The courtly love tradition brings with it a view of love and accompanying literary forms ready made to describe as much as is humanly possible these extremes and paradoxes of the experience of love: the experiences of loving God and being loved by God, and of Love itself.

Conclusion: Contingencies

Throughout this work I have challenged the ideals of the dominant model of moral philosophy as they get played out in the designation of certain forms as "philosophical" or "non-philosophical." In the case of *The Flowing Light*, these ideals get played out in more complex and subtle ways. For its form is "non-philosophical" not so much because of the particular shape or literary structure, or because of the forms Mechthild uses to express her moral thought, but because of the ambiguity of its authorship. The concept of authorship in *The Flowing Light* conflicts with the ideals of the dominant model of moral philosophy as they get played out in its concepts of the "philosophical" author. The ideal of the normative subject as an independent, autonomous individual requires an identifiable author of a work (even if they remain anonymous), while—in contrast—the ideal of divine love of *The Flowing Light* requires that it is written from or through this love.

What Mechthild is offering the audience of *The Flowing Light* as "moral knowledge" is essentially an understanding of God's love. Obviously this is not something that can be directly understood, and instead her audience learns through Mechthild's descriptions of her love for God and her experiences of God. This concept may be problematic for modern philosophers of whatever stripe to grasp. Reading *The Flowing Light* shows us that there can be other ways of delineating the scope of morality, other ways of thinking about morality, and thus other views about how to do moral philosophy. Indeed in order to understand completely Mechthild's view of moral knowledge, we need to recognize the different view of morality and the moral world within which it is framed. For Mechthild, morality is understood in terms of developing an appropriate response and an appropriate relationship to God/God's love. Yet while divine love lies at the heart of Mechthild's moral thought, it would be a mistake to see it as some kind of foundation stone on which her view is developed. Every corner of Mechthild's universe is permeated with divine love; we must recognize that every fiber of her being, every aspect of her life, is aimed towards loving God and being loved. While she certainly uses literary forms as a way of bringing out or "analyzing" this divine love, the purpose of this analysis is for Mechthild and her audience to become more at one with the all encompassing divine love. It is a widening rather than a narrowing, for the more we love, the more we can know.

We may be inclined to wonder whether there is something circular in her account of moral knowledge and love of God, and we may find it difficult to grasp that this may not be the problem, that this is precisely the point. For Mechthild, everything ties back, and is connected to, the all encompassing divine love. While—on the dominant model of moral philosophy—philosophical analysis exists precisely for the purpose of removing such things as circularity in the initial conception of morality and in thinking about morality, Mechthild's poetry and her way of writing with one form slipping into another with no particular order to the book brings out the significance for her moral and spiritual thought of this circularity. Any coherence we find in Mechthild's moral view is not in spite of this circularity, but because of it. Coherence in someone's moral view need not be identified with the presence of a set of explicitly formulated, systematized interconnected principles or beliefs, produced through such intellectual capacities in the agent as derivation, deduction, etc. In Mechthild's case, coherence in her moral thought is produced by the all-connecting love of God.

In order to understand this claim, however, we must recognize the connections between Mechthild's moral epistemology and the conceptual scheme of her world. Mechthild's concept of morality is dictated by her view of the world, and this is something we also saw with Eliot's view of morality in relation to her deterministic view of the universe. In Mechthild's case it is crystal clear that certain moral judgments, specifically about the presence of divine love, and a certain way of seeing the world, are involved in her conception of morality.[15] Similarly if we find this claim problematic or incoherent, we must recognize that this may be due to a clash of her conceptual scheme with ours, rather than to any fundamental incoherence in Mechthild's writing. Any sense of alienation or confusion we may experience in accepting this claim should not be attributed to the fact that her writing is "not philosophical," or that she has not grasped what morality "is," or that her concept of moral knowledge is "not really knowledge."

Even though we, as her modern audience, may not be able to accept Mechthild's conceptual scheme, an examination of it is useful for it illuminates the contingency of our own definitions of philosophy. For what is to count as moral philosophy is not ahistorical and unchangeable. Reading *The Flowing Light* challenges us to see the contingency of our modern conceptions of moral philosophy as well as their possibilities for change. But we must recognize that in making these changes, we are making moral judgments, and accordingly are morally responsible for the subsequent form of moral philosophy we produce, something which I emphasize in the concluding chapter. For we are now in a position to recognize that the assumption of the dominant model of moral philosophy that the notion of morality that *it* begins from is somehow an ahistorical, universal, neutral "given" is questionable. Indeed the very desire for and valuing of the neutral, the universal, and the abstract, themselves comes from a particular moral perspective. And it is here that I want to leave my argument, with its indication of the possibilities of different ways of conceiving of moral philosophy, and its claim that the inability of the dominant model of moral philosophy to treat some of these possibilities as moral philosophy comes not just through its theoretical ideals and methods of assessment, but from its very origins. Origins that, as I argued in the introduction, are inherently male-biased.

Notes

Mechthild of Magdeburg: *The Flowing Light of the Godhead* translated and introduced by Frank Tobin. © by Frank Tobin. Reprinted by permission of Paulist Press, Inc.

1. I shall be using Frank Tobin's 1998 translation of the critical edition.
2. See Howard 1984: 153.
3. Caroline Bynum in *Jesus as Mother: Studies in the Spirituality of the High Middle Ages* also lists historians who appear to base their work on the assumption of women's inherent affectivity (see Bynum 1982, 172–3).
4. Klaus Grubmüller (1992), in particular, comments on the way no other writer claims God's authorship to the extent that Mechthild does.
5. See, for example, Frank Tobin's fn 58 for Book II in Mechthild (1998).
6. This point is drawn from Waithe 1989, 2: 33.
7. See, for example, Tobin 1998, fn 56 for Book VI in Mechthild (1998).
8. There is some disagreement as to who is the speaker of the first part of the prologue, but it is clear that God is the speaker of the second part that I am quoting. It is also not clear when the prologue was added, and who by. Nellmann argues that it was probably done by Mechthild. Certainly the prologue seems to be fashioned from the two main arguments given to justify the writing of the book (V 34, II 26) (see Nellmann 1989).
9. Although Hans-Georg Kemper (1979) does try to demonstrate an order.
10. Although Schmidt (1987) offers a reading using Mechthild's imagery of wine etc. that brings out the complexity of the notion.
11. Some theologians in the twelfth century also emphasized love over the intellect. For example, William of St. Thierry desired to know God as more than an

abstraction, and he held that the only way he could reach this knowledge of God was through love. In this way, for him, love becomes knowledge. According to Zum Brunn & Epiney-Burgard (1989), St. Thierry was an influence on the Beguines.

12. Given Mechthild's task of communicating God's message to all Christians, her use of such a wide variety of forms is hardly surprising.

13. For an interesting account of the use of the courtly love tradition by Mechthild and other Beguines, see Barbara Newman, *From Virile Woman to WomanChrist*. (Philadelphia: University of Pennsylvania Press, 1995).

14. See also, for example, how repetitive the poems associated with earth are in I 44.

15. See my comments on Iris Murdoch in the introductory chapter.

7

Conclusion

Philosophical Genre and the Boundaries of Philosophy

Having looked at the work of these five philosophers it becomes clear, not simply that the types of form within which they wrote are excluded from dominant paradigms of "the philosophical" but also what underlies this exclusion. On the most immediate level, if we adhere to dominant paradigms of what is to constitute a philosophical text—whether in terms of its form, what sort of assessment it requires, or some such thing—then this may result in the automatic exclusion of works of many women philosophers. This exclusion simply in itself should be a cause for concern, especially in light of the fact that the use of these excluded forms was historically prevalent among women philosophers. Obviously these forms were not exclusively used by women, but we must not forget how sex can affect the categorization of a work or attempts to take the work seriously.

Even if the work is not automatically excluded on the grounds of its form, and it is examined for its philosophical content using dominant paradigms of the philosophical, this examination may result in the devaluation or misinterpretation of the work. For example, it can lead to the conclusion that Catharine Macaulay's intellectual contribution is only to the subject of childhood education, or that a search for the philosophical content of the novels of George Eliot is a search for her replication of the thought of an established philosopher. Further still, a lack of recognition of the potential philosophical status of certain forms can mean that their significance for the philosophical content of certain works themselves can be lost. We shall not be able to see, for example, how the allegorical city of Christine de Pisan's *The Book of the City of Ladies* can aid the female reader in a development of moral agency, or how the assumption that God is the author of *The Flowing Light of the Godhead* is important for understanding its moral thought.

My starting point was to ask why certain genres, styles, and forms are devalued on, or are excluded from, what I have been calling the dominant model of moral philosophy.[1] It is not that certain forms are inherently "unphilosophical," although it might seem that way from the standpoint of this model. Instead the ideals of the dominant model of moral philosophy get played out in the designation of certain forms as "philosophical" or "unphilosophical." Ideals of the moral agent and the activities of this agent will, for example, play out in the ways that a text should be written or read in a philosophical manner; and thus, by definition, exclude or devalue other possibilities. Similarly, this model's methods of assessment of philosophical arguments can only deal easily with work that apparently fits the ideals of this model; work that is, for example, abstract and objective. Ultimately, I believe that this exclusion of certain types of philosophical writing from the dominant model can be traced back not just to its ideals and methods of assessment, but to its very foundations: the initial delineation of morality, or the view of the moral world, it begins from.

I have endeavored to show throughout this work that the different forms employed by the five philosophers I study are in fact philosophical, and in what ways they are philosophical. However in order to allow for certain forms as philosophical forms, and thus not automatically exclude philosophers (male or female) who wrote in these forms, we are required to rethink and expand upon what counts as philosophical genre forms for moral philosophy. This ultimately means that we must be prepared to engage in critiquing the dominant model of moral philosophy itself.

I began by challenging the standard expectations of the form that a work of moral philosophy should take. An examination of Catharine Macaulay's *Letters on Education* can show us that non-traditional forms such as letters—or even novels or poetry—cannot be *automatically* excluded from the domain of the philosophical on the grounds that the structure itself does not allow them to maintain or contain a sustained philosophical argument. The assumption that the *Letters* does not contain a sustained philosophical argument seems to be created in part by the way that the epistolary form encourages us to read the *Letters* as made up of independent units, but mainly by the association between this type of form and "feminine" domestic writing. It is in this way that we can see that the designation of work due to its form as "non-philosophical" is not somehow neutral, or a "given," but related to other factors, in this particular case to the devalued social spheres and moral concerns associated with women.

In the third chapter, my discussion of Christine's *The Book of the City of Ladies* raised the issue of the importance of the presentation to the philosophical content of the work and the related issue of the way that the work is to be read. For Christine, philosophical truths are complex matters that require metaphorical expression through layers of meaning. The self-reflective reader then enters into the allegorical form of the work, and in this way the reader does not simply have a better grasp of Christine's arguments for the moral defense of women, the reader will become defended herself. Wollstonecraft also emphasizes the importance of the presentation of ideas, but she holds that honesty and genuine sensibility on behalf of the writer—rather than subtle disguises—are necessary for significant philosophical content. While, for Eliot, the moral and philosophical content of a work is dependent on the realistic and sympathetic depiction of human life; a depiction that will produce a corresponding reflective sympathy in the reader.

These issues of the importance of the presentation of an argument, the skills or emotional capacities of the author, and the corresponding capacities in the reader are integral to philosophical work like *The Book of the City of Ladies* or Eliot's novels. It is not simply that the objective critical reader of the dominant model of moral philosophy has not been trained to read allegorical work like Christine's, it is rather that Christine's way of reading and writing philosophy does not embody ideals of moral agency and activity employed on this model, nor does it need to do so.

The ideals of the type of rationality practiced by the moral agent of the dominant model come into play in a provocative way in an examination of the work of Mary Wollstonecraft. It has traditionally been assumed that *A Vindication of the Rights of Woman* takes the form of an Enlightenment treatise: essentially that it is a rational argument for the rights of women based on their capacity for rational thought. But this then leaves certain problematic anomalies, such as her frequent emotional outbursts and her fiction, to be explained away or ignored. I claimed that in order to gain a complete understanding of Wollstonecraft's moral thought, we need both to integrate her fictional work into what has traditionally been seen as her "philosophical" work and to recognize the philosophical and moral importance of the form—understood in this case as style—of her writing. Once we have done this then we can see how Wollstonecraft offers different—but still equally coherent—possibilities for both philosophical argument and for defining the sphere of the philosophical. Wollstonecraft holds that rational philosophical argument for social and political reform must be grounded upon a reflective principled sensibility, and in so doing she breaks down the disciplinary boundaries between "the poetic" and "the philosophical."

In giving an account of the philosophical content of Wollstonecraft's fictional work, this did not mean that I used it just to support the main

themes of her non-fictional work or that points and arguments were extracted from them to add to these main themes. For there are other approaches to the philosophical assessment of a text. This issue was
brought out more thoroughly in my discussion of the novels of George
Eliot where I showed the failure of standard approaches to philosophical
assessment of her work. Given that the notion of what is to count as
philosophical assessment is both bound up with, and reinforces, the notion of what is to count as moral philosophy itself, this challenge to dominant paradigms of philosophical thought must be taken seriously.

Mechthild of Magdeburg's *The Flowing Light of The Godhead*, discussed
in the previous chapter, is in many ways challenging even for someone
like myself who is open to the different forms that moral philosophy can
take. The notion that the overall form of the work is a message written by
God was something that, as a distinctly secular philosopher, I found hard
to know how to approach. Moreover the highly literary forms of the conventions of courtly love are in many ways so distant from courtship rituals at the new millenium, that initially it was hard not to treat them as little more than a curiosity. However, once the overall form and the
constituent forms of *The Flowing Light* are framed within Mechthild's
own worldview, they take on moral and philosophical significance. In
this way, a study of *The Flowing Light* indicated not only that there can be
other ways of thinking about morality, but the contingency of our own
ways of conceptualizing moral philosophy.

The issues raised by Mechthild's *The Flowing Light* can indicate what
might be the underlying problem with what I have been calling the dominant model of moral philosophy. This model fails to deal with the work
of these five women philosophers because it is too narrow in what it allows to count as moral philosophy; and my interest is specifically in how
this narrowness gets played out in what is to count as philosophical
genre. This narrowness then results in the exclusion—or the potential exclusion—of a lot of work by fascinating women moral philosophers. This
narrowness means that Macaulay's philosophical contributions will be
ignored, while Christine's will be misunderstood. Even though Wollstonecraft's work will not be ignored, her contribution will be greatly undervalued because we shall not be able to see how wide ranging and
complex her philosophical view really is. This narrowness also means
that attempts to assess the philosophical content of Eliot's work—while
no doubt worthy—will fail, for we shall not be able to recognize other
ways of seeing morality and doing moral philosophy.

But we need to recognize that this exclusion of certain forms is not accidental, that the narrowness of the dominant model of moral philosophy
is not simply a bald fact, nor is it a neutral fact. For we should not forget
the male-biased origins of this model. If we reflect on the problems, or

even the possibility, of trying to open up this dominant model to include work of the kind I have been discussing, we can see that there will be tensions and conflicts. The ideals of this model, of impartiality, abstract theorizing, and universality, for example, are in tension with forms that express the concrete or autobiographical, or can elicit love or sympathy from the reader. Yet it is these ideals that explicitly or implicitly get played out in the designation of certain forms as "philosophical" and in the exclusion of others as "unphilosophical."

In order to argue against the exclusion of these five women philosophers—and others like them—we can criticize these ideals and instead show the value of such concepts as Christine's partiality and particularity, Eliot's emphasis on concreteness for morality, or Mechthild's notion of morality as love and devotion. But even though this type of investigation is important, it does not explain the underlying problem with these ideals. For the problem does not, strictly speaking, lie just in the theoretical ideals of the dominant model of moral philosophy. The problem also lies in the original delineation of the scope of morality from which these ideals are developed, although this delineation is *itself* based on pre-reflective versions of these ideals. This original delineation directs not only the theoretical and refined ideals and concerns of moral philosophy, but—albeit more indirectly—the categorization as "philosophical" of particular forms. Philosophical genre forms did not just "happen." The forms, ideals, and concerns generated by this initial delineation of the subject area analyzed by moral philosophy, in their turn, reinforce this delineation.

The mistake is to believe—and this is something I have aimed to bring out in this work—that this original delineation of the sphere of morality underpinning the dominant model of moral philosophy is somehow morally neutral, or does not involve moral judgments in any way. In the case of Eliot's moral philosophy, it is clear how it rests on a particular view of morality and ultimately on a view of human life. Similarly, Mechthild's moral epistemology stems from a view of morality that is a part of her cosmology. Both these views are probably so different from our own that we are unlikely to be tempted to adopt either of these different notions of morality. But this sense of distance is helpful because it allows us to stand back and observe the way or ways that a particular model of moral philosophy can get constructed. Furthermore, faced with these possibilities of alternative delineations of the sphere of morality, it cannot be maintained that the delineation of the sphere of morality underpinning the dominant model of moral philosophy is a delineation of *the* (only) sphere of morality.

To attempt to argue that—unlike Eliot or Mechthild—this initial delineation of the sphere of morality at least comes from a neutral or objective standpoint is also mistaken. The implications that this makes it "better," or that this makes it more "suitable" for philosophical analysis, is to assume what I am questioning. It is true that the moral judgments grounded in Eliot's pessimistic view of the determinism of human life that carve out the sphere of morality for her are neither neutral nor objective; the same follows for those judgments grounded in Mechthild's view of the cosmos suffused with divine love. But this is to fail to see that the valuing of, and desire for, neutrality and objectivity are themselves moral judgments grounded in a particular view of the world, a view that—as I claimed in the introduction—is male biased.

Thus I hold that when we construct our feminist ethics, we should not simply construct it in a way that allows for the work of our foremothers. I am not just arguing that the boundaries of the subject of whatever we want to call "the philosophical" must be opened up so that these forms can be included. Rather we should recognize the potential significance of the forms in which they wrote both for the interpretation of their own work and for the way that these forms can be of significance to the task of moral philosophy itself (whatever that might be). Moreover in the construction of our feminist ethical theories, we must be prepared to deal consciously with the moral judgments that underlie our ethical thinking and recognize that we are morally responsible for those judgments and thus our theorizing itself.

A Few Comments on Content

Yet evidently the work of these five women philosophers is not philosophically interesting simply because of the challenge presented by the forms which they employed. They are our philosophical foremothers, and as such, we should consider what philosophical interest their thought itself may have for present day feminist ethics (and I recognize here that feminist ethics is no one thing). Given the fact that form and philosophical content are often related in their work, indeed sometimes even the form *is* philosophical content, the philosophical interest or significance of their work is obviously something that I have indicated throughout this work. I can only deal with these issues briefly here, but I do want to highlight what seems to be of particular interest in the work of these five particular female philosophers for the construction of feminist ethics and what moral insights and philosophical contributions they might have to offer.

However tempting it might be, I do not want to try and create some sort of "tradition" from the work of these five philosophers. Although it does seem clear that their moral thinking has its roots in their experience as women of their awareness of themselves as women, or of their awareness of the social limitations of their sex. Indeed all of these three aspects quite clearly underpin the work of both Christine de Pisan and Mary Wollstonecraft. In George Eliot's case, she makes it quite clear that women have to bear an even more determined and limited life than men, and it is certainly tempting to speculate how much her moral thought grew out of her own experiences of such limitations. Yet, and this is one reason why I do not want to try and create a "tradition" from the philosophers I have examined, Catharine Macaulay's work—despite her recognition of the oppression of women—is underpinned by sex-neutral moral principles that are drawn from her "perfectionist" moral view.

Two of the themes raised by these five philosophers that appear to be of particular interest to feminist ethical study are the notions of moral understanding as moral response and the importance of personal moral development. Eliot's notion of moral understanding as the moral response of sympathy is interesting not because she is simply arguing for the moral significance of sympathy, but because she offers an example of a fully worked out philosophical system that has sympathy at its core. Wollstonecraft's notion of sensibility and Mechthild's notion of love are provocative in that these moral responses may start with the particular (love for friends, or love of the divine bridegroom), but they are universal in their scope and aim. In the case of Mechthild, the particular love she feels for God is part of the universal, all encompassing love of God. Whereas Wollstonecraft's notion of sensibility is tied in to the improvement of society and the liberation of women. It is through this love or this sensibility that the agent comes to know God or to understand the moral importance of true civilization.

Each of the five philosophers has a distinctive notion of what constitutes personal moral development. These notions range from Macaulay's argument that moral development is produced by education based on immutable principles and the increased perfection of society, to Mechthild of Magdeburg's call for divine love (both from and for God) to make the soul fulfill its potential. Perhaps the two most fascinating accounts are George Eliot's concept of the relationship between the limitations of a life and moral growth, and Christine de Pisan's attempt to create moral agency for women using the very evidence, arguments, and examples that have been used to deny agency to them. Even if our modern feminist ethics cannot find a use for any of these notions, we can learn from their variety. There are other possible ways of framing our contemporary discussions of moral development and moral maturity than in terms of autonomy (or lack thereof), or in terms of creating a balance between care for others and care for self.[2]

However, I do not want to claim that we should include the work of these five philosophers uncritically. Simply because they were women does not guarantee the value or validity of their work. While Christine and Eliot should be admired for their achievements and their talents, we cannot assume that simply by virtue of their sex they can offer insights valuable for the construction of feminist ethics. Used uncritically, the moral thought in works such as those of Christine or Eliot may not enlarge or challenge the domain of the ethics. Instead it may serve to value supposedly "feminine" virtues that have contributed to the oppression of women, such as obedience and passivity.

In my discussion of Christine de Pisan, I showed that, despite her intentions to defend women, ultimately this defense was limited to the development of moral agency at the expense of other skills and dispositions that the modern reader may find vital for personal fulfillment. Whereas, given George Eliot's notion of the moral significance of limitations and suffering, it is not surprising to find that while she recognizes that of the two sexes "woman seems to have the worst share in existence," she does not criticize the injustice of this fact.[3] Instead, Eliot believes that this difference should be the "basis for a sublimer resignation in woman and a more regenerating tenderness in man."[4] Both Eliot and Christine recognize that, due to the limitations of the female lot in life, the moral life of women is correspondingly harder. Yet—whether it is through caring for an ungrateful husband or being more resigned to the frustrations of their life—the virtue of women for both these philosophers is ultimately tied into their acceptance of these greater hardships.

Used critically, however, Christine's and Eliot's concepts of moral activity that grow out of these problematic notions of moral agency can provide an interesting study for an examination of the relationship between the concepts of moral agency and activity.

We can see that if moral agents are restricted or limited, in the way that they are for Eliot and Christine, then moral activity becomes less about what we do, and more about how we see the world. On Eliot's account this means that clear perception and resignation to the limitations of human life are then among the constituents of moral activity; indeed many of her good characters actually "do" very little. In Christine's case, virtue is connected far more to attitude than action. Given the restrictions on the moral agent, and her corresponding lack of action, moral freedom for Christine then becomes the personal salvation women achieve in the city. While, for Eliot, moral freedom is the embracing of these restrictions as the way towards a sympathetic interconnectedness with our fellow beings. In this way, for both Eliot and Christine, moral freedom then becomes less a question of capacity for choice, but something closer to a spiritual liberation.[5]

What is further fascinating about the work of some of the philosophers I have examined is the way that often the philosophical content and arguments of their work focus on moral concerns that are typically devalued or excluded by the dominant model of moral philosophy: care, emotion, relationships, and the related or contextualized self. An assessment of these devalued or excluded concerns is often seen as part of the modern feminist ethical enterprise broadly understood, and a study of the work of historical women philosophers may find that they can contribute to this work. Although again I want to stress that simply because the work is by a woman philosopher does not entail that it will focus on these concerns. Moreover I think, on the whole, we should be cautious in searching for prototypes of modern ethical thought in the work of these historical figures; for example, Christine seems to share much with Sarah Ruddick's maternalist ethics, while Eliot's thought seems to exemplify the conventional stage of what Carol Gilligan has identified as the ethic of care.[6] While this type of comparison work can be interesting, it has the potential for the same problems that we encountered with a search for the philosophical thought of Comte and Spinoza in Eliot's novels. Instead, I believe we should use the work of these philosophers as providing examples— potentially illuminating ones I hope—of different ways of thinking about and conceptualizing these devalued and excluded moral concerns.

Let me briefly give an example of the sort of thing I am thinking of here. Both Christine and Eliot—albeit in different ways—stress the importance of our responsibility to care for particular others. For Christine, this care for others is specifically played out in the wife's caring for her husband, yet this care can be as valuable to the wife as to the husband because it can become part of her moral agency and her personal salvation. While ultimately we saw the problems inherent in Christine's moral thought, her notion that care for others is a sign of moral strength and wisdom is an interesting one. For Eliot, however, care for particular others is part of our only possible response to the world in which we live and the fate of humanity as suffering. There is an unusual cognitive element in Eliot's notion of care, for not only do we need to develop a perceptive sympathy that will allow us to recognize those in need, but— given the restrictions of human life—our response to them may not involve action, but simply be not to judge.

Perhaps the most fascinating view of our responsibilities to care for particular others can be found in Macaulay's *Letters on Education*. For Macaulay shows us that the care of infants and children is central to the moral improvement of human society as a whole. In this way discussions of the correct way to care for children, and the justifications for such care, become as integral a part of her principled moral theory as her discussion of the practices of government. Indeed there is a sense in which what we think of as the concerns of the private and public spheres are no longer separate, for they are both part of the moral perfection of humanity.

Eliot's notion of caring for others brings with it a specific notion of our relationships to these particular others. For Eliot, human relationships are so intertwined that not to acknowledge this or to try and stand apart from them is to fail in one's humanity. Moreover, the moral self can only be understood in terms of these relationships and the limitations they can put on our choices and actions. It is important to notice that, for Eliot, this notion of the interconnectedness of human beings means that we must recognize our moral responsibilities to humanity itself, not just to those individuals we know. However, she believes that our sphere of moral action in practice will rarely be the sphere of the "heroic" or on a grand moral scale. Most of us will act as moral agents only within the small group of individuals for whom we are responsible because their lives are so interconnected with ours. Indeed Eliot ties the moral sphere so closely into what we think of the private sphere, that the public almost drops out of sight. We find in her novels that one of the reasons she distrusts Christianity is that it claims we should act for the good of all humankind, while she constantly criticizes those who think that our moral lives can be dealt with through generalizations, abstractions, and principles, rather than with individuals.

The notion of the interconnectivity of human life and the universe can be seen to play out in a far more challenging way in Mechthild's *The Flowing Light*. There is a sense in which the individual self becomes subsumed into the all-encompassing notion of divine love, and here divine love is understood as the soul's love for God, God's love for the soul, and Love itself. In this way Mechthild is making an emotion—albeit a divine emotion—central to moral agency and moral activity, indeed central to morality itself.

However it is not simply that philosophers such as Wollstonecraft, Eliot, and Mechthild value certain emotions, or place them as central to their philosophical thought, they offer us different ways of conceiving moral emotions themselves. True sensibility for Wollstonecraft is not simply a benevolent emotion, it is a reflective, principled, emotion; one that is integrally connected not just with arguments for social and political reform, but with this reform itself. With Eliot we not only saw the centrality of the emotion of sympathy to morality and moral philosophy, but we saw that an emotion was equated with morality itself.

As I said, this is merely to indicate potential areas of interest for modern feminist ethical thought in the work of the five philosophers I have studied. And obviously, I believe that contributions can be made—and in different ways—by many other of our forgotten or undervalued foremothers. It would seem possible, therefore, that once we have recovered the work of our philosophical foremothers properly, their moral thought may be of help in our ethical theorizing. But at present, I am content in the aim of showing that an argument for *the initial inclusion* of the work of some of these philosophers can *in itself* provide a critique of the dominant model of moral philosophy. If I have succeeded in doing just this, then I have shown that we must take our philosophical foremothers seriously.

Notes

1. This question seems to connect ultimately with questions about why certain philosophical styles and forms lost favor. Unfortunately the latter issue is too large for the present moment. However this is something that is part of a fascinating discussion in Eileen O'Neill (1998).

2. Although attempts have been made to try and place both Christine (Green 1996) and Eliot (Gilligan 1982) within a care ethics framework, these attempts, in my opinion, do not bring out all the nuances of their moral views.

3. George Eliot to J. Morley, 14th May 1867. L.W. Smith Collection, Morristown, New Jersey.

4. George Eliot to J. Morley, 14th May 1867. L.W. Smith Collection, Morristown, New Jersey.

5. Something similar is claimed by Iris Murdoch in "Vision and Choice in Morality": "moral freedom looks more like a mode of reflection which we may have to achieve, and less like a capacity to vary our choices which we have by definition." This is something that, she adds, "I hardly think is a disadvantage" (Murdoch, 1956, 55).

6. See for example, Sarah Ruddick (1980) "Maternal Thinking." *Feminist Studies* 6(2): 342–67; Carol Gilligan (1982) *In a Different Voice* (Cambridge, Mass.: Harvard University Press).

References

Allen, Prudence. 1997. *The Concept of Woman: The Aristotelian Revolution, 750 BC–AD 1250*. Grand Rapids, MI: W.B. Eerdmans Publishing.

Barrell, John. 1986. *The Political Theory of Painting from Reynolds to Hazlitt: "The Body of the Public."* New Haven: Yale University Press.

Boos, Florence. 1976. "Catharine Macaulay's *Letters on education* (1790): An early feminist polemic." *University of Michigan Papers in Women's Studies* 2 (2): 64–78.

Boos, Florence, and William Boos. 1980. Catharine Macaulay: Historian and political reformer. *International Journal of Women's Studies* 3 (6): 49–65.

Bromwich, David. 1995. "Wollstonecraft as a Critic of Burke." *Political Theory* Vol. 23 No. 4: 617–634.

Burke, Edmund. 1790. *Reflections on the Revolution in France*. London: J. Dodsley.

Bynum, Caroline Walker. 1982. *Jesus as Mother: Studies in the Spirituality of the High Middle Ages*. Berkeley: University of California Press.

Cameron, Kenneth Neill, ed. 1970. *Shelley and His Circle*. Vol. 4. Cambridge: Harvard University Press.

Card, Claudia. 1991. *Feminist Ethics*. Lawrence, KS: University Press of Kansas.

Chapone, Hester. 1773. *Letters on the Improvement of the Mind, Addressed to a Young Lady*. London: Printed by H. Hughs for J. Walter.

Christine de Pisan. 1982. *The Book of the City of Ladies*. Earl Jeffrey Richards, trans. New York: Persea.

———. 1985. *The Treasure of the City of Ladies or The Book of the Three Virtues*. Sarah Lawson, trans. Harmondsworth: Penguin.

———. 1994. *The writings of Christine de Pizan*. Charity Cannon Willard, ed. New York: Persea.

Christine de Pisan. 1995. *L'Avision-Christine*. (Catholic University of America Studies in Romance Language and Literature, No. 6). New York: AMS Press.

Clifford, Gay. 1974. *The Transformation of Allegory*. London, Boston: Routledge and K. Paul.

Comte, Auguste. 1975. *A General View of Positivism*. J.H. Bridges, trans. New York: Robert Speller and Sons Inc.

Coole, Diana. 1988. *Women in Political Theory*. New York: Wheatsheaf.

Delany, Shelia. 1987. "'Mothers to think back through': Who are they? The ambiguous example of Christine de Pisan." In *Medieval Texts and Modern Readers*. L. Finke and M. Schictman, eds. Ithaca: Cornell University Press.

Diamond, Cora. 1995. *The Realistic Spirit*. Cambridge: MIT Press.

Dronke, Peter. 1984. *Women Writers of the Middle Ages*. Cambridge: Cambridge University Press.

_____. 1988. _A History of Twelfth Century Western Philosophy_. Cambridge: Cambridge University Press.

Eliot, George. 1855. Review. _The Leader_ VI: 474–5.

_____. 1861. _Silas Marner_. Edinburgh: W. Blackwood.

_____. 1883. _Wise, Witty, and Tender Sayings_. Alexander Main, selected. London: William Blackwood and Sons.

_____. 1954–78. _The George Eliot Letters_. Gordon Haight, ed., 7 Vols. New Haven: Yale University Press.

_____. 1970. _The Writings of George Eliot_. New York: AMS Press.

_____. 1984. _Daniel Deronda_. Oxford: Oxford University Press.

_____. 1985a. _The Mill on the Floss_. Harmondsworth, Middlesex: Penguin Books.

_____. 1985b. _The Sad Fortunes of the Reverend Amos Barton_. Oxford: Oxford University Press.

_____. 1993. _Romola_. Oxford: Oxford University Press.

_____. 1999. _Middlemarch_. Oxford: Oxford University Press.

_____. n.d. _Adam Bede_. New York: Bernard Clarke and Co.

Elshtain, Jean Bethke. 1992. "Introduction." _Politics, Gender, Genre_. Margaret Brabant, ed. Boulder, CO: Westview Press: 1–6.

The European Magazine. 1783. London. November: 332–4.

Ferguson, Moira. 1984. _Mary Wollstonecraft_. Boston: Twayne Publishers.

Fordyce, James. 1766. _Sermons for Young Women_. London: Printed for A. Millar and T. Cadell.

Gatens, Moira. 1991. "'The Oppressed State of My Sex': Wollstonecraft on Reason, Feeling and Equality." In _Feminist Interpretations and Political Theory_. Carol Pateman and Mary Lyndon Shanley, eds. University Park: Pennsylvania State University Press. 112–128.

Gilligan, Carol. 1982. _In a different voice: Psychological theory and women's development_. Cambridge: Harvard University Press.

Green, Karen. 1995. _The Woman of Reason: feminism, humanism and political thought_. New York: Continuum.

_____. 1996. "Christine de Pisan and Thomas Hobbes." In _Hypatia's Daughters_. Linda Lopez McAlister, ed. Bloomington, IN: Indiana University Press: 48–67.

Gregory, John. 1774. _A Father's Legacy to His Daughters_. London: Printed for W. Strahan, T. Cadell, W. Creech.

Grimshaw, Jean. 1989. "Mary Wollstonecraft and the Tensions in Feminist Philosophy." _Radical Philosophy_. 52: 11–17.

Grubmüller, Klaus. 1992. "Sprechen und Schreiben: Das Beispiel Mechthild von Magdeburg." In _Feschrift für Walter Haug und Berghart Wachinger_. Tübingen: Niemeyer. Vol 1: 335–48.

Gunther-Canada, Wendy. 1996. "Mary Wollstonecraft's "Wild Wish"" Confounding Sex in the Discourse on Political Rights." In _Feminist Interpretations of Mary Wollstonecraft_. Maria J. Falco, ed. University Park: Pennsylvania State University Press. 61–83.

Harvey, W. J. 1962. _The Art of George Eliot_. New York: Oxford University Press.

Held, Virginia. 1999. "Feminist Ethical Theory." In _Proceedings of the Twentieth World Congress of Philosophy_. Klaus Brinkman, ed. Bowling Green, OH: Philosophy Documentation Center.

Hicks, Eric. 1992. "The Political Significance of Christine de Pizan." In *Politics, Gender, Genre*. Margaret Brabant, ed. Boulder, CO: Westview Press: 7 –15.

Hill, Bridget. 1992. *The Republican Virago: The Life and Times of Catharine Macaulay, Historian*. Oxford: Clarendon Press.

Holmes, Richard. 1987. *Mary Wollstonecraft and William Godwin, A Short Residence on Sweden and Memoirs of the Author of "The Rights of Woman"*. Harmondsworth, Middlesex: Penguin Books.

Honig, Edwin. 1960. *Dark Conceit: The Making of Allegory*. Cambridge, MA: Walker-deBerry.

Howard, John. 1984. "The German Mystic: Mechthild of Magdeburg." In *Medieval Women Writers*. Katharina M. Wilson, ed. Athens: University of Georgia Press: 153–85.

Hulme, H. M. 1967. *Middlemarch: Critical Approaches to the Novel*. New York: Oxford University Press.

Hume, David. 1783. Letter. *The European Magazine*. London. November: 331–2.

Jacobus, Mary. 1986. *Reading Woman: Essays in Feminist Criticism*. New York: Columbia University Press.

Jaggar, Alison. 1991. "Feminist Ethics: Projects, Problems, Prospects." In *Feminist Ethics*. Claudia Card, ed. Kansas: University of Kansas Press. 78–104.

James, Henry. 1984. *Literary Criticism*. 2 Vols. New York: Literary Classics of the United States: Viking Press.

Kaplan, Cora. 1986. *Sea Changes: Essays on Culture and Feminism*. London: Verso.

Kelly, Gary. 1993. *Women, Writing, and Revolution 1790–1827*. Oxford: Clarendon Press.

Kelly, Joan. 1984. *Women, History and Theory: The Essays of Joan Kelly*. Chicago: Chicago University Press.

Kemper, Hans-Georg. 1979. "Allegorische Allegorese: Zur Bildlichkeit und Struktur mystischer Literatur." In *Formen und Funktionen der Allegorie*. Symposium Wolfenbüttel, 1978. Walter Haug, ed. (Germanistische Symposien 3.) Stuttgart. 90–125.

Khin Zaw, Susan. 1998. "The Reasonable Heart: Mary Wollstonecraft's View of the Relationship Between Reason and Feeling in Morality, Moral Psychology, and Moral Development." *Hypatia*. Vol. 13. No. 1: 78–117.

Lanson, Gustave. 1965. *Essais de méthode, de critique et d'histoire littéraire*. Paris: Librarie Hachette.

Levine, George. 1962. "Determinism and Responsibility in the Works of George Eliot." *PMLA* lxxvii: 268–279.

Lévy, Jean-Philippe. 1965. "L'Officialité de Paris et les questions familiales à la fin du XIVe siècle," *Etudes de droit canonique dédiées à Gabriel LeBras*. Paris: Sirey. II: 1265–1294.

Lewis, C. S. 1953. *The Allegory of Love*. London: Oxford University Press. 1936. Reprint.

Locke, John. 1690. *An essay concerning human understanding*. London: Tho. Basset.

Macaulay, Catharine. 1763–83. *History of England, From the accession of James I to that of the Brunswick line*. 8 vols. London: J. Nourse. Vol. 4, 1768.

_____. 1769. *Loose remarks on certain positions to be found in Mr. Hobbes's "Philosophical rudiments of government and society," with a short sketch of a democratical form of government, In a letter to Signor Paoli*. London: printed for T. Davies.

———. 1770. *Observations on a Pamphlet entitled 'Thoughts on the Cause of the Present Discontents.'* London: Printed for Edward and Charles Dilly.

———. 1774. *A Modest Plea for the Property of Copyright.* Bath: R. Cruttwell, for Edward and Charles Dilly.

———. 1775. *Address to the People of England, Scotland, and Ireland on the Present Important Crisis of Affairs.* London: Dilly.

———. 1778. *History of England from the Revolution to the Present Time in a Series of Letters to a Friend.* Bath: R. Cruttwell.

———. 1783. *A Treatise on the Immutability of Moral Truth.* London.

———. 1790. *Observations on the Reflections of the Right Hon. Edmund Burke, on the Revolution in France, in a Letter for the Right Hon. The Earl of Stanhope.* London.

———. 1974. *Letters on Education with observations on Religious and Metaphysical Subjects.* 1787. Reprint. London: Garland.

MacIntyre, Alasdair. 1995. "The Relationship of Philosophy to Its Past." In *Philosophy in History.* Richard Rorty, J.B. Schneewind, and Quentin Skinner, eds. Cambridge: Cambridge University Press. 31–48.

Mackenzie, Catriona. 1996. "Reason and Sensibility." In *Hypatia's Daughters.* Linda Lopez McAlister, ed. Bloomington and Indianapolis, IN: Indiana University Press.

Martin, Jane. 1985. *Reclaiming a Conversation: The Ideal of an Educated Woman.* New Haven: Yale University Press.

Mechthild of Magdeburg. 1998. *The Flowing Light of the Godhead.* Frank Tobin, trans. New York: Paulist Press.

Le Ménagier de Paris. [1393]. Jérôme Pichon, ed. 2 vols. Paris: Techener. Reprint. 1846.

Mohr, Wolfgang. 1963. "Darbietungsformen der Mystik bei Mechthild von Magdeburg." In *Märchen, Mythos, Dichtung: Festschrift zum 90. Geburtstag Friedrich von der Leyens,* Hugo Kuhn and Kurt Schier, eds. Munich: Beck. 375–99.

More, Hannah. 1777. *Essays on Various Subjects, Principally Designed for Young Ladies.* London: Printed for J. Wilkie and T. Cadell.

Murdoch, Iris. 1956. "Vision and Choice in Morality." *Proceedings of the Aristotelian Society,* supp. Vol. 30: 32–58.

Nellmann, Eberhard. 1989. "'Dis buoch . . . bezeichent alleine mich.' Zum Prolog von Mechthilds 'Fließendem Licht der Gottheit.'" In *Gotes und der werlde hulde: Literatur in Mittelalter und Neuzeit. Feschrift für Heinz Rupp zum 70. Geburtstag.* Rüdiger Schnell, ed. Bern/Stuttgart: Francke. 200–205.

Neumann, Hans. 1964. "Beiträge zur Textgeschichte des "Fließenden Lichts der Gottheit'und zur Lebensgeschichte Mechthilds von Magdeburg." In *Altdeutsche und altniederländische Mystik.* Kurt Ruh, ed. Darmstadt: Wissenschaftichte Buchgesellschaft. 175–239.

Newman, Barbara. 1995. *From Virile Woman to WomanChrist.* Philadelphia: University of Pennsylvania Press.

Nietzsche, Friedrich Wilhelm. [1889] 1998. Oxford: Oxford University Press.

O'Donoghue, Bernard. 1982. *The Courtly Love Tradition.* Manchester: Manchester University Press.

O'Neill, Eileen. 1998. "Disappearing Ink: Early Modern Women Philosophers and Their Fate in History." In *Philosophy in a Feminist Voice.* Janet Kourany, ed. Princeton: Princeton University Press. 17–62.

Palmer, Nigel. F. 1992. "Das Buch als Bedeutungsträger bei Mechthild von Magdeburg." In *Bildhafte Rede in Mittelalter und früher Neuzeit: Probleme ihrer Legitimation und Funktion*. Wolfgang Harms and Klaus Speckenbach, eds. Tübingen: Niemeyer. 217–35.

Pennington, Sarah. 1761. *An Unfortunate Mothers Advice to Her Absent Daughters*. London: S. Chandler.

Petroff, Elizabeth Alvilda. 1986. *Medieval Women's Visionary Literature*. New York: Oxford University Press.

Poston, Carol H. 1996. "Mary Wollstonecraft and 'The Body Politic.'" In *Feminist Interpretations of Mary Wollstonecraft*. Carol Pateman and Mary Lyndon Shanley, eds. University Park: Pennsylvania State University Press. 85–104.

Prasad, Thakur Guru. 1968. *Comtism in the Novels of George Eliot*. Lucknow: Hindustani Book Depot.

Quilligan, Maureen. 1979. *The Language of Allegory: Defining the Genre*. Ithaca: Cornell University Press.

_____. 1991. *The Allegory of Female Authority: Christine de Pizan's Cité des dames*. Ithaca: Cornell University Press.

Raphael, D.D. 1983. "Philosophy and rationality: A response to Cora Diamond." *New Literary History*. 15: 171–7.

Reno, Christine. 1992. "The Preface to the *Avision-Christine* in ex-Phillipps 128." In *Reinterpreting Christine de Pizan*. Earl Jeffrey Richards, ed. Athens, GA: Georgia University Press: 207–227.

Ruddick, Sarah. 1980. "Maternal Thinking." *Feminist Studies* 6(2): 342–67.

Sapiro, Virginia. 1992. *A Vindication of Political Virtue*. Chicago, IL: Chicago University Press.

_____. 1996. "Wollstonecraft, Feminism, and Democracy: 'Being Bastilled'." In *Feminist Interpretations of Mary Wollstonecraft*. Mary J. Falco, ed. University Park: Pennsylvania State University Press. 33–45.

Schmidt, Margot. 1987. "'Minne dú gewaltige kellerin.' On the Nature of *minne* in Mechthild of Magdeburg's *fliessendes licht der gottheit*." Susan Johnson, trans. *Vox Benedictina* 4: 100–125.

Scholl, Edith. 1987. "To Be a Full-Grown Bride: Mechthild of Magdeburg." In *Medieval Religious Women*. Vol. 2: *Peace Weavers*. Kalamazoo, MI: Cistercian Publications. 223–37.

Seaton, William. 1984. "Transforming of Convention in Mechthild of Magdeburg." *Mystics Quarterly* 10: 64–72.

Sklair, Leslie. 1968. "Comte and the Idea of Progress." *Inquiry* 11: 321–331.

Solente, Suzanne, ed. 1936–1941. *Le Livre des faits et bonnes meurs du sage roy Charles V*. 2 Vols. Paris: H. Champion.

Staves, Susan. 1989. "The liberty of the she-subject of England": Rights, rhetoric and the female Thucydides. *Cardozo Studies in Law and Literature*. 1 (2): 161–83.

Sulloway, Alison G. 1989. *Jane Austen and the Province of Womanhood*. Philadelphia, PA: University of Pennsylvania Press.

Tobin, Frank. 1994. "Mechthild von Magdeburg and Meister Eckhart: Points of Coincidence." *Meister Eckhart and the Beguine Mystics: Explorations in Vernacular Theology*. Bernard McGinn, ed. New York: Continuum. 44–61.

_____. 1995. *Mechthild von Magdeburg: A Medieval Mystic in Modern Eyes*. Columbia, SC: Camden House.

Todd, Janet. 1986. *Sensibility: An Introduction*. London; New York: Methuen.

_____. 1996. Introduction. *Female Education in Age of Enlightenment*. 6 Vols. London: Pickering and Chatto.

Vogeler, Martha S. 1980. "George Eliot and the Positivists." *Nineteenth Century Fiction* 35: 406–31.

Wainwright-deKadt, Elizabeth. 1980. "Courtly Literature and Mysticism: Some Aspects of Their Interaction." *Acta Germanica* 12: 41–60.

Waithe, Mary Ellen. 1987–1995. *A History of Women Philosophers*. 4 Vols. Dordrecht: Kluwer.

Walker, Margaret Urban. 1989. "Moral Understandings: Alternative "Epistemology" for a Feminist Ethics." *Hypatia* Vol. 4, No. 2: 15–28.

_____. 1998a. "Moral Epistemology." In *A Companion to Feminist Philosophy*, Alison M. Jaggar and Iris Marion Young, eds. Oxford: Blackwell Publishers Ltd. 363–71.

_____. 1998b. *Moral Understandings: a feminist study in ethics*. New York: Routledge.

West, Jane. 1806. *Letters to a Young Lady*. New York: O. Penniman & Co.; I. Riley & Co.

Willard, Charity Cannon. 1984. *Christine de Pizan: Her Life and Works*. New York: Persea.

Williams, Bernard. 1985. *Ethics and the Limits of Philosophy*. Cambridge: Harvard University Press.

Withey, Lynne E. 1976. "Catharine Macaulay and the uses of history: Ancient rights, perfectionism, and propaganda." *Journal of British Studies* 16: 59–83.

Wollstonecraft, Mary. 1976. *Mary, a Fiction and the Wrongs of Woman*. Gary Kelly, ed. London: Oxford University Press.

_____. 1977. *Letters written during a short residence in Sweden, Norway, and Denmark*. In *A Wollstonecraft Anthology*, Janet Todd, ed. Bloomington: Indiana University Press.

_____. 1983. *A Vindication of the Rights of Woman*. 1792. Reprint, Harmondsworth, Middlesex: Penguin Books.

_____. 1989. *The Works of Mary Wollstonecraft*. Janet Todd and Marilyn Butler, eds. 7 Vols. New York: New York University Press.

_____. 1996. *A Vindication of the Rights of Men*. New York: Prometheus Books.

Zum Brunn, Emilie and Epiney-Burgard, Georgette. 1989. *Women Mystics in Medieval Europe*. Sheila Hughes, trans. New York: Paragon House. Original: *Femmes Troubadours de Dieu*. Belgium: Brepols, 1988.

Index

Wollstonecraft, Mary, 1, 81–121,
123–124, 146, 150
biography of, 84–89
Cave of Fancy, 86
The Female Reader, 87–88
*An Historical and Moral View of the
Origin and Progress of the French
Revolution and the Effects It Has
Produced in Europe,* 88
*Letters Written during a Short
Residence in Sweden, Norway, and
Denmark,* 88
Macaulay's influence on, 19–22,
25–26
Mary, 86, 94, 99–101, 105, 110, 118,
120
on morality, 83
Original Stories from Real Life, 86–87,
94
on sensibility, 13, 98–121, 181,
184
style and content in, 82–83, 95–101
*Thoughts on the Education of
Daughters,* 85–86, 87
use of Enlightenment treatise form
by, 83, 89–95, 101–104

A Vindication of the Rights of Men, 82,
84, 88
A Vindication of the Rights of Woman,
13, 19, 20, 21, 27, 34, 81–121, 177
on virtue, 90, 94, 98–99
The Wrongs of Woman, or, Maria, 88,
93, 107–108, 110, 111, 115, 120
See also Enlightenment treatise,
form of; Sensibility
Women
education of, 21, 29–34
emancipation of, 20–21
equality of, 21, 22, 28, 29–35, 35–36,
42–43, 44, 85
and marriage, 58–62
misogynistic criticism of, 48, 51–55,
71
and moral agency, 57–58, 64, 68, 70
oppression of, 49
prudence of, 62–68, 70
and social reform, 35–36, 37–44
virtue of, 36, 37–42, 49, 52–55,
59–68, 70–71, 72, 182

Zum Braun, Emilie, *Women Mystics of
Medieval Europe,* 162